Jewish Stories
from *Heaven*
and Earth

Inspiring Tales to Nourish
the Heart and Soul

Edited by
Rabbi Dov Peretz Elkins

For People of All Faiths, All Backgrounds

JEWISH LIGHTS Publishing
Woodstock, Vermont

Jewish Stories from Heaven and Earth:
Inspiring Tales to Nourish the Heart and Soul

2008 Quality Paperback Edition, First Printing
©2008 by Rabbi Dov Peretz Elkins

Library of Congress Cataloging-in-Publication Data
Jewish stories from heaven and earth : inspiring tales to nourish the heart and soul / compiled and edited by Rabbi Dov Peretz Elkins.
p. cm.
Includes bibliographical references.
ISBN-13: 978-1-58023-363-7 (quality pbk.)
ISBN-10: 1-58023-363-5 (quality pbk.)
1. Jewish way of life—Anecdotes. 2. Judaism—Anecdotes. 3. Jews—Anecdotes. I. Elkins, Dov Peretz.
BM723.J53 2008
296.7092'2—dc22
2008025715

10   9   8   7   6   5   4   3   2   1

Manufactured in the United States of America
❀ Printed on recycled paper
Cover Design: Melanie Robinson
Cover Art: Melanie Robinson

For People of All Faiths, All Backgrounds
Published by Jewish Lights Publishing
A Division of LongHill Partners, Inc.
Sunset Farm Offices, Route 4, P.O. Box 237
Woodstock, VT 05091
Tel: (802) 457-4000   Fax: (802) 457-4004
www.jewishlights.com

To the newest members of our family:

Arthur Benjamin Stadlin
and
Lily Belle Elkins

with love

May the Lord bless you from Zion;
may you share the prosperity of Jerusalem
all the days of your life,
and live to see your children's children.
May all be well with Israel!
—Psalm 128:5–6

Contents

$\mathcal{H}$ope and $\mathcal{E}$ndurance   25

$\mathcal{C}$ontinuity and $\mathcal{T}$radition   55

Introduction

As my friend Rabbi Mark Greenspan once remarked, if there's something that Jews enjoy, it's a good story. We are the original storytelling people. Long before we studied philosophy or theology and wrestled with God, long before we even began praying to God, we told stories about our Creator. Long before Steven Spielberg came to Hollywood, Jews were telling stories to the world. Maybe it's not surprising, then, that so many Jews are drawn to the movie industry. For thousands of years we Jews have been seeing movies in our mind's eye, and telling them, writing them, singing them, and passing them from generation to generation.

Nobel Laureate Elie Wiesel once wrote that God created humans in order to listen to their stories. Without creatures on earth, what tales could be spun to bring God the joy, intrigue, curiosity, celebration, and sanctification that are ensconced in each and every Jewish story?

The stories selected for this volume include tales that reflect both the glory and grief, the humor and pride of Jewish life. If Jews have survived for four thousand years, from the ancient patriarchs and matriarchs to David Ben-Gurion, Golda Meir, Ariel Sharon, and Albert Einstein, it is because no assembly of Jews has ever lived without carrying a bag chock-full of parables, anecdotes, and narratives to share with family, neighbors, and anyone who loves a good story (and who doesn't?!).

The tales told in this book emerge out of the Jewish tradition, but can undoubtedly be read and enjoyed by people of all faiths. They are Jewish, but also very human stories, universal in content and theme in the same way as *Fiddler on the Roof* was understood and enjoyed by people from every walk of life.

These Jewish stories are not simply stories, not mere legends spun out of the mysterious minds of a talented muse. Rather, they are tales of courage, devotion, and passion; narratives of commitment to education, perseverance, piety and familial love, community solidarity, heroic behavior, and extraordinary achievement. They come from the muse of the famous, and the not so famous. We include stories from Nobel Laureate Elie Wiesel, the late Israeli Prime Minister Yitzhak Rabin, and other world-renowned figures, as well as by little-known people such as elderly folks who participated in a writing contest.

For a decade prior to the publication of my former collection of Jewish stories, *Chicken Soup for the Jewish Soul,* I have sought out exciting, inspiring, and hair-raising Jewish stories. The present collection, *Jewish Stories from Heaven and Earth,* is the fruit of two decades of searching every corner of the world—in books and libraries, squeezing tales from friends, colleagues, and, yes, even from strangers who heard of my passion for uplifting stories.

One cannot come away from reading these amazing chronicles of life at its heights and depths without experiencing a surge of pride in our Jewish heritage. We have withstood the shame of slavery and the pain of persecution, and enjoyed the bliss of creativity and the sigh of liberation. From exile to rebirth, from degradation to renaissance, the Jewish people have undergone every human experience and emotion that God has created.

In these tales are the best and the worst of God's creations: people who are gentle, kind, compassionate, audacious, and heroic; and others who have tried to extinguish from the planet that glowing ember of spirituality called the Jewish People. You will be lifted to the highest mountaintop and plunged into the darkest abyss in the course of reading about the lives of people who are simply trying to eke out a living.

In our time, no collection of Jewish tales would be complete without sections on the Holocaust (*Shoah*) and the miraculous rebirth of the third Jewish commonwealth—the State of Israel. Along the way are stories of kindness, hope, goodness, faith, love of tradition, relations with our non-Jewish neighbors, the discovery of profound wisdom, divine providence, and every other human experience.

Taken together, these tales exemplify what it means to be the Jewish People, whose history is as old as Babylon and as new as Tel Aviv. Having read about all these incredible events, no one can put this book down without saying, with Mark Twain, that the Jew, "a nebulous dim puff of stardust lost in the blaze of the Milky Way ... exhibit[s] no decadence, no infirmities of age, no weakening of his parts, no slowing of his energies, no dulling of his alert and aggressive mind. All things are mortal but the Jew; all other forces pass, but he remains."

Rabbi Dov Peretz Elkins

Simple Goodness

Some forty years ago, when I was associate rabbi of Har Zion Temple of Philadelphia, the senior rabbi, David A. Goldstein, of blessed memory, officiated at the funeral of a Jewish educator who had devoted his life to the young charges in the religious school. The late teacher never wrote any famous books, never became known nationally or internationally, but carried out his day-to-day tasks with consummate skill and passion. One thing that Rabbi Goldstein said about this kind of unsung hero has stayed with me, and I have referred to his idea in many eulogies I have delivered. He said that the true heroes of the world are not the ones who march to the beat of loud drums and blaring horns, in a great parade, with confetti raining down upon them. True heroism is that of the simple folk who do their daily job without fanfare or fame, but whose influence is like a pebble in a pond that creates ripples that spread far and wide.

The people in this section are such heroes. A woman who decides to "pass on" a coin so a stranger will not be embarrassed; a merchant who empties his cash register and contributes his entire day's earnings to help another human in need; a group of kids who cheer a special-needs child and make him feel great about himself; a Roman Catholic man whose humanity and sense of decency were too strong to comply with anti-Semitic directives; a Jew who helped a drunken Nazi see the humanity of his victims; a former soldier whose life was so turned around that he died a saint instead of a miser; and others like them.

These people are all the simple, unheralded folk whose compassion exemplifies the mitzvah of *tikkun olam* (repairing the world).

Pass It On

Several years ago I was shopping at a local grocery store and when my purchases were tallied, I was surprised and embarrassed to discover that I was ten cents short. I quickly surveyed what I had bought to determine what I could leave behind to buy another day. As I was about to make this decision, the woman behind me suddenly offered me ten cents to cover the shortfall. Now I was also humiliated!

I quickly explained that I couldn't accept her money and that I had no problem leaving something behind. "Oh," she exclaimed, "I'm not giving it to you. Just take it and pass it on." That sounded reasonable, so I accepted the ten cents and left the store with all my purchases, inspired by the whole idea.

Exactly two weeks later, I was in the same store and this time I was second in line when the woman in front of me realized that she was ten cents short. The replay of the episode from my previous visit to the grocery store was uncanny. I offered her the ten cents, which she graciously refused. I explained that I was not giving it to her but that she should take it and pass it on, and only then did she agree to accept the money.

I've often wondered how many times that ten cents has traveled the world! The entire experience confirmed for me that even a small gesture of help could have broad consequences. It reinforced the recognition that countless people have assisted me, often in ways unknown to me, and I have an obligation to pass on whatever I can to help others. The Jewish values I learned from my parents and from my Jewish studies have stood me in good stead once again!

Irene Goldfarb

Tzedakah (Charity)

When Pa was about sixteen, his family fled the Russian pogroms and settled in Brooklyn. As a boy in the shtetl, he studied all day, memorizing the Torah and the Talmud. Here in America, Pa had to earn a few dollars working in a sweatshop.

Ma's family had come to Brooklyn from Romania. When she met Pa, she was seventeen and working as a seamstress. Ma was a beauty. Pa loved her, and she loved the gentle scholar. They were married in 1912. I was born in 1913.

Together Ma and Pa worked and scrimped, and saved enough money to buy a knitting machine and start up a business making sweaters. For a few years they were moderately prosperous, lived a bit easier, and along the way had another child, my sister, Shirley. Intent on expansion, Pa went into debt and didn't put aside any reserve funds. Of course, the Depression wiped us out. Pa's spirit broke. I still remember the terrible crying jags. Ma was a constant source of comfort, hope, and love unlimited. Her repeated "It will be all right" kept us intact and gradually healed Pa. Eventually Pa managed to borrow $200 to buy a little candy store. For the rest of their working years, Ma and Pa spent eighteen-hour days, seven days a week, fifty-two weeks a year (excluding Rosh Hashanah and Yom Kippur) in their candy store, sustained only by their hopes for their children's future. From behind his soda fountain, Pa explored the universe. "Ah," he would say, "God created such wonders—the skies, the mountains, the oceans. Such beauty, if only people wouldn't spoil it." And yet to him a human being was the most marvelous creation of all. "I'll never understand how even God could make us."

One morning Pa was at the soda fountain as usual, waiting for the rare customer. I was off in a corner reading a magazine. About ten o'clock a short, thin, middle-aged man came in out of the scorching sun and walked very slowly to the soda fountain. He was neatly dressed in a well-worn blue suit and tie. He asked Pa if he might have a drink of water, apologizing because he didn't have the two cents to pay for a glass of seltzer.

"Here, take the seltzer," said Pa. "You'll owe me two cents." Sipping slowly, the man began to tell Pa in a low, halting voice how he had walked here all the way from the Bronx, hoping to find work in a tailor shop down the street. It was a temporary job, but it paid a full $10 a week. He'd read the advertisement in the evening edition of the paper and had left his home long before dawn. Our store was in a section of Brooklyn close to Coney Island—miles and miles from the Bronx. By the time he got to the tailor shop, the job had been taken. Now he had to walk all the way home to tell his family.

"When will I ever get a job?" he sobbed.

I'll never forget Pa's face as he cried silently with his fellow man. He went to the register, took out $2 and change—the whole morning's receipts—and gave it all away. Afterward, he never said a word about it, never spoke of it at all. It was done. It was gone. To Pa, nothing rare or unusual. It was just Pa.... Now long gone, but still with me today, in all I do.

Sam Fishman

My Great-Grandfather's Partner

L ike many immigrants, my great-grandfather came to the United States with nothing but hope, faith, and determination. Settling in the Lower East Side, he worked diligently, finally saving enough money to bring his wife and children over from the old country. The family reunited, he and his wife would have one more son; this son, the only child born in the United States, would become my grandfather.

My great-grandfather decided to form a partnership with his best friend. Although times were extremely difficult, they worked hard, combining dedication to their craft with keen insight and intelligence. Encouraging and helping each other, they slowly began to realize financial success in their work; while not accumulating a fortune by any means, they made a fine living, enough to support their families and inspire dreams of still-better times to come.

But all that changed one night. That was the night my great-grandfather's partner disappeared, taking with him all the assets of their business, stealing all the money they had worked so hard to save. I don't know why he left. I don't know why he betrayed his best friend and his best friend's family. I don't think even my great-grandfather ever knew. All he knew was that his partner was gone.

Times were hard again. Money was scarce again. But my great-grandfather refused to give up; he formed a new business, put his heart and his hope into it, rededicated himself to the betterment of his family. And in time, he found success once more; not as much as he had shared with his best friend, perhaps, but enough.

And then his best friend returned.

I don't know the details of the reunion. I imagine a knock at the door in the middle of the night, a cold night, raining. I imagine my great-grandfather opening the door, his sleep-filled eyes widening as he stared at his once-best friend, now thinner, soaking wet, shivering.

What I do know is that my great-grandfather's best friend came back, shamefaced and needy. I know that he looked up at my great-grandfather, the man he had cheated, and pleaded for money. I know that my great-grandfather gave him money and asked for nothing in return.

Still a little boy, the man who would become my grandfather watched quietly. He asked his father why he would unquestioningly give money to the man who had betrayed him.

"He must have been in desperate need to return to the friend he had cheated and ask for money," my great-grandfather said. "And you must never turn away a man in desperate need."

My great-grandfather was not a clergyman, but his gravestone bears the title RABBI. It is not hard to understand why.

Rabbi Elaine Rose Glickman

God's Perfection

In Brooklyn, New York, there is a school, *Chush*, for learning-disabled Jewish children. One evening, at a fund-raising dinner for the school, the father of one of the Chush children stood up, extolled the school and its dedicated staff, and then cried out: "We are taught that God is perfect and all that God does is done with perfection. But what about my son, Shaya? He cannot understand things as other children do. He cannot remember facts and figures as other children do. Where is the divine perfection in Shaya?"

Shocked by the question, pained by the father's anguish, the audience sat in silence as he went on. "Perhaps," he continued, "I have found the answer to my own question." And he told a story:

One Sunday afternoon, Shaya and his father came to the yeshiva where Shaya studies in the morning. The yeshiva boys were playing baseball.

"I would like to be in the game," Shaya whispered to his father. His father was worried—he knew Shaya was not athletic at all, that he didn't even know how to hold a bat properly, let alone hit it—and that most of the boys understandably wouldn't want Shaya on their team.

Nevertheless, he approached one of the boys in the field and asked if Shaya might join them. The boy shrugged. "We're losing by six runs, and we're already in the eighth inning. So I guess it's okay if he joins our team and goes up to bat for us in the ninth."

Shaya and his father were both ecstatic. But by the bottom of the eighth, Shaya's team had managed to hit three runs, and by the bottom of the ninth they scored again. When Shaya's turn at bat came up, there were two outs and the bases were loaded. Would they really let Shaya go to bat in this crucial situation?

They did. The first pitch came in. Shaya swung clumsily and missed. One of the teammates came up to Shaya and helped him hold the bat. The pitcher took a few steps forward. He threw the ball softly—and the two batters together hit a slow grounder.

The pitcher caught the ball and could have easily ended the whole game by throwing it to the first baseman. Instead, he threw it on a high arc to right field, way beyond the first baseman's reach.

"Shaya, run to first! Run to first!" all the boys yelled. Never in his life had Shaya ever had to "run to first." Wide-eyed, startled, he scampered down the baseline. By the time he reached first, the right fielder had the ball. He could have easily thrown it to the second baseman who in turn could have tagged Shaya out ... but instead he threw it far over the third baseman's head.

Everyone started yelling again, "Shaya, run to second! Run to second!"

Shaya ran to second base as the runners ahead of him deliriously circled the bases toward home. When he got to second base, the other team's shortstop ran up to him, turned him toward third base, and shouted, "Shaya, Shaya, run to third!"

And then as he rounded third, all the boys from both teams ran behind him screaming, "Shaya, run home! Shaya, run home!"

And Shaya ran home. No sooner had he stepped on home plate, than all the boys from both the teams raised him high in the air on their shoulders. He had just hit a "grand slam" and won the game for his team. "That day," said the father, who by now had tears rolling down his face, "I learned about God's perfection. For when God brings a child like Shaya into the world, the perfection God seeks is in how other people treat him."

Rabbi Paysach J. Krohn

Leica Freedom Train

I carry my Leica camera a bit more proudly these days.

The reason? A story I had never heard before—a tale of courage, integrity, and humility that is only now coming to light, some seventy years after the fact.

The Leica is the pioneer 35mm camera. From a nitpicking point of view, it wasn't the very first still camera to use 35mm movie film, but it was the first to be widely publicized and successfully marketed.

It created the "candid camera" boom of the 1930s.

It is a German product—precise, minimalist, utterly efficient. Behind its worldwide acceptance as a creative tool was a family-owned, socially oriented firm that, during the Nazi era, acted with uncommon grace, generosity, and modesty.

E. Leitz Inc., designer and manufacturer of Germany's most famous photographic product, saved its Jews.

And Ernst Leitz II, the steely-eyed Protestant patriarch who headed the closely held firm as the Holocaust loomed across Europe, acted in such a way as to earn the title, "the photography industry's Schindler."

As George Gilbert, a veteran writer on topics photographic, told the story at a convention of the Leica Historical Society of America in Portland, Oregon, Leitz Inc., founded in Wetzlar in 1869, had a tradition of enlightened behavior toward its workers. Pensions, sick leave, health insurance—all were instituted early on at Leitz, which depended for its workforce upon generations of skilled employees—many of whom were Jewish.

As soon as Adolf Hitler was named chancellor of Germany in 1933, Ernst Leitz II began receiving frantic calls from Jewish associates, asking for his help in getting them and their families out of the country.

As Christians, Leitz and his family were immune to Nazi Germany's Nuremberg laws, which restricted the movement of Jews and limited their professional activities. To help his Jewish workers and colleagues, Leitz quietly established what has become known among historians of the Holocaust as "Leica Freedom Train," a covert means of allowing Jews to leave Germany in the guise of Leitz employees being assigned overseas.

Employees, retailers, family members, even friends of family members were "assigned" to Leitz sales offices in France, Britain, Hong Kong, and the United States. Leitz's activities intensified after Kristallnacht in November 1938, during which synagogues and Jewish shops were burned across Germany.

Before long, German "employees" were disembarking from the ocean liner *Bremen* at a New York pier and making their way to the Manhattan office of Leitz Inc., where executives quickly found them jobs in the photographic industry.

Each new arrival had around his or her neck the symbol of freedom—a new Leica. The refugees were paid a stipend until they could find work. Out of this migration came designers, repair technicians, salespeople, marketers, and writers for the photographic press.

Keeping the Story Quiet

The Leica Freedom Train was at its height in 1938 and early 1939, delivering groups of refugees to New York every few weeks. Then, with the invasion of Poland on September 1, 1939, Germany closed its borders.

By that time, hundreds of endangered Jews had escaped to America, thanks to the Leitzes' efforts.

How did Ernst Leitz II and his staff get away with it?

Leitz Inc. was an internationally recognized brand that reflected credit on the newly resurgent Reich. The company produced range finders and other optical systems for the German military. Also, the Nazi government desperately needed hard currency from abroad, and Leitz's single biggest market for optical goods was the United States.

Even so, members of the Leitz family and firm suffered for their good works. A top executive, Alfred Turk, was jailed for working to help Jews and freed only after the payment of a large bribe.

Leitz's daughter, Elsie Kuhn-Leitz, was imprisoned by the Gestapo after she was caught at the border, helping Jewish women cross into Switzerland. She eventually was freed but endured rough treatment in the course of her interrogation.

She also fell under suspicion when she attempted to improve the living conditions of seven hundred to eight hundred Ukrainian slave laborers, all of them women, who had been assigned to work in the plant during the 1940s.

(After the war, Kuhn-Leitz received numerous honors for her humanitarian efforts, among them the Officier d'honneur des Palmes Academiques from France in 1965 and the Aristide Briand Medal from the European Academy in the 1970s.)

Why has no one told this story until now? According to the late Norman Lipton, a freelance writer and editor, the Leitz family wanted no publicity for their heroic efforts. Only after the last member of the Leitz family was dead did the Leica Freedom Train finally come to light.

James Auer

We Need to Be Hugged and Held

Joel Osteen, senior pastor of one of America's largest congregations, tells the following story:

"I heard an amazing story about a set of twins who were just a few days old. One of them had been born with a serious heart condition and wasn't expected to live. A few days went by and the baby's health continued to deteriorate; she was close to death. A hospital nurse asked if she could go against hospital policy and put the babies in the same incubator together, rather than in individual incubators. It was a big ordeal, but finally the doctor consented to allow the twins to be placed side by side in the same incubator, just as they had been in their mother's womb. Somehow, the healthy baby managed to reach over and put his arm around his sick sister. Before long, and for no apparent reason, her heart began to stabilize and heal. Her blood pressure came up to normal. Her temperature soon followed suit. Little by little she got better, and today they are both perfectly healthy children. A newspaper caught wind of the story and photographed the twins while still in the incubator, embraced in a hug. They ran the photo with the caption 'The Rescuing Hug.'"

Perhaps the point of the story is that there are many times in life when we need to be hugged and held. May each one of us be the sustaining hand for those who turn to us for spiritual strength and support.

Rabbi Joseph Potasnik

A Righteous Person

On the tenth of December 1996, I went to La Honda, California, a small, isolated town on the spine of the last mountain range before the Pacific Ocean, and planted a redwood tree in memory of Hugo Burghauser, taking care to select a Sequoia that would someday produce the largest, most noble, longest-living member of the species, and choosing a site not likely ever to see a lumberjack's chain saw. Since I don't know Burghauser's exact date of birth, I chose the anniversary of his 1982 date of death for the ceremony, one at which I was the only attendee. My effort was not as a result of some formal action but was self-motivated because of my conclusion that Burghauser was a righteous person, deserving of the honor. His behavior in 1938, though modest in scope, required great personal sacrifice and strength of character. Let me tell you about him.

On a Saturday morning in 1966, when I was still living in New Jersey, I received a phone call from the personnel manager at the Metropolitan Opera House, asking if I were free to play that afternoon's performance of Richard Strauss's one-act opera, *Elektra*. When an orchestra member gets sick at the last moment, as had the orchestra's bass clarinetist, someone must be engaged to fill in and, since I played at the Met from time to time, my name was on the substitute list, which is how I came to be called that day.

Accepting the engagement, I called Herb Blayman—my friend and then first-desk clarinet at the Met—in the nearby town of Tenafly to ask if I could catch a ride with him to the matinee performance. He agreed but with the caveat that he was playing both matinee and evening performances that day and would not be able to leave until after 11 p.m. That meant I either had to wait until he finished or take the bus home.

"What's the second show?" I asked.

"*Così fan Tutte*," he said.

I needed to know nothing else. A day when one can play *Elektra* in the afternoon and then see Mozart's *Così fan Tutte* in the evening is a gift from God.

It was while warming up backstage that Blayman introduced me to Hugo Burghauser. He was a neatly dressed man who appeared to be in his mid-seventies. "There will be a seat on your left for Hugo to occupy and watch the opera. He used to play bassoon with the orchestra but is now retired," said Blayman.

"I'm very glad to meet you," Burghauser said to me, his German accent noticeable at once. "I hope you don't mind me sitting next to you, but since your seat looks directly at the conductor's right-hand side, it is a good place for a view of the stage. You recognize, of course, that, in the pit, the closer one gets to the lip of the stage, the less one sees of it. I will be sure not to inconvenience or disturb you."

"Mr. Burghauser, your presence will not bother me in the least," I replied. "You realize that I am kept very busy during the opera so I won't be able to see much of it with you."

"I know," he said. "One really works hard in *Elektra*. I once told Strauss that the work exhausted the musicians physically, emotionally, and intellectually."

That stopped me cold.

"Mr. Burghauser," I said, respectfully, "you knew Richard Strauss?"

"Very well," he replied. "I was privileged to work with him many times in Vienna and elsewhere. He was a marvelous conductor." And then, pausing for a moment, Burghauser added, "though a terrible card player." Much later I was to learn that Strauss's "Concertino for Clarinet and Bassoon with String Orchestra and Harp" was written for and dedicated to "Hugo Burghauser, *dem Getreuen* [the faithful]." In the world of music, to have someone of the magnitude of Richard Strauss write and dedicate a work to a performer makes the recipient of that honor very special indeed.

At that point the orchestra began to file into the pit, tuned up, and got ready to open with the muscular "A-GA-MEM-NON!" theme that pervades the entire opera. On my left, with his chair turned ninety degrees—placing his back directly against the audience separation wall, which gave him a face-front view of the stage—sat Burghauser. The lights dimmed, the conductor made his entrance, we rose and bowed to the audience, seated ourselves, and, with a flick of the wrist, were into the story of matricide among the ancient Greeks.

For the next hour and thirty minutes—the length of the opera—it became obvious to me that Burghauser knew every detail of the work. He flicked a finger when Klytemnestra missed an entrance by an eye-blink. And when, for the arrival of Orestes, a trumpet overshot a cue by a millisecond, Burghauser's hands, folded and resting on his lap, imperceptibly rose up, as if to give the player a helpful cue. It was just a tiny movement, but I saw it out of the corner of my eye.

After the performance, I asked him if he might join me for supper, explaining that I was finished playing but was coming back for the evening's performance. And that is how I got a small piece of Hugo Burghauser's remarkable story. It took a long time to get all of it. He was so modest and self-effacing that he chose not to speak of himself. The details came from others much later.

It is not wild hyperbole to state that, until 1938, Hugo Burghauser was the most powerful musician in the world. During that time, he was the president of the Vienna Philharmonic—as well as the principal bassoon—which means that he was the most influential person in the world's most influential symphony orchestra. Ergo, he was the most dominant musician in Vienna, in Austria, in Europe, and, therefore, in the world.

There is no orchestra quite like the Vienna Philharmonic. Proud, haughty, brilliant, though, by today's standards, unforgivably sexist and inflexible. But in early 1930, it stood at the pinnacle of symphony orchestras, a law unto itself. The VPO is completely self-governing. Unlike the vast majority of professional orchestras, this one did not have two faces; that is, the musicians on one hand and management on the other. On the contrary. The orchestra manages itself, inviting whomever it wishes, ignoring those with whom it chooses not to be involved. As royalty is not told what to do, one does not dictate to the VPO. They can be pressured, to be sure—as was the case of the scandal caused by their obstinate refusal to hire women—but they are a law unto themselves, with vast record sales, a large government subsidy, completely sold-out subscription concerts, and the world's most prestigious summer festival in Salzburg. Thus, the VPO can and does thumb its nose at demands that, in any other orchestra, would be political suicide. It is a private club. (I do not defend its attitude, only report it.)

And in the 1930s, Hugo Burghauser was the president of this most influential body.

After the Anschluss, or occupation of Austria by Germany, Burghauser was requested to appear at the headquarters of the Austrian Nazi Party. There he was directed to dismiss all Jewish players from the orchestra and, further, to block the hiring of all artists and conductors who were Jewish or whose politics were not in accord with Nazi philosophy.

Burghauser, a Roman Catholic, refused to comply, stating that he would not participate in such an immoral act. Storming out, he went back to work. Called in for a second meeting where he was threatened, Burghauser again refused to obey. Ordered to appear a third time, he refused to go. Two days later he was summarily fired from the presidency of the VPO and his more amenable replacement immediately terminated the employment of every Jew in the ensemble. A later and very public disagreement with a Nazi Party member in the cello section resulted in Burghauser's resignation from the orchestra.

Burghauser did not have to do any of this. Had he concurred with the request made of him, he would have continued in his important and well-paying job, perhaps facing criticism at the end of the war, but who knows? However, Burghauser's ethics were such that he gave it all up rather than be a prisoner to the Nazi view of who should not be permitted to play in Austria's most important symphony orchestra.

Now, being without a job, he approached his friend Arturo Toscanini, who recommended him to Sir Ernest MacMillan, then-conductor of the excellent Toronto Symphony, an orchestra that was searching for a principal bassoon. On the basis of Toscanini's endorsement, Burghauser was offered the position.

Strangely, Burghauser had no idea where Toronto was and thought that he had been engaged to play in Taranto, Italy. Since his mother was Italian—his grandfather had played flute under Verdi—he was fluent in the language and looked forward to living there. But soon, the misunderstanding was clarified and he was on his way to Canada with his bassoon and exactly ten marks, the maximum allowable on leaving Austria.

Arriving in Paris on his way to Cherbourg, where his boat journey was to begin, it was his intention to finance his trip from a French bank account he maintained. However, a bank moratorium, caused by expectations of an imminent war with Germany, prevented him from making any withdrawal. Overnight Burghauser had gone from being the most powerful musician in Europe to being indigent in a foreign country. He was also advised by the French police that, without a steamship ticket, his tourist status would be revoked in one week and this would immediately be followed by expulsion from France. Alone and without resources, Burghauser chose the only avenue available to him: He joined the French Foreign Legion. By the most incredible coincidence, on the day of his induction—the last day before he would have been expelled from France and the day before his scheduled-but-unpaid-for boat trip to New York—he ran into Mrs. Carla Toscanini on a Paris street. Like Burghauser, the Toscaninis were fleeing Europe and scheduled to take the same boat from Cherbourg, for which he was ticketed but without money to pay for the trip. Mrs. Toscanini lent him the amount needed for the boat fare, and he was on his way to New York and Toronto, sharing the ocean voyage with his old friend, a conductor who also had thumbed his nose at fascism.

Ensconced in the first-bassoon chair, Burghauser spent three seasons in Toronto before departing for New York, where he played first with the NBC Symphony and later assumed the second bassoon/contrabassoon chair at the Metropolitan Opera House. A vignette about an event during his time with the Toronto Symphony reveals the magnitude of his prestige and reputation. The TSO had hired a world-famous guest conductor who appeared for rehearsal at the appointed time. He took one look at the orchestra, saw Burghauser, and left the stage, ashen-faced.

"Do you realize who it is you have playing first bassoon?!" he said to the orchestra manager. "That is the most powerful musician in all Europe. What is he doing here?!!"

"He is playing the bassoon," came the response.

Hugo Burghauser was a righteous person. Unlike Oskar Schindler and Raoul Wallenberg, Burghauser did not directly save lives, but his actions and behavior in the face of a hostile, ferocious, and oppressive government were consistent with the highest ethical principles of humankind. The behavior of a few people like him saved whatever honor Austria retained following the events of 1938–1945.

The last time I played *Elektra*, it was with the San Francisco Opera and, as I played it, I thought of this gentle, kind, brave, and righteous man. It was later that I decided to plant a tree in his memory.

Daniel N. Leeson

The Blankets

In the 1930s, my mentor, Rabbi Meier Schimmel, was a young man growing up in Frankfurt-am-Main, Germany. His was a religious family, originally from Poland, but one that stood out for the broad-minded way in which Rabbi Schimmel's parents, Rabbi Jehuda and Civia Schimmel, raised their eight children. If there was a way to experience God's goodness, or to bring God's goodness into the world through some experience, then it was likely that it would be encouraged—a visit to services at a Reform temple to learn how other Jews worshipped, sharing their Sabbath and holiday meals with all different types of Jews, from Vladimir Jabotinsky to emissaries of the Gerer rebbe. The gentile cleaning girl was already referred to by her name, never as "the *shikseh*." The children were even allowed to go to the movies if they reported on the messages (or lack thereof) in the films they saw. Rabbi Schimmel's parents wanted their children to see all around them opportunities to better know and better serve God and God's creations.

While this approach encouraged some humorous tales from time to time—like when my rabbi, as a boy, refused to eat in the home of a family that did not accept the community's kashrut standards, as a sign of protest against such unctuous zealotry—a true test of the Schimmel family's open-mindedness came one night in the mid-1930s. It was an experience that Rabbi Schimmel remembered a lifetime later, one that had shaped his thinking from that time forward.

One night, a Brownshirt, or some other Nazi sympathizer given to playing dress-up in the pseudomilitary uniform of his new political party, could be heard loudly carrying on, banging around in the street outside of the Schimmel home. While things would grow much worse in time, already what even a noisy drunk wearing the Nazi armband represented to the Jews was clear. No doubt anxious tension filled the Schimmel home while the man kept up his ranting. Finally, however, the man quieted down. Opening the door to investigate, my rabbi's father, Jehuda Schimmel, quietly crept outside to find that the man had passed out their front steps. Seeing that the man was not likely to get up and move anytime soon, the elder Rabbi Schimmel made a decision about how to handle the situation. He went back inside and came out again after a few moments, this time bringing with him a pillow and some blankets. He carefully arranged them around the man so he might be warm and somewhat comfortable where he lay.

In the morning, the Nazi awoke. He banged on the door and my rabbi's father answered it. The man, apparently even sober, had lost none of the rabid anti-Semitism he had displayed the night before. He barked, "Hey, Jew-boy, why didn't you call the police? Why'd you do all this for me?"

With a twinkle in his eye that his son would also grow up to have, and just a bit of a smile, one more inwardly pleased for having done something good than outwardly aimed at the yelling man, the senior Schimmel answered, "If I had called the police, would they have treated you any better than I did?"

"God damn you Jews, you are something else ..." The man didn't know what to say, but the hatred in him seemed to have lost its direction and purpose for a moment. He left the doorway.

Rabbi Aaron Benson

The Just

All things change when we do …
—KUKEI, THE ZEN POEMS,
EIGHTH CENTURY CE JAPAN

He was a good man. I was fresh from fellowship, with a pregnant wife and a small child, and Tom (who lived across the street) was the first one to show up the day we moved to the neighborhood. We had been there only ten minutes when he introduced himself, gray-haired with a broad grin, with a "Hi-yah-there" and a firm handshake. Within moments he was helping us unpack, giving my wife directions to the supermarket, and instructing me on the finer points of lawn care. A retired businessman, he had a down-home humor and good nature that made him seem like a modern-day Will Rogers.

I soon learned that we were not the only recipients of his kindness. The children in all the surrounding neighborhoods all referred to him as "Grandpa." They would gather round his feet to listen to his stories of the war and life in the Pacific. When anything broke, Tom was the first person you would ask about it. He somehow seemed to know everybody, and with a single phone call he could have a repairperson there in minutes. When a baseball shattered the glass of the front door, Tom helped my wife pick up the broken pieces, disappeared with the frame, and reappeared later with a new window made of high-impact plastic. When I offered to pay, he only winked. "The storeowner owes me a few favors," he said. When there was a local blood shortage, he was the first in line. When a windstorm left the area covered with broken tree branches, he was there to help clear away the debris. When I got too busy to mow the lawn, he did it. He was a regular at the corner coffee shop, where he often "held court." If you needed someone to talk to (about anything), he would listen. I marveled at the man. He seemed to be the very embodiment of goodness. But it was not always so.

One afternoon, sitting on the back porch sipping iced tea, he told me that for a long time he had been anything but saintly. Severely wounded in the Pacific campaign of the Second World War, he had lost sight in one eye and hearing in one ear. Often in pain from his wounds, he became a heavy smoker, a hard drinker, and a ruthless businessman. He was not, as he put it, "a nice man." Yet things changed dramatically one day when he attended the funeral of a friend from his childhood. His friend had been a kind and caring person, beloved by family and friends. Hundreds of people had shown up to pay their respects, with heartfelt feelings of grief.

"I realized that if it were my funeral, at that moment few people would have bothered to show up." He paused and took a sip of tea.

"Then the strangest thing happened. Suddenly I realized what I had become. A drunk, cruel brute. It was as if I had just woken up from a long sleep."

He stopped smoking and drinking that day, sold his business, and devoted himself to the community with a passion that made those who had known him question his sanity.

"I had a lot of lost time to make up for," he reflected. Miserly before, he gave away great sums to charity after what he referred to as "the change." He joined every civic organization in town. His one wish was that at least a few people would some day show up at his funeral.

Yet as good as he was, the years of cigarettes and alcohol caught up with him, and he suffered a massive heart attack while helping an elderly neighbor clear away a fallen tree. He died the following day. The community was stunned, and my children cried incessantly. On the weekend of the funeral the bell of a small nearby church next to the cemetery began to ring in a slow rhythmic tolling. On and on it tolled.

Slowly, one by one, people stopped what they were doing and began to walk to the graveyard. Stores closed, restaurants emptied, and the playgrounds fell silent. Soon a multitude of people had gathered around the side of Tom's grave. And more continued to come. The police showed up to keep order, but they were not needed. Indeed, they joined the throng. As the pallbearers went by, people reached out to touch the casket. People I have rarely seen show any emotion wept openly. The bell continued to toll unendingly till nightfall, and the crowd did not dissipate for hours. I smiled through my own tears as I realized that Tom had gotten his wish.

There is a legend from the Kabbalah that the world is sustained through the actions of thirty-six just and righteous people. Referred to as the *Lamedvovnick* (the "thirty-six" or simply the "Just"), their goodness sustains our world, and without them all would soon fall into chaos. No one knows exactly who they are, but they are out there, among us, sustaining us all. It is said that when one of them dies, their soul passes to another, who then takes up the job of *tikkun*, restoring and redeeming the world.

I think of that now, as I sit on the porch where I once would spend evenings chatting with Tom, and I wonder to whom his spirit may have passed, for surely he was one of the Just. Perhaps it is someone you know who lives nearby or right across the street, and maybe, just maybe, it is you....

Blair P. Grubb, MD

Hope and Endurance

One of my favorites among the 150 psalms is Psalm 90. In it the writer asks God, "How long must we suffer? Have compassion upon Your servants.... Match days of sorrow with days of joy, equal to the years we have suffered" (90:13–15).

There is much suffering in our unredeemed world. The psalmist asks God for relief, for hope, for the ability to endure what life metes out to us. The stories in this section speak of that hope in the face of cruelty—wrought by humans and by nature. Hope by people who are ill, and for whom the Jewish tradition offers comfort; hope of people who are confined to prisons of anti-Semitism; and hope of dedicated physicians whose care for their patients goes beyond the professional services for which they are engaged.

I am reminded of the words of Emily Dickenson in "Hope":

> Hope is the thing with feathers
> That perches in the soul
> And sings the tune—without the words
> And never stops at all.

For Everything a Blessing

When I was an elementary school student in yeshiva—a Jewish parochial school with both religious and secular studies—my classmates and I used to find amusing a sign that was posted just outside the bathroom. It was an ancient Jewish blessing, commonly referred to as the *asher yatzar* ("who formed") benediction, that was supposed to be recited after one relieved oneself. For grade-school children, there could be nothing more strange or ridiculous than to link the acts of micturition and defecation with holy words that mentioned God's name. Blessings were reserved for prayers, for holy days, or for thanking God for food or for some act of deliverance, but surely not for a bodily function that evoked smirks and giggles.

It took me several decades to realize the wisdom that lay behind this blessing, which was composed by Abayei, a fourth-century Babylonian rabbi.

Abayei's blessing is contained in the Talmud, an encyclopedic work of Jewish law and lore that was written over the first five centuries of the Common Era. The Jewish religion is chock-full of these blessings, or *brachot*, as they are called in Hebrew. In fact, an entire tractate of Talmud, 128 pages in length, is devoted to *brachot*.

On page 120 (Brachot 60b) of the ancient text it is written: "Abeyei said, when a person comes out of a privy, that person should say: Blessed is God who has formed us in wisdom and created in us many orifices and many cavities. It is obvious and known before Your throne of glory that if one of them were to be ruptured or one of them blocked, it would be impossible for a person to survive and stand before You. Blessed are You that heals all flesh and does wonders."

An observant Jew is supposed to recite this blessing in Hebrew after each visit to the bathroom. We young yeshiva students were reminded of our obligation to recite this prayer by the signs that contained its text that were posted just outside the restroom doors.

It is one thing, however, to post these signs and it is quite another to realistically expect preadolescents to have the maturity to realize the wisdom of and the need for reciting a sixteen-hundred-year-old blessing related to bodily functions.

It was not until my second year of medical school that I first began to understand the appropriateness of this short prayer. Pathophysiology brought home to me the terrible consequences of even minor aberrations in the structure and function of the human body. At the very least, I began no longer to take for granted the normalcy of my trips to the bathroom. Instead, I started to realize how many things had to operate just right for these minor interruptions of my daily routine to run smoothly.

I thought of Abayei and his blessing. I recalled my days at yeshiva and remembered how silly that sign outside the bathroom had seemed. But after seeing patients whose lives revolved around their dialysis machines, and others with colostomies and urinary catheters, I realized how wise the rabbi had been.

And then it happened: I began to recite Abayei's *bracha*. At first I had to go back to my *siddur*, the Jewish prayer book, to get the text right. With repetition—and there were many opportunities for a novice to get to know this blessing well—I could recite it fluently and with sincerity and understanding.

Over the years, reciting the *asher yatzar* became for me an opportunity to offer thanks not just for the proper functioning of my excretory organs, but for my overall good health. The text, after all, refers to catastrophic consequences of the rupture or obstruction of any bodily structure, not only those of the urinary or gastrointestinal tract. Could Abayei, for example, have foreseen that "blockage" of the "cavity," or lumen, of the coronary artery would lead to the commonest cause of death in industrialized countries some sixteen centuries later?

I have often wondered if other people also yearn for some way to express gratitude for their good health. Physicians especially, who are exposed daily to the ravages that illness can wreak, must sometimes feel the need to express thanks for being well and thus well-being. Perhaps a generic, nondenominational *asher yatzar* could be composed for those who want to verbalize their gratitude for being blessed with good health.

There was one unforgettable patient whose story reinforced the truth and beauty of the *asher yatzar* for me forever. Josh was a twenty-year-old student who sustained an unstable fracture of his third and fourth cervical vertebrae in a motor vehicle crash. He nearly died from his injury and required emergency intubation and ventilatory support. He was initially totally quadriplegic, except for weak flexion of his right biceps.

A long and difficult period of stabilization and rehabilitation followed. There were promising signs of neurological recovery over the first few months that came suddenly and unexpectedly: movement of a finger here, flexion of a toe there, return of sensation here, adduction of a muscle group there. With incredible courage, hard work, and an excellent physical therapist, Josh improved day by day. In time, and after what seemed like a miracle, he was able to walk slowly with a leg brace and a cane.

But Josh continued to require intermittent catheterization. I knew only too well the problems and perils this young man would face for the rest of his life because of a neurogenic bladder. The urologists were very pessimistic about his chances for not requiring catheterization. They had not seen this occur after a spinal cord injury of this severity.

Then the impossible happened. I was there the day Josh no longer required a urinary catheter. I thought of Abayei's *asher yatzar* prayer. Pointing out that I could not imagine a more meaningful scenario for its recitation, I suggested to Josh, who was also a yeshiva graduate, that he say the prayer. He agreed. As he recited the ancient *bracha*, tears welled up in my eyes. Josh is my son.

Kenneth M. Prager, MD

Standing Up to the Fires of Hate: Sacramento, 1999

"I have bad news," my mother-in-law said to us as Jan and I returned from an early morning walk. "Your synagogue has been torched. The rabbi left his cell phone number. Call him right away."

Our son Max's Bar Mitzvah was to be held the next morning. One hundred and sixty friends and family were either already at the hotel or arriving within the next few hours to celebrate this milestone in our lives. You would think we'd be overcome with tears, but there wasn't time, no time even to go into shock. Immediately we had to start thinking about notifying our guests, caterers, florists. But we had no idea what to tell them. Where, when, and especially how were complete unknowns.

I called the rabbi. "I have Max's Torah," he said immediately. In that one kind sentence, our rabbi communicated to us that our family's simcha, Max's milestone, was foremost in his mind and would go on as planned. "We are working on a change of place right now," he continued.

Within half an hour we learned that the Sacramento Convention Center would be made available to us to hold services and the celebration afterwards. By eleven we were meeting with the center's representatives. They rolled out the red carpet for us, temporarily voiding their contract with their own caterer so that ours could come in. They gave us two beautiful rooms that were more than enough to hold our services and the celebration that would follow. Our Chavurah began calling our guests to inform them of the change in plans. That accomplished, next on the list was Max's final rehearsal.

When Lou Anapolsky, our temple president, got news of the attack, he and his wife, Marlene, rushed to the building and found the firefighters in the last stages of extinguishing the fires in the temple library/administration building. At that point everyone thought the fire was contained in that part of the building. Lou received permission to enter the chapel at the other end of the building and remove the Torah from the chapel ark. Torah scroll safely in the trunk of his car, he watched as the firefighters wound the last of the hoses into their truck. Suddenly, the shrieking of a second alarm split the predawn air.

Racing to the sanctuary, Lou tried to enter to save the Torah scrolls but was pushed back by a wall of thick black smoke. The entire space was lit by the dull orange glow of fire. "Fire in the sanctuary!" he shouted to the firefighters, who immediately began unrolling the hoses they had just stowed into their truck. Once he explained to the fire chief the importance of the Torahs and the need to protect them, if at all possible, from smoke and water damage, all he could do was wait until he was given permission to enter the sanctuary.

The piano at the front of the room was black and charred. The reading table on the bimah, the platform in the synagogue from which the Torah is read, was partially burned, as were the red velvet bimah chairs. The prayer books, Plaut Torah commentaries, and the wooden pews were drenched with accelerant. But the Torahs were safe. For some miraculous reason the fire on the bimah had changed course and traveled away from the ark and the trio of Torah scrolls within. Thanks to Lou's quick thinking, the firefighters were able to rescue all three. Max would still be able to read from one of his temple's Torahs.

It is surreal to think that with calamity all around us, we were still holding to our schedule. I don't think Max really understood the impact of everything that had happened and what it would mean for him over the next twenty-four hours. The cantor welcomed us into his home for the final rehearsal, and at that moment Jan and I were totally overcome. The enormity of what had happened was beginning to sink in. The scroll in the cantor's home was a survivor Torah. It had been brought to the temple by a Holocaust survivor from a synagogue in Czechoslovakia, and you could still see the imprint of a Nazi boot on it.

When the cantor unrolled the Torah, the smell of smoke filled the room. Jan and I were moved to tears. And then Max began chanting. His voice was strong and sure. If ever a statement of invincibility could be made, that was it. At three-thirty in the morning that survivor Torah had been rescued from a burning sanctuary. Barely eight hours later its words were coming to life.

Then, in the time it takes to say *L'hadlik ner shel Shabbat* ("who commanded us to light Shabbat candles"), sunset arrived. We headed to the Convention Center theater for services. Because the other two synagogues in the area had also been firebombed, the service was communitywide. Thousands of people, of different religions and races, had made it their business to worship with us that night. Not only were congregants from three synagogues there, but also our rabbi emeritus, who had flown in from Phoenix, and various dignitaries from the City Council. Also present were many Methodist ministers who were in Sacramento for a convention. They came as a show of strength, and one of the ministers presented the rabbi with a check for $2,500 that had been raised during the day.

Jan, her mom, and my mom rose to light the candles. "May God bless us with Shabbat joy. May God bless us with Shabbat holiness. May God bless us with Shabbat peace." The power of those words reverberated in every corner of the theater. God had blessed us with so much that day. No lives had been lost. In the face of irreparable damage, caring and immediate outreach had been the order of the day.

We were looking forward to this day on so many levels. Our son was about to take his place in a long chain of tradition. My brothers have married non-Jewish women, and so on my side, I am the strongest link in the chain. For Jan, Max's Bar Mitzvah was a statement to her mother that her unbreachable commitment to giving Jan and her brother a Jewish education had not been in vain. My mother-in-law was raised in a small Mississippi town that probably doesn't even exist any more. Despite her own modest Jewish education, she had persevered in passing along to her children their Jewish heritage. Max's becoming a Bar Mitzvah was another tribute to her dedication to her faith.

Our son had had no idea of the number of people who would be at the Friday night service. The numbers overwhelmed him. We knew Saturday would be more manageable and we, and our rabbi, were determined to preserve that sense of a family service. Saturday would be Max's day, the time for him to read his Torah and Haftarah, deliver his talk.

But when we arrived at the Convention Center Saturday morning, Max totally lost his equilibrium. A dozen or so cameramen and news reporters were outside the building interviewing people, angling for shots. A half-dozen Sacramento police officers and a bomb-sniffing dog were present for security. There were chairs set up for five hundred people. We delayed the service a bit to allow Max to steady himself; then the rabbi asked the media to lay low. It was Max's time.

Max did beautifully. You cry at any Bar Mitzvah. You certainly cry at your own child's. Considering what we had been through in the past twenty-four hours, our tears had special impact. Max looked so grown up. He was relaxed, companionable even, with the rabbi. You could feel the warmth flowing between them. Max rose to the challenge of Bar Mitzvah—he mastered his texts and did all that parents hope their children will do, and he did them under extraordinary circumstances.

Ascending the bimah to give our speeches to Max, we were overcome. Through my tears all I could see, in my mind's eye, were the ashes in the library, how they had sparkled in the sunlight as the wind blew them up through the rafters. The rabbi was wearing a kittel, a robe of mourning, instead of his tallis. The tallis, along with the glass *yad* ("hand," pointer used for Torah reading) we were to present to Max, had been destroyed in the fire. Jan said to me later that the kittel was the perfect expression of so much that is Jewish life. We mourn and we celebrate, and sometimes we do both at once.

The weekend of Max's Bar Mitzvah, joy and grief danced on the head of a single pin. Max was the symbol that the hatemongers hadn't won. A few days later over three thousand people of all races, religions, and ages attended a unity rally. We were one. Sacramento, 1999 was not Berlin, 1938.

In addition to the unity rally, a memorial service was held in a park across the street from our synagogue. Days after the fire, people were still shoveling the ashes of the books into boxes to be buried in the cemetery. The air was still filled with the acrid smell of smoke. As we walked, Max found a page from a book. It was singed around the edges and showed a picture of a boy and girl with their arms around each other, walking away from the camera. "It's a symbol, Mom," Max said as he picked it up. "They can burn our books but they can't break our unity." Max now keeps the picture in his room as a reminder.

The vandals reduced our synagogue's entire library—the video collection of Holocaust interviews, the children's section, everything—to a three-foot pile of ash. Prayer books and Torah commentaries, whole offices and precious artifacts were all burned. But as Max recognized, they didn't destroy our community. They failed to gut our faith. If anything, the neo-Nazis' terrorism only strengthened the very community they targeted in their hate-filled crosshairs.

The day after the fires, a Sacramento newspaper printed the Chai ("Life") sign as part of a full-page ad in support of the city's Jews. Readers were urged to cut the Chai out and display it as a sign of solidarity with the Jewish community. Six months after the firebombing, we still see newsprint Chai signs taped to an occasional storefront door or peeking from the windows of a private home. Out of something so unfathomably evil, humanity's goodness blossomed. In the face of great tragedy the people of our city came out by the thousands to show that hate has no home in Sacramento.

As Max grows into manhood, and then fatherhood, the story of his Bar Mitzvah might well become the stuff of legend. "Tell me, Daddy," my grandchild may say one day, "tell me about how they burned your synagogue on your Bar Mitzvah day." And what I hope Max tells my grandchildren is not only the story—the panic, the triumph, the fear, and the joy—but the underlying message. Evil may never be eradicated, but as long as people have courage and stand up to hate, peace and goodness will triumph every time.

Debra B. Darvick

The Clarion Call of Hope

Just a little over five hundred years ago, the Spanish Inquisition was raging. Torquemada, the grand inquisitor, was rounding up hundreds of Jews and burning their bodies in order to save their souls. Many Jews continued their Jewish practices in secret, in closed rooms, and in damp cellars. Though they longed to be in the synagogue to hear the somber blasts of the shofar on Rosh Hashanah, the Jewish New Year, they knew that it would be impossible because the agents of the hated Torquemada were everywhere, and any display of Jewish custom or ritual could betray family and friends. The Jews of 1492 Spain knew that they could not fulfill the sacred commandment to hear the shofar.

But then a rumor began to spread in the street: "Shhh, keep it to yourself." It was in the city of Barcelona that word began to spread of a special concert to be given to Spanish royalty and church officials. Jews bristled at the thought of spending Rosh Hashanah eve, one of the most sacred days of the year, in the Royal Concert Hall, but it was also an opportunity to pretend to their tormentors that no ties remained to the despised religion, Judaism.

An undercurrent, a whisper went around, "Just go, you won't be sorry." The hall was filled to capacity and there were huge crowds outside. Spanish royalty believed that the full house was due to the prominence of the composer, Don Fernando Aguilar. Don Fernando, himself a secret Jew, had announced that on Rosh Hashanah eve he would present a concert featuring instrumental music of various peoples. The compositions were many and the instruments unusual. At the crescendo of one very moving piece came shofar sounds, in full keeping with Jewish tradition.

None of the dignitaries was aware of the significance of the shofar sounds to their Jewish compatriots. All the royalty and the leading figures of the Inquisition were present—they all heard, and saw, but they understood nothing. They could not sense the hidden emotion that electrified the air all around them. Do you wonder why these Jews imperiled their lives to hear this call that we can listen to in this land of freedom?

There have been other times in Jewish history when Jews risked death to hear the sound of the shofar. Among the many things that it has come to signify, it is a reminder of the indomitable spirit that struggles to survive all attempts at subjugation and repression. But there is more to the call of the shofar than just a reminder of the will to survive in a hostile world.

When the shofar sounds, I have listened and I have heard the echoes of our lives. The shofar has spoken to Jews across the span of time and the bridge of years. In the shofar's blasts I have heard the voice of childhood, the dialogue of youth, the wisdom of adulthood, and the sagacity of old age. The shofar is a call to life; it sounds the clarion call of hope.

Rabbi Stephen S. Pearce

A Most Interesting "Amen"

President George W. Bush awarded the Medal of Freedom to Natan Sharansky, among others, at a Hanukkah reception at the White House. After the event at the White House, Sharansky attended a reception at the Israeli embassy, where he told a story about one particular Hanukkah he had spent in the Soviet gulag.

During the year in question, Sharansky celebrated the first few nights of Hanukkah with some non-Jewish prisoners who helped him create a menorah and some candles. However, eventually, the prison guards confiscated his menorah and candles, and he was forbidden to celebrate the holiday further on the theory that "a camp is not a synagogue." Sharansky promptly went on a hunger strike. As he explained today, he would not have done so if he had not already started celebrating the holiday, but once you exercise a freedom you cannot give it back.

Fortunately, the prison officials were expecting the visit of state inspectors from Moscow and did not want Sharansky to be on a hunger strike when the visitors arrived. So the head of the prison asked him what it would take to get him to stop. Sharansky said he would eat only if he were allowed to celebrate the one remaining night of Hanukkah. Sharansky also insisted that he be permitted to do so in the chief's office (a much warmer place than Sharansky's freezing quarters), that the chief bow his head while Sharansky prayed, and that he say "Amen" with Sharansky at the end. The chief asked how long this would take. Sharansky assured him it would not take long.

The chief agreed and the menorah reappeared. Sharansky then said a lengthy prayer, part of which he made up, and which he repeated to keep the service going as long as possible. Since he was praying in Hebrew, the prison chief didn't realize that Sharansky was repeating himself. Soon wax from the candles was dripping onto the chief's beautiful desk.

At the end, Sharansky prayed that he would soon be able to celebrate Hanukkah with his family in Jerusalem and added, "May the day come when all our enemies, who today plan our destruction, will stand before us and hear our prayers and say 'Amen.'" On cue, the chief, relieved that the service had finally ended, echoed "Amen."

Anonymous

Anne Frank's Tree

Trees and agriculture played an important role for the ancient Jewish people. But trees still play an important role in modern Jewish history as well. Twenty-five million people who have read *The Diary of Anne Frank* know what I mean. In her diary, Anne Frank describes how she would look out from the attic—the only window that was not blacked out to prevent anyone from seeing movement in the apartment where the family lived—and there was a tree, a chestnut tree, in front of it. Anne writes in her diary: "Nearly every morning I go to the attic to blow the stuffy air out of my lungs. From my favorite spot on the floor, I look at the blue sky and the bare chestnut tree, on whose branches little raindrops shine, appearing like silver … and at the sea-gulls and other birds as they glide on the wind … as long as this exists, I thought, and I may live to see it, the sunshine, the cloudless skies, while this lasts I cannot be unhappy." It was that tree that gave Anne Frank hope to carry on. Well, you know what happened? That tree, which some estimate to be over 150 years old, developed a disease and this past December it had to be cut down. But one person stepped forward and said, "Let's take a sampling from the old tree and replant it." The sampling has precisely the same DNA as the old tree. It will take many years to match the glory and beauty that Anne Frank's tree possessed, but it keeps alive the memory of Anne Frank and it keeps alive the hope.

When I read this story I thought of a story in the Talmud that tells of a man who was journeying on the road and saw a man planting a carob tree (the carob is one of the popular food items that are eaten on Tu B'Shvat). He asked the man how long it took for the tree to bear fruit. The man replied, "Seventy years." He then further asked him, "Are you certain that you will live another seventy years?" And the man replied, "I found carob trees in the world. As my forefather planted these for me, so I, too, plant these for my children."

Rabbi Mitchell Wohlberg

Tools of the Trade

I grasped the list of patients, fingering the crispness of the sheet that represented my first day of service on the medical wards. I knew that the sheet would soon be crumpled and covered with scrawl, as I scurried about, meeting thirty-six patients, two residents, four interns, and six medical students. But for now, the paper felt cool, controlled, and reliable in my grip.

I was ashamed to admit it, but I was perversely thankful for the numerous comatose patients on my service, because they made rounds faster and left me more time to concentrate on the active GI bleeders, the patients in diabetic ketoacidosis, the ones with gram-negative septicemia, and the ones who spoke English. Mrs. Millstein was one such comatose patient, an elderly woman with Alzheimer's disease who had been sent from her nursing home in Brooklyn after falling and hitting her head. An overflowing hospital census and pure bad luck conspired to land Mrs. Millstein on 7-East, galaxies away, for all practical purposes, from the medical wards on the sixteenth and seventeenth floors. The combination of her flatline mental status and her location in the hinterlands of the hospital ensured that my visits would be brief and infrequent.

The previous attending had told me that he'd spoken with the patient's sister in Florida, the social worker from the nursing home, and the patient's rabbi. All had assured him that Mrs. Millstein would not want any aggressive measures. A Do Not Resuscitate (DNR) order had been signed, and the plan was to put a permanent feeding tube into her stomach and then return the patient to her nursing home.

I poked my head into Mrs. Millstein's room on that first day of service. I saw a white-haired elderly lady, either sleeping or unconscious, but clearly comfortable. She was breathing well and her vital signs were stable. The pen was already in my hand as I stood in the doorway, and I jotted the briefest of notes in the chart. I nodded to myself, checked off the box on my now slightly rumpled list of patients, and continued with my rounds.

I had no plans to call the sister—or to do any additional work for this patient—since the previous attending had settled the main issues. But then the question arose of whether Mrs. Millstein would consider the planned permanent feeding tube to be too invasive; this decision would require consultation with the family. So I dialed the number, and a heavily Eastern European–accented voice met my ears. "Yes, I am Goldie. I am her sister."

My fingers leafed through a medical journal as I explained to Goldie that I was taking care of her sister, that I was the new doctor on the service. She told me that Dora would never want any painful or invasive procedures. We agreed that a permanent feeding tube would not be necessary, that the temporary tube was OK, given Mrs. Millstein's comatose state and probably abbreviated life expectancy, and that the patient would not have any IVs inserted or blood drawn.

The transfer process moved along. Papers were signed and stamped. Transportation services were arranged. Necessary authorizations were obtained. On the day of transfer, as I readied myself to cross one more patient off my now well-worn list, the social worker noted the last set of vital signs. There was a fever.

The great machinations of interhospital transfer ground to a halt: Nobody, it seemed, could be transferred anywhere, anytime, at any stage of illness with a core body temperature other than 98.6°F. Despite my protestations that the patient was already receiving oral antibiotics, that she would not undergo blood cultures or be given IV antibiotics, that she had a DNR order, that the medical team would not do anything about this fever, that in fact it was actually expected that this patient would have a fever, the social worker's rule was ironclad. I would not be able to cross Mrs. Millstein off my list.

It was already quite late in the day, but I decided to call Goldie. I assumed that we could have a quick conversation and that she would agree with my judgment that her sister could indeed return to her nursing home, despite the fluctuations in her body temperature. I glanced at my watch as I dialed her number. Goldie sounded delighted to hear from me. While I packed my stethoscope and crumpled patient list in my bag to leave for the evening, she asked me if Dora looked comfortable. I said yes.

"Dora had such a hard life," Goldie said. "I am much younger, and she was like a mother to me." In the casual voice of someone recounting her afternoon shopping, she added, "We went through the camps together, you know. She took care of me after we lost our parents. She is the reason I survived."

My hands abruptly ceased their activity and drew together with interlocked fingers, awkwardly making their way down into my lap. Goldie and I proceeded to talk for the better part of an hour. Goldie told me about Dora's escape in Europe, their harrowing experiences in the forest, their long journey to America.

After the phone call, I went back to Mrs. Millstein's room. I put down my bag, pulled up the empty visitor's chair, and sat next to Mrs. Millstein. Next to Dora. The sun had already set over the East River, and the darkness from the windows formed a rigid wall of black behind me. I looked at Dora under the fluorescent bed light for what seemed like the first time all month. Her white hair was neatly brushed, and someone had tied it with a fanciful green bow. Her parchment skin folded in fine wrinkles over a tranquil, sleeping face. There was not a trace of agony or stress. Dora's left arm lay open on the bed, atop the neatly tucked white sheet.

There were the numbers.

I hadn't seen them before, but only because I hadn't looked closely. Blue-green numbers, faded with time, but still legible. I had never seen tattooed numbers up close, and I wasn't prepared for the reflexive chill that they would cause. Haltingly, I placed my index finger on the numbers. I had never before touched tattooed numbers, and I feared—I don't know exactly what I feared; the numbers were simply frightening to touch.

I rubbed my fingers over her skin tentatively, and the silkiness of this soft side of her arm—the part that had remained free of a lifetime of sun damage—calmed me. The numbers, of course, did not smudge or disappear with my rubbing, despite my irrational thought that they might. I let out the breath that had been caught inside me and leaned in closer. Her fragrance—a combination of baby powder, Betadine, and the vague sourness of the sick—enveloped me and froze me in that moment.

I was touching Dora's skin, the same skin that had been wrenched by a Nazi soldier, stabbed with a metal plate of tattoo needles, and then abraded with blue ink rubbed into the wounds. I could almost feel the shivers and gooseflesh that must have rippled through the supple skin of a teenage girl, one hand stiffened in a soldier's clench, the other gripping the hand of her little sister.

More than a half-century later, I was standing in the same position and handling the very same flesh as that Nazi. I shuddered to think of the connection that my fingers were making and to know that I now had a link with that German soldier whose name I would never know but whose features and touch, I imagined, were seared into Dora's now-quiescent mind. I was grateful that, between then and now, this skin had at least felt decades of loving touch from a devoted sister and a husband—sixty years of caresses to mitigate, somewhat, the vicious touch that had assaulted the tender underside of this arm and branded it with these numbers. And now I was part of that chain of touch.

The next morning, as I girded myself for battle with the bureaucracy to get my patient transferred back to her nursing home despite her unruly temperature, the intern came up to me and told me that Mrs. Millstein had died at 8:20 the previous night. 8:20 p.m.—thirty minutes after I had left her bedside. I stared at my fingers, rubbing the pads, suddenly entranced by the whorls and creases. Of all the thousands of fingers that had touched Dora in her eighty years of life, from the first that had brought her into this world as a fragile infant, through the many that had touched her with either violence or affection, could mine have been the last? These callused bits of skin that I scrub daily and unthinkingly with desiccating antimicrobial soap, that I sheathe and unsheathe with airless latex gloves, that casually grasp my ever-crumpling list of patients may have been the end of this particular chain.

Many industries have been automated, and medicine is no exception. I can't deny the increased efficiency provided by computerized lab results, telemetry monitoring, and wireless e-mail. But no matter how much our field is pushed to streamline and to maximize efficiency, there is an asymptotic limit. In the end, medicine will always be about one patient and one physician together in one room, connecting through the most basic of communication systems: touch. In an age of breathless innovation, this system is almost antediluvian. But medicine simply cannot be automated beyond this point.

Every so often, when the chaos of clinic and ward life becomes overwhelming, I dump my computerized list of patients, the review article I've been reading, my Palm Pilot, my triplicate prescription pad, and whatever else I happen to be carrying onto the nearest table. I place my hands flat on the surface, absorb its comforting smoothness, then spread my fingers and contemplate their outlines. These—more than our stethoscopes, more than our textbooks, more than our clinical practice guidelines—are our most fundamental diagnostic and therapeutic tools. I realize that I am grateful for the inefficiencies of medicine and for their steadfast ineradicability.

And then I gather up my other tools, sigh, and move on.

Danielle Ofri, MD, PhD

Enough

It was near the end of the war, maybe late 1944 or early 1945. After all the time in the concentration camps, I couldn't tell you what year it was, let alone what day or month. But it was near the end, and I was in Bergen-Belsen. I had also been in Auschwitz for a short while. I had spent the first two years of the war making uniforms and clothes for the Germans in Plaszow, the labor camp near Krakow, where I grew up. I was young and in good physical shape then. Otherwise I would have been killed.

In Bergen-Belsen I got very weak and was put in a typhus block with about two thousand other girls. All around me everyone was sick. We slept on the cold, hard floors, we ran high fevers, and we were dying. The Germans hadn't fed us for a long time, and everyone was starving.

But I never felt hungry. My mother, who was a holy woman, I always thought, had been killed by the Germans earlier in the war, along with my father, my first husband, and my eight brothers. She was dead, but she was still able to help me, as she always did. At night, maybe because I had such a high fever, maybe not, I would dream that my mother came to me and fed me. She gave me all the wonderful foods I loved. I ate and ate till I was full. In the dream, she even told me to give some of the extra food to my youngest brother. There was so much. Those dreams kept me alive. The Germans finally began feeding people. They gave everyone a soup of carrots, potatoes, and ground glass, which they made to seem like flour. I think by then they knew they were going to lose the war and they wanted to destroy the evidence of what they had done before the Allies came.

You needed a cup to put your soup in. I didn't have a cup. A friend of mine said she would get one for both of us. I told her, "No, thank you, my mother gives me enough food."

My friend died the next day. So did most of the other girls in the block. After one cup, they suffered great pains. With two cups, they dropped dead.

I was lucky. I didn't eat. I survived. My mother gave me enough.

Frieda Friedman

I Danced at the Wedding of Sharansky's Daughter

It was a dream come true. There beneath the *chuppah* (wedding canopy) stood Rachel Sharansky, daughter of Natan and Avital Sharansky, with her beloved, Micha Danziger.

The hills of Jerusalem encircled us, like a wedding ring around the whole city. Jerusalem's chilly winter days took a respite as the sun shone brightly; even the weather knew it was the time to feel the warmth and love of bride and groom.

Attending the wedding were many heroes of the Soviet Jewry movement, proud Jews who had struggled against the Soviet regime. There was Zev Dashevsky, the great Moscow Hebrew teacher, and Yosef Begun, one of the longest-serving prisoners of Zion.

Activists from the West who did all they could to free Soviet Jewry were there as well: former Union of Councils president Stuart Wurtman; Jerry Stern, who took out the first ad publicizing Natan's plight; Gordy Zacks, a friend of the elder George Bush, who intervened on many occasions for Avital.

Also taking part in the great joy was the team of unknown Israelis who, while never seeking glory, were active throughout the struggle. Rabbi Zvi Tau, who orchestrated the team. Eli Sadan, the brilliant ideologue who inspired Avital. And Avi Maoz, Avital's indefatigable and savvy right hand.

There, too, were the souls of those who had made this moment happen but were sadly not present to join in the simcha. Ida Milgrom, Natan's mother, the woman who never caved in to Soviet brutality and who gave Natan the strength never to give up. And Avital's brother, Mikhail Stieglitz, a forceful figure for Natan throughout the world, an Israeli army officer who died at too young an age.

Beneath the *chuppah* Natan recalled his wedding to Avital thirty-four years earlier. It was held in a small room with barely a *minyan* (quorum of ten) present. Natan recounted that it had all seemed incomprehensible to him as the rabbi read the blessings and carried out the wedding ceremony, but when the time came to break the glass, it all became clear.

"The dream of immigrating to Israel, building Jerusalem, was our hope," he explained.

Turning to Rachel and Micha, both just twenty-one years old, Natan pointed out that in certain ways the struggle today is much greater than the one he and Avital experienced, since the dream of Jerusalem and the responsibility to protect and defend the holy city is more complex.

The wedding took place at Kibbutz Ramat Rachel just before the Shabbat on which we read the refrain that resounded throughout the Soviet Jewry movement: "*Shalach et Ami*—Let My People Go."

The last blessing under the *chuppah*, sung to Shlomo Carlebach's tender tune, was the Shabbat welcome prayer "*Lecha Dodi*—Come my beloved to greet the bride."

This time the words of that blessing jumped from the page. The hills of Jerusalem resonated with song, and the countless words describing joy of bride and groom, which at times seem repetitious, all made sense; no words were sufficient to express that happiness.

As we sang, Avital shed tears. Not the tears of sadness she shed when advocating for Natan, tears and resolve that moved the world. Tears of joy and happiness.

And then we danced. First the men and women were separated by a *mechitza* (divider), but soon Natan and Micha joined Rachel and her sister Chana, and Avital and Micha's parents, and all danced together.

What a far cry from that wedding thirty-four years ago in Moscow when Natan and Avital were forcibly separated the following day. They would not see each other for another twelve years, including nearly nine that Natan spent in the gulag.

When they were finally reunited, Natan's first words to Avital were, "I'm sorry I'm late." For their children there would be no such separation, no such apologies.

Avital was once asked whether she had ever written to Soviet officials after Natan's release. She replied that she had sent them pictures of each of the girls after they were born. One wonders if Avital had also sent to any of the tormentors over whom Natan had triumphed an invitation to Rachel's wedding. For those blessed to be there, the Sharansky wedding was a microcosm of Jewish history. There have been many forces of evil that have bedeviled *Am Yisrael,* and yet, the good has prevailed.

Off to one side in the wedding hall, in a wheelchair, was Yeshayahu Nebenzahl, an accomplished professor in Israel. We danced a bit, total strangers but brothers in joy.

He whispered to me: "When I come to heaven they'll ask me, "What have I done in life?' I'll be able to answer, 'I danced at the wedding of Sharansky's daughter.'"

Rabbi Avi Weiss

The following remarks were given by Natan Sharansky under the chuppah *(wedding canopy) of his daughter, Rachel, at her wedding.*

In Jewish tradition after *kiddushin* ("betrothal") and *chuppah* we take one step back, look at our personal simcha from a broader perspective, and break a glass in memory of Jerusalem. And here I want to say a few words.

This moment takes me back to our *chuppah,* Avital's and mine, thirty-four years ago. It was in a small, one-room Moscow apartment where four friends held a sheet above our heads. The number of guests hardly reached a *minyan*.

It was the first *chuppah* in our lives that we ever saw and all that we could do was simply repeat after the rabbi every move and every word—while hardly understanding many of them.

But when it came to breaking the glass, the rabbi spoke about Jerusalem and we became instantly reconnected to our reality. It was so obvious to us that we were in the very last stages, the final meters, of the thousands of years of struggle to return to Jerusalem. And this *chuppah*, ours, invigorated our determination to win this battle and made us feel powerful.

Today, we are standing here: You, Rachel, are the first sabra in the Sharansky family, and you, Micha, the first new immigrant in the Danzinger family. And we are in Jerusalem! The dream has come true.

But if we are here already, in the unified capital of the reborn Jewish state, what is the meaning today of breaking the glass? What is the dream we still yearn for? What is our—your—challenge?

When I compare your *chuppah* and our *chuppah*, I think that the challenge that you face is much more difficult. Our aim was so simple and so clear. We had to win the battle and nothing could deter us.

Today, on the one hand you have to be builders and guardians of Jerusalem, and at the same time guardians of the idea of Jerusalem. You have to physically build the earthly Jerusalem and keep alive the power, energy, and uniqueness of the heavenly Jerusalem.

The power of unity and connection to the generations of our people is in heavenly Jerusalem, in *Yerushalayim shel ma'ala*.

The two of you met a year ago and immediately starting talking, and haven't stopped talking till today. And it was clear to all of us who enjoyed watching the beauty and intellectual and spiritual power of your talks that this union was made in the heavens.

Now that you are turning this union into a material and physical one and building your home in Jerusalem, keep the spiritual power of this past year throughout your life.

For Baba Ida, your birth, Rachel, was the most powerful proof of our victory over our enemies. She wanted to send your picture to the whole world, but first and foremost to the enemy.

I am sure that for Savta Ida and Savta Grace—who was excited to get the news about the impending wedding just before she left us—as well as for all the generations of the Danzinger, Horowitz, Sharansky, Stieglitz, and Milgrom families—this *chuppah* is their victory. It is the victory of all the generations who were true to the Jewish people's oath of Jerusalem.

Now let's break the glass.

Continuity and Tradition

*O*ne of the touching ceremonies that occurs on the pulpit of a synagogue, on a Shabbat morning when a young person becomes a Bar or Bat Mitzvah, is the moment when the scroll of the Torah is removed from the Holy Ark, and passed from generation to generation. The rabbi passes it to the grandparents, from them to the parents, and finally to the Bar or Bat Mitzvah. Often there are tears in the congregation as they witness this symbolic transmission of tradition.

This is the theme of this section—honoring the past and paying tribute to those whose turn comes next. It is found when a parent sings a Yiddish lullaby to their child, which in turn is sung to the next generation, and so on and so on. It is the memories that sanctify each Jewish home that have made Jewish history glow with holiness and sweetness. The sights, sounds, and smells of the Old World transform our present universe into a brave new world filled with love, attachment, and community.

The Lullaby

Here is a story of remembrance—a lullaby I learned from my father. Lullabies are very special songs. They stay with us throughout our lives and bring back to us warmth, good feelings, our childhood homes, and our parents' voices.

Elie Wiesel wrote a beautiful essay, called "Echoes of Yesterday," for the Yeshiva University Centennial, in which he recalls a lullaby, *"Oifn pripitchik."* He writes: " '*Oifn pripitchik brennt a feierl.*' I remember the lullaby, so beautiful and moving. It accompanies me and haunts me. Thanks to it, words start singing on my lips and on my pen.

"I recall my teacher and his pupils. I recall their shadows on the wall. Their melancholy and fervent voices reach me from far, very far away, from the other side of a vanished world. I look there for my own voice with an inexpressible anguish."

In the nineteenth century, Yiddish lullabies were numerous and expressed the dreams and aspirations of the Jewish mother in the Czarist Pale of the Settlement. The lullaby that my father's mother sang to him in Lithuania was called *"Az ikh volt gehat dem Keiser's oitzres"*—If I could have had all the king's treasure." It was written by the folk poet Mikhl Gordon (1823–1890), who was born in Vilna. Gordon sometimes combined his own melodies with his poetry; at other times he set the written text to music. Whichever may be the case, the lullaby appeared as a folk song in his first anonymous collection in 1868 and was sung throughout Russia during the later part of the nineteenth century.

This is my family lullaby story.

My father, Cantor Samuel E. Manchester, came to America at the turn of the twentieth century. He was born about 1878 in Sapieshok, a village near Kovno, in Lithuania, and later studied with his father, who was a *hazen-shohet-mohel* (cantor, ritual slaughterer, and circumcisor). At sixteen, my father married, had children soon after, and came to America, where he served as *hazen-shohet-mohel* in several cities. In 1929, he became a widower. The following year he met and married Dora Markman, an immigrant from Lepl in White Russia. When they married, they moved to New London, Connecticut, where I was born four years later.

When I was about eight years old, I began to take piano lessons. The first piece of music my father put on the piano for me to learn was Beethoven's *Moonlight Sonata*. I did learn to play it but not for another few years.

Then one day, I remember, my father returned from a trip to New York City, where he had gone to buy some music at the Metro Music Company on Second Avenue and to bring them more copies of his book of cantorial compositions, *Kol Rinah Utfilah*. With great excitement he took a book out of his suitcase, *Jewish Folk Songs*, opened it to page 29, and announced, "This is the lullaby my mama sang to me when I was a child. It's a lullaby that's almost a hundred years old." And he sang the lullaby in Yiddish:

> *Az ikh volt gehat dem keiser's oitzres,*
> *Mit zain ganze melikhe.*
> *Volt dos bai mir nit geven azoi nikhe.*
> *Vi du bist bai mir nikhe, main kind, main shain.*
> *Az ikh derzei dikh, dukht zikh mir,*
> *Di ganze velt iz main.*
>
> *Shlof main kind, shlof main kind,*
> *Zolst lang leben un zain gezunt.*

> *If I could have had all the king's treasure*
> *And all of his dominions,*
> *It would never bring me as much pleasure*
> *As you now bring me pleasure, my child, my*
>   *light!*
> *When I see your face, then I feel*
> *The whole wide world is bright.*
> *Sleep, my child, sleep, my child;*
> *May life be long and fortune ever smile.*

He sang it with his eyes closed, as if he were back in his childhood once again, with his mama singing it. When he had finished, he opened his eyes, reoriented himself, and just smiled. Then he said to me, "Peninnah (my name is also his mama's name), bring this to your piano teacher; she should teach you to play it on the piano."

I brought the piece to my teacher, and I soon learned to play it and to sing it. I would often play it for my father on our mahogany Marshall and Mendel upright piano, which stood majestically in our living room, so he would sing it for me, over and over. I loved the words and the tune—the lullaby of a grandmother I never met.

Years later, after I had finished college and married, I sang this lullaby to my two children, Rebecca and Michael, as I tucked them in and kissed them good-night. Even when they had grown beyond early childhood, they still wanted to hear the lullaby, especially when they didn't feel well or needed some extra attention. I would sit on the edge of their beds to talk, and they would say, "Sing *der zade's* lullaby to me—sing Grandpa's lullaby." And I would sing it to them.

Years later, when my son had come home from college, he came to my bedroom one morning. Seeing that I was asleep, he tiptoed into the room. I sensed someone was there, but I kept my eyes closed and pretended to be asleep. Michael sat on the edge of my bed, pulled the blanket up closer under my chin, and sang, *Shlof main kind, shlof main kind, Zolst lang leben, un zain gezunt.*

That lullaby is now his, and it's my daughter's, too. And someday, God willing, it will belong to their children, and to their children's children, and it will live for another hundred years—and hopefully for hundreds of years and even longer. And so must our stories!

Peninnah Schram

Kaddish in Cambodia

On the eighteenth day of the Hebrew month of Shevat I found myself in the dusty, noisy village of Aranyaprathet, on the border between Cambodia and Thailand, searching desperately for nine more Jews.

I had *yahrzeit* for my father, and I needed a *minyan* so that I could say *Kaddish*. I would have found a *minyan* easily enough in Bangkok. There are about fifty Jewish families in the community there, plus twenty Israeli embassy families, so there would have been no problem about finding ten men for *Minchah*. But in Aranyaprathet?

I had gone there to take part in a March for the Survival of Cambodia organized by the International Rescue Committee and Doctors Without Borders. There were philosophers, novelists, parliamentarians, and journalists—myriad journalists. But how was I to find out who might be able to help me with my problem?

I would have liked to telephone one of my rabbi friends in New York or Jerusalem and ask his advice on the halachic aspects of the matter. What did one do in such a case? Should one observe the *yahrzeit* the following day, or the following week? But I was afraid of being rebuked and of being asked why I had gone to Thailand precisely on that day, when I should have been in synagogue.

I would have justified myself by saying that I had simply been unable to refuse. How could I refuse when so many men and women were dying of hunger and disease? I had seen on television what the Cambodian refugees looked like when they arrived in Thailand—walking skeletons with somber eyes, crazy with fear. I had seen a mother carrying her dead child, and I had seen creatures dragging themselves along the ground, resigned to never again being able to stand upright. How could a Jew like myself, with experiences and memories like mine, stay at home and not go to the aid of an entire people? Some will say to me, Yes, but when you needed help, nobody came forward. True, but it is *because* nobody came forward to help me that I felt it my duty to help these victims.

As a Jew I felt the need to tell these despairing men and women that we understood them; that we shared their pain; that we understood their distress because we remembered a time when we as Jews confronted total indifference....

Of course, there is no comparison. The event which left its mark on my generation defies analogy. Those who talk about "Auschwitz in Asia" and the "Cambodian Holocaust" do not know what they are talking about. Auschwitz can and should serve as a frame of reference, but that is all.

So there I was in Thailand, in Aranyaprathet, with a group of men and women of goodwill seeking to feed, heal, save Cambodians—while I strove to get a *minyan* together because, of all the days of the year, the eighteenth day of Shevat is the one that is most full of meaning and dark memories for me.

Rabbi Marc Tanenbaum was a member of the American delegation. Now I needed only eight more. Leo Cherne, the president of the International Rescue Committee, was there as well. Only seven more to find.

Then I spotted the well-known Soviet dissident, Alexander Ginsburg, and rushed over to him. Would he agree to help me make up a *minyan*? He looked at me uncomprehendingly. He must have thought I was mad. A *minyan*? What is a *minyan*? I explained: a religious service. Now he surely did not understand. A religious service? Here, by the mined bridge separating Thailand and Cambodia? Right in the middle of a demonstration of international solidarity? I began all over again to explain the significance of a *minyan*. But in vain. Alexander Ginsburg is not a Jew; he is a convert to the Russian Orthodox Church. I still had seven to find.

Suddenly, I caught sight of the young French philosopher Bernard-Henri Levy, who was making a statement for television. Only six more to find. Farther on, I found the French novelist Guy Suares. Then a doctor from Toulouse joined us, followed by Henry Kamm, of the *New York Times*. Another doctor came over. At last there were ten of us. There, in the midst of all the commotion, a few yards from the Cambodian frontier, we recited the customary prayers, and I intoned *Kaddish*, my voice trembling.

Then, suddenly, from somewhere behind me, came the voice of a man still young, repeating the words after me, blessing and glorifying the Master of the Universe. He had tears in his eyes, that young Jew. "For whom are you saying *Kaddish?*" I asked him. "For your father?" "No." "For your mother?" "No."

He grew reflective and looked toward the frontier. "It is for them," he said.

Elie Wiesel

A Grandfather Remembers

I had slept fitfully. Periodically, every fifteen minutes or so, I checked the luminous dial to see if it was time to get up. Of course I had set the alarm, but who can trust a mechanical contraption when a crucial appointment has to be met punctually on the morrow? It was to be one of the biggest assignments I had carried in a long time. I was going to drive Elisha and two of his nursery school classmates to Solomon Schechter Day School (a religious all-day Jewish school for intensive Jewish education). Elisha is special at Solomon Schechter School. He is the first student who is a child of a graduate of the same school. With him, Solomon Schechter begins educating a second generation of Jewish youngsters to know and love their heritage. Being Elisha's driver would be no small honor.

After several hours of "wait-watching"—waiting and watching—I finally decided it wasn't worth the struggle and got up. There was enough time to perform all my exercises, physical and spiritual, at a leisurely pace and still ring the doorbell of the first five-year-old passenger at 7:30 a.m.

"Who are you?" a mother shouted at me through the windowpane of the door she kept suspiciously bolted.

"I'm Elisha's grandfather," I shouted back. "I'm the carpool driver today." Jeremy Schneider whimpered reluctantly, and finally agreed to go with the stranger only when I promised him a special surprise in the car, a surprise that he would be the first to see. I kept my promise to Jeremy. I showed him an etrog (the citron fruit used at the Jewish holiday of Sukkot) that we had kept from the previous year. It had shrunk to one-fifth its size, its skin was wrinkled and shriveled, its color had turned from golden yellow to mournful brown. Jeremy admitted he had never in his "whole life" seen such an etrog.

As we moved along toward Elisha's house, I learned a lot about Jeremy. He would rather stay home. He loved his toys. He enjoyed playing with his younger sister, but he also enjoyed playing by himself. "I like myself," he explained matter-of-factly. I could not suppress the silent prayer that he would go through life liking himself. "You're lucky," I said to Jeremy. "It's important to like yourself because wherever you go, you are going to take yourself along with you." "I know," said Jeremy, sounding much older than his years.

Elisha's door was open, announcing to the driver that his arrival was not unexpected. He greeted me with a casual wave of the hand. I tried very hard to be equally casual, as though I had been doing this every morning for twelve consecutive years. I tried not to betray the excitement of doing for Elisha for the first time what I had done for his mother not so many years before. A last-minute check of his lunch bag, a reminder to take along the birthday present for a classmate, a soft hug and kiss from his mother, and the passenger was tucked into the back of the car.

Susie Spodek was the third stop. She was quite surprised to find me at her door so early in the morning. When I told her that I was the driver of the day, a smile broke on her beautiful face and joyously she joined the men in the back of the car. Susie had a lot to tell us about life in India. She had been born there and spent the last two years there. The only problem that Susie could find with India was that there were a lot of kids who didn't speak English, but otherwise it was really nice and friendly and there was even a synagogue there.

The subject quickly changed to little sisters and, wonderful to relate, all three passengers had one and were all rather proud of their younger siblings. They took turns boasting of their sisters' most recent accomplishments.

A little probing revealed that they each knew the Hebrew prayer-song about peace, *"Oseh Shalom,"* and the singing of it occupied the rest of the trip. We were in the middle of the fourteenth round when we pulled into the school driveway. I released my passengers and they were quickly swallowed up by their classmates. Elisha never turned around. It was just as well. He wouldn't have understood why his grandfather was crying.

Rabbi Sidney Greenberg

My Father and the Priest

Almost thirty years ago, my father, Rabbi Dovid Schochet, was asked to lecture to a group of Jewish and non-Jewish people in the neighboring city of Buffalo. He decided to focus his lecture on the theme of charity, due to its universal application to both Jews and gentiles.

My father began with the following story.

A wealthy individual who never contributed to charity lived during the time of Rabbi Yom Tov Lipman Heller, universally known as the "Tosfos Yom Tov," the name of his most distinguished publication, a popular commentary on the Mishnah. After this miser died, the Chevra Kaddisha (the society responsible for the burial and performing the rites on the body) felt that he was unworthy of being interred next to any upright and respectable individual and buried him, instead, in the area of the cemetery called *hekdesh*, reserved for society's outcasts and destitute.

A few days after the funeral, a tumult developed in Prague. The butcher and baker, two prominent members of the community, who had hitherto been extremely charitable, suddenly stopped distributing their funds. The poor people, who had relied on the benevolent pair for their sustenance, now were in a state of uproar.

Emotions ran so deep that the matter was finally brought before the Tosfos Yom Tov. He asked the two why they had so abruptly terminated their worthy acts. They replied: "In the past this 'miser' would continuously supply us with funds for charity. He strongly warned us, however, not to disclose our source, since he wanted the great merit of performing the mitzvah in a hidden manner. Now that he is dead, unfortunately, we are no longer able to continue."

Awed by the unassuming "miser's" behavior, the Tosfos Yom Tov requested that he be buried next to this humble individual, even though this meant being interred in a disreputable section of the cemetery.

As my father concluded his lecture, a member of the audience, who happened to be a priest, approached him and requested that he repeat the story. My father suggested they meet the following day.

Thinking that the matter would be forgotten, my father was surprised when, at the appointed hour, the priest actually arrived at my father's hotel. The priest, once again, pleaded with my father to repeat the story.

My father obliged, but was astounded when, after concluding the story a second time, the priest seemed terribly distraught and begged him to repeat it yet again. At this point, the priest was nervously pacing back and forth across the room.

Finally, he divulged the reason for his agitation. He turned to my father and confessed, "Rabbi Schochet, that charitable man in the story was my ancestor."

Skeptically, my father calmed the young man, saying that there was absolutely no connection between him and the story, which took place over one hundred years ago. "Furthermore," he told him, "you are a gentile, while this man was Jewish."

The priest looked intently at my father and whispered, "Rabbi, now I have a story to tell you!" He began by describing his background. He had grown up in the State of Tennessee. His father was a major in the U.S. Army during the Second World War. Overseas, in Europe, his father had met a Jewish girl and fallen in love. He brought her back home as his war bride and no one knew of her background. A short time after their marriage, the couple was blessed with a child, whom they devoutly raised in the Catholic tradition. The child grew up and attended a seminary, where he eventually trained to become a priest.

In his early adulthood, the priest's mother died prematurely. At her deathbed, she disclosed her secret identity to her completely baffled son. After reciting the *Shema* prayer, she confessed, "I want you to know that you are Jewish." She informed him of his heritage and that his great-grandfather was buried next to a great sage called the Tosfos Yom Tov. She then recounted, almost verbatim, the story that my father had told in his lecture.

At the time, the priest imagined that his mother was delirious. Although he felt uneasy by his mother's parting words, it was only a temporary, fleeting emotion. As he got on with his life, he soon forgot the entire episode and lost interest in the subject.

"Rabbi," cried the priest, in a state of complete emotional upheaval, "you have just repeated this story, detail for detail. You have reminded me of my mother's parting words, and that the story must be true. Yet what am I to do? I am a reputable priest with a large congregation of devoted followers."

My father offered to assist him in any way. He emphasized to him, however, that, according to Judaism, he was indeed Jewish. He encouraged him to explore his heritage, and put him in contact with people in his city who could guide him. With that, the weary, newly found Jew departed. My father had no future correspondence with this man, and heard no further from him.

Several years ago, on a visit to Israel, a bearded, religious Jew approached my father at the Western Wall, the Kotel, and wished him "Shalom Aleichem." My father didn't recognize the individual and was completely taken aback when the man exclaimed, "Don't you recognize me, Rabbi Schochet? I am the former priest whom you met in Buffalo!" He continued, "A Jew is never completely lost from his people."

Chana Weisberg

The Cardinal Who Spoke Yiddish

The following commentary was given by Scott Simon on NPR radio, Saturday morning, August 11, 2007.

"There used to be a joke in Paris, what is the difference between the chief rabbi in France and the cardinal of Paris?"

The cardinal speaks Yiddish!

Jean-Marie Cardinal Lustiger was buried yesterday; he died this week of cancer. He was born almost eighty-one years ago to Polish parents who ran a dress shop in Paris. When the German army marched in, his parents sent him and his sister into hiding with a Catholic family in Orleans. Their mother was captured and sent to Auschwitz.

In 1999, as cardinal of Paris, Jean-Marie Lustiger took part in reading the names of France's day of remembrance of Jews who had been deported and murdered. He came to the name Gesele Lustiger, paused, teared, and said, "My mama."

The effect in France during a time of revived anti-Semitism was electric.

He was just thirteen and in hiding when he converted to Catholicism, not to escape the Nazis, he always said, because no Jew could escape by conversion, and not out of trauma, he said. Among his most controversial observations: "I was born Jewish and so I remain, even if that is unacceptable for many. For me the vocation of Israel is bringing light to the goyim. That is my hope and I believe that Christianity is the means for achieving it." There were a great number of rabbis who consider his conversion a betrayal.

Especially after so many European Jews had so narrowly escaped extinction, Cardinal Lustiger replied, "To say that I am no longer a Jew is like denying my father and mother, my grandfathers and grandmothers. I am as Jewish as all other members of my family who were butchered in Auschwitz and other camps."

He confessed to a biographer that he had a spiritual crisis in the 1970s, provoked by persistent anti-Semitism in France. He studied Hebrew, and considered emigrating. He said, "I thought that I had finished what I had to do here," he explained, "and I might find new meaning in Israel." But just at that time the pope appointed him bishop of Orleans. He found purpose, he said, in the plight of immigrant workers. Then he was elevated to cardinal.

The Archbishop of Paris

Jean-Marie Lustiger was close to the pope. They shared a doctrinal conservatism. He also battled bigotry and totalitarianism. For years Cardinal Lustiger's name was among those considered to succeed John Paul. Without putting himself forth, the cardinal joked that few things would bedevil bigots more than a Jewish pope. They don't like to admit it, he said, but what Christians believe, they got—through Jews.

The funeral for Cardinal Lustiger began at Notre Dame Cathedral yesterday, with the chanting of *Kaddish*, the Jewish prayer for the dead.

Scott Simon

Five Gold Bangles and a
World of Difference

The morning of my wedding day, my mother called me into her bedroom. "Come sit with me," she said quietly, patting the spot next to her on the bed. I sat down beside her, the softness of the mattress causing our shoulders to touch. She turned her face toward mine, looking happier than I had seen her look in years. I attributed it to the fact that her almost-thirty-year-old daughter was finally getting married. Smiling, she handed me a box.

"Open it," she urged. Inside the box were five beautiful, gold-filigree bangle bracelets of different patterns. The gold was unlike any I had ever seen and the bracelets warmed as I held them in my hands. They were not new, their shapes having been altered from perfect circles to imperfect ones by the wrists they had adorned.

I turned them over in my hands and, one by one, slid them on my right arm. They were truly lovely. "Oh, Mom, I love them! Where did you get them?"

She answered by telling me a story about my great-grandmother, Jamilla Danino, who, at the age of twelve, married a man more than three times her age to become his second wife. Born in 1882 to a poor family in Alexandria, Egypt, she had no choice but to respect the marriage arrangement her parents had made. One afternoon her intended arrived with gifts, and a week later she left on a ship with her new husband for Haifa, never to see her parents again. The bracelets on my arm were the same ones that Jamilla had received from her husband as an engagement gift.

Living in the twenty-first century, it is hard to fathom an arrangement like the one Jamilla's parents made for her. I barely get to meet the boys my daughter, Lauren, dates, let alone have the deciding vote as to whom she chooses to marry. And I quiver at the idea that I might never see Lauren again or be able to cuddle my grandchildren on my lap.

Yet as recently as the early 1900s, my great-grandmother was forced to live side by side with the other woman who shared her husband's bed but could not give him a child. For Sephardi Jews who lived in communities influenced by Islam—such as Egypt, Yemen, Morocco, and Turkey—a polygamous marriage like Jamilla's was an accepted practice.

The Bible is filled with stories of unhappiness and the problems that exist in a polygamous marriage: Sarah was derided by Hagar because she couldn't have a child, Leah was jealous of Rachel because Jacob loved her more, and Solomon's many wives brought idolatry into the Land of Israel. Jamilla suffered a similar fate when, at the tender age of thirteen, she gave birth to a son, Albert. She was scorned by the first wife and suffered terribly at her hands. What saved Jamilla during those difficult years were her wit, her wisdom, and her undying love for her son, my grandfather.

The laws on polygamy, which often created hardship and injustice for women throughout Jewish history, have thankfully changed. In Eastern Europe, Rabbi Gershom decreed a ban on polygamy in the tenth century, but Sephardi Jews did not accept it. When Israel was created in 1948, in order to accommodate its Sephardi immigrants, the government honored existing polygamous marriages but forbade future ones. Today, the ban on polygamy is universally accepted in the Jewish world.

I treasure wearing my gold bracelets for many reasons. They help me remember my great-grandmother, a woman whose courage, strength, and devotion carried her through a lifetime of struggle. They remind me of my mother, who wore them as a young girl when she was raised by Jamilla as a result of her own parents' untimely deaths. And they give me a sense of optimism about our future as Jews. For it is through the wisdom of the Jewish tradition and its ability to change laws that are patently unfair or result in hardship and injustice that our greatest hope for the future lies.

Amy Hirshberg Lederman

The Reunion

The reunion was planned for four years. Two cousins and I outlined ambitious plans to collect Wolpes for an unprecedented family gathering. The relationship of the three of us illustrated, in microcosm, the peculiar structure of our family. Don, Myra, and I had no idea how we were related except that we had mutual relatives. Although now very close, we had connected by chance only in our adult years. For some reason, the first generation of immigrant Wolpes did not keep in touch. There were small pockets of close family members, but the wider ties were missing.

The reunion was designed to re-create that connection. The uniqueness of our name aided our search. We utilized the magic of the Internet and the network expanded dramatically. Replies poured in from throughout the world. Our reunion would consist of Wolpes from the United States, Canada, Israel, Australia, South Africa, Europe—all over. Some carried the family name and others identified through the memory of a Wolpe grandparent or maternal relative. Washington, D.C., was chosen as the venue for the gathering.

A full program was created and it included one unique feature. We would be the first family to have our concluding session at the Holocaust Museum. That was permitted, as the major exhibition at the time in the museum dealt with the city of Kovno, Lithuania. Our family originated in a suburb of Kovno and one of our cousins was being honored. Marcia was an honoree, as she was among a small group of Jews who had survived the entire Nazi horror in the Kovno ghetto.

The first days of the reunion were spectacular. Connections were made and we rejoiced in our expanding relationships. A young man had utilized interviews and genealogical studies to create family trees. We looked for common features, names, and characteristics among the group that was changing from strangers to "new relatives" of interest and affection.

As one unit, we gathered in the museum's auditorium for a farewell session. The three chairpeople made appropriate remarks, and then Marcia was introduced. She stood for a moment at the podium, waiting for the receptive applause to subside. Small in stature, she exhibited a quiet charm and command that soon captured the listeners. She began with a description of the Kovno of her childhood. The family was large and prominent; its history in that area went back many centuries. Kovno was a center of Jewish piety and culture, while it suffered from the familiar story of shtetl poverty and bigotry. It all came to a horrible end with the arrival of Nazi forces.

The terror began immediately. Mass killings at the hands of the Nazis and their Lithuanian allies resounded in the surrounding fields. Deportations to the death camp soon followed, and the Kovno ghetto retained only those Jews who were strong enough for manual labor. Those few included Marcia and her sister. The daily horrors are familiar stories and almost beyond description. For amusement, the demonic Nazis would march the Kovno Jews before a firing squad. Most of the time, their rifles contained blanks, and the victims survived. However, to maintain the tension and authenticity of the lethal game, there were sporadic executions.

We listened with morbid fascination. Racing through every mind was the realization that our children and we could have suffered the same horrors. The good fortune of immigration had spared us Marcia's fate.

The Russian armies began their sweep westward in late 1944. They approached the Baltics, and it was clear that in a short amount of time they would reach Lithuania. The Germans were determined to leave no witnesses. One morning, they took Marcia, her sister, and other survivors onto boats from which they were cast into the North Sea. A British gunboat was in the area and rushed to the rescue. The Nazis fled, and the rescuers began to pull the struggling Jews from the water. Marcia held her sister in her arms. As she was being helped into the boat, her sister slipped from her arms and drowned.

The silence in the room was broken only by audible sobs. No eye was without mist. Marcia's pause was dramatic.

"I then had to figure out how I could take revenge on these monsters."

Our attention was complete.

"I decided to become a Hebrew teacher."

Rabbi Gerald I. Wolpe

December Dilemma? Humbug!

I must admit that I love December, this thirty-one-day excursion into a time when all of a sudden, everyone seems to love one another. Shopping malls are decked out with colorful holiday decorations. And I love the music, too: "Joy to the World," "Chestnuts Roasting on an Open Fire …"

Oh, wait a moment; it's my phone.

"Hi, Mrs. O'Cohen. Have you spoken to the teacher? OK, I'll see what I can do. I'll get back to you as soon as I can."

Gee, it seems that every year I receive the same phone calls. Math teachers ask students to create geometric designs, which will be used as ornaments on that seasonal pine tree, and the Jewish parents call me. Oh, the phone again.

"Yes, Mrs. O'Bromovitz. Why don't you speak with the choral director and request that Amber not have to sing 'Silent Night'?"

To be a rabbi in the month of December is no easy task. Forever it feels that we, as Jews, have been confronted with the issues relating to Christmas. It usually starts right around Thanksgiving. Many Jews try holding their breath during this month, hoping that they or their children won't be placed in too uncomfortable a position.

Well, let's face it. Jews are a minority living in a Christian world. Maybe it's good that we feel a bit uncomfortable. Maybe our discomfort will make us appreciate more the fact that we have a rich Jewish heritage. And while we can appreciate our Christian neighbors' holidays, we don't have to feel bad about not celebrating them.

I know, I know: "But rabbi, I don't want my son or daughter singing Christmas carols or making decorations." And I'm not suggesting that we just sit back and allow our children to be subjected to such activities in a public school.

Contact the school and calmly (unemotionally) express your concerns that such activities violate the principle of the separation of religion and state. In my experience, most school principals and teachers have been receptive to such calls, although know that there are some who will not be.

We Jews have coined the term *December Dilemma*, suggesting that Christmas is a problem for us. But we need to get away from looking at this holiday season as a "dilemma" and see it as just another celebration of diversity. We should feel some pride, for had it not been for the Jews, there would be no holiday called Christmas.

And while we all enjoy Hanukkah, which coincidentally usually falls around the same time, let us remember that it is a minor holiday and not allow it or any other Jewish holiday to "compete" with the religious traditions and celebrations of our neighbors.

Allow me to conclude with a true story. I remember when our oldest son was three. My wife, Judy, had taken him to Chris-Town Mall in Phoenix one Friday afternoon in December. As they were sitting on a bench in the mall, eating ice cream, Judy noticed our son Avi intently looking at the scene of children lined up to sit on the lap of Santa Claus.

As they were leaving the mall, Judy felt a sense of relief that our son expressed no desire to join the line. Then, as they were exiting the mall, all of a sudden, Avi said, "Eema [Mother], I'll be right back." He then ran over to the display where Santa Claus was sitting, and as Judy ran after him, she heard him yell at the top of his lungs, "Santa, Santa"—everyone in line stopped to look—and then he yelled: "Santa, Santa! Shabbat Shalom, Santa!"

Rabbi Reuven Taff

The Real Jew

From the day of the Revelation on Sinai, it was an accepted fact that Jews lived according to the mitzvot of the Torah. But Mendele Sokolover was not satisfied with the mere observance of mitzvot. He was searching for more than that. He was searching for what he called a "real Jew."

Mendele Sokolover had grown up and had been educated in Kotzk, where he learned what a real Jew was capable of doing. He spent all of his formative years trying to find such a person. He traveled around the Pale of Settlement, from shtetl to shtetl. The people he met were fragmented: Something was missing. True, he found Jews who were observant of every detail of Halachah; he found Jews who studied day and night; he found Jews who were dedicated to mitzvot; he found Jews who devoted their lives to acts of kindness. But somehow, none of these Jews measured up to his image of a real Jew. They did not portray what he knew a real Jew was capable of doing. One day, he found Moshele, a poor, illiterate, downtrodden water carrier. This is the story that Mendele Sokolover told about Moshele the water carrier, the real Jew.

I was passing a dilapidated hut one night. As I peered into the window, I noticed a lone man clutching a worn volume of Tehillim (the biblical Book of Psalms). He seemed to be praying fervently. I stood outside the window for a long time, watching. I did not want to intrude. He never raised his eyes from the pages: His lips never ceased moving.

I returned many nights and found the same scene each time. One night, I hesitantly knocked on the door. I wanted to talk to him. I wanted to find out if he had that special quality, that spark of holiness for which I was searching.

He opened the door. I asked him his name. He told me: "My name is Moshele the water carrier."

I tried to draw him into conversation, but he shook his head from sided to side. I asked him how he was and he answered: "Good, thank God."

Many years passed, and I became the rebbe of Sokolov, the shtetl where Moshele the water carrier lived.

One night, as I walked, I saw that Moshele was not reciting Tehillim as he usually did. There was a party in his dilapidated hut. The shtetl's shoemakers, tailors, and water carriers were dancing around Moshele. It seemed to me as if the Divine Presence radiated from his face.

I wanted to know why everybody was celebrating, so I walked in. Moshele was the first one to notice me.

"Rebbe," he asked, "what are you doing here?"

"I was walking by," I said, "and I saw that you were having a party. I wanted to find out why everybody was celebrating." At first, Moshele refused to answer my question, but I persisted. Finally he began.

"This is my story, rebbe. I was orphaned at a very young age. I remember neither my father nor my mother. I grew up on the streets of this shtetl. I had very little education. There was an old man who took a liking to me, and he taught me how to recite Tehillim. I married a most beautiful girl, but she is not beautiful anymore. We had seven children. They were born angels, but we can't bear to hear them crying anymore. It is impossibly difficult to eke out a living as a water carrier. Most of the time, we go to sleep hungry. Since I can't sleep when I am hungry, I spend the night reciting Tehillim, the only prayers I know.

"A week ago, I ran to the shul (synagogue) in the middle of the night. I could not bear to hear my wife and children crying anymore. I stood before the Holy Ark and I pleaded from the depths of my soul: 'Master of the universe! I can't stand to see my wife and children suffering so much anymore. Please help me. Give me enough money to ease their pain.' I did not know if the Almighty heard my prayer. Nothing unusual happened. Two days ago, before I delivered water to my usual customers, I decided to stop in the shul. I was carrying two buckets attached to a yoke across my shoulders. I placed the buckets on the ground and entered. I stood once again before the Holy Ark, and I said: "Please help me! Please help me! If You do not help me, then we are through!

"I walked out of the shul, and bent to pick up the heavy buckets. From their weight, my shoulders were stooped, and my eyes gazed at the ground. I noticed one thousand rubles lying on the ground. I picked up the money and lifted my head in thanksgiving: 'You do listen to prayers, Almighty, don't You,' I exclaimed gratefully.

"I finished my deliveries and started to run home. I dreamed that my wife would appear beautiful again, that I could buy her lovely clothing, that my children would greet me joyfully each night when I returned from work, that they had become angels again, like when they were born. I was bursting with joy.

"But as I passed Channele, the widow's house, I heard bitter crying. 'Don't stop, Moshele. Today is your day of joy. Someone else's trouble is not your problem.' I could not quiet my conscience. I could not proceed. I knocked on Channele's door, entered and found her sobbing uncontrollably. She had lost one thousand rubles that the water carriers, the shoemakers, and the tailors had raised to help her when her husband passed away.

"I ran out of her house.

"'Why did You have to give me Channele's rubles?' I demanded. 'Couldn't You find one thousand rubles someplace else for me? What kind of compassionate God are You anyway? I don't want anything to do with You anymore. No more *Shema*, no more *bentching* [Grace after Meals], no more *n'telat yadayim* [washing hands before the blessing over bread]. We are finished.'

"I ran home, the money still in my pocket. I hated the whole world. I was angry at God and at man. I lay on my bed for a whole day.

I cried and I cursed. I ranted and I raged. I was heartbroken and dis-traught. I didn't know much, but I did know that if a person finds money in the street, and it has no symbols on it, then he doesn't have to return it. The money is not hers! I denied that the money belonged to Channele. But a few hours later, I was in touch with my soul. 'What happened to you?' my soul asked. 'All your life you prayed. Why did you stop praying now? All your life you lived as a Jew? Are you going to stop living as a Jew now?' I knew what I had to do with the money.

"I stood up from my bed, left my hut, and began walking toward Channele's house. On the way, I stopped in the shul. I stood again before the Holy Ark. I proclaimed, 'I stood at Sinai.' I heard, 'I am the Lord your God.' I raised my voice loudly and said: 'Thank You, Almighty God, for having given me the privilege of finding that money. Had someone else found it, they may not have returned it.'

"I headed for Channele's hut and handed her the money.

"I found her, sitting at a broken-down table. She was still crying, so bitterly, as if the Holy Temple had been destroyed once again. I placed the money on the table. She looked up and smiled weakly. She could not believe that I had found her money. She could not believe that anyone would return one thousand rubles. Gradually, her smile returned to her face, as if the Holy Temple had been rebuilt. I felt so good at that moment. I knew that my life would never change. I knew that my children would never look like angels, that they would still have to wear used clothing. I knew that there would never be enough food on our table. But I knew how good it felt to be a Jew. My friends are making a party in my honor. They are celebrating how good it feels to listen to God's voice."

Rebbe Mendele Sokolover joined the shoemakers, the tailors, and the water carriers in their celebration. He knew he had found a real Jew. He told the story of Moshele the water carrier, the real Jew, each year on his *yahrzeit*, the anniversary of his death.

Rabbi Eugene Labovitz and Dr. Annette Labovitz

Lessons Learned

"Teach them diligently to your children," proclaims the Torah in the well-known *Shema* liturgy. While some medieval leaders signed their name with an X because they were illiterate, little Jewish children from simple homes were taught the *alef-bet*, the Hebrew alphabet, and the songs from the Bible like "Moses commanded us a Torah, the inheritance of the congregation of Jacob." "Jewish learning is equal to all the other commands combined," teaches the Talmud.

In this section we read of how the moral values of Judaism were transmitted from one generation to the next—with humor, with love, and with great patience. This learning has helped make the Jewish people conscious of our ethical duties in all aspects of our life. "In all your ways, know God," teaches a biblical proverb. In waking and in going to sleep, we recite and practice the ancient, time-tested teachings of our people, to purify our lives and our hearts.

Pencil It In

Broadway and 17th Street. High up in the luxurious penthouse, the executive board had convened for a special meeting. The conference room was adorned with a plush, deep-pile carpet that was so thick it had to be waded through. Traversing from one side of the sanctum to the other, a person emitted enough static electricity to illuminate lower Manhattan. The mirrorlike finish of the massive rosewood conference table reflected both opulence and power, and bore witness to the felling of a major forest. And the leather-upholstered chairs, coordinated to match the elaborate furnishings, added to the atmosphere of total elegance and comfort.

No one seated in the chamber that afternoon, however, felt the least bit elegant or comfortable. Everyone knew that the CEO was in a fury and the ax was poised to strike. Trepidation hovered over the conference room like an enormous plume of steam in a bathhouse. The CEO was cutting into his employees with facts and figures that spelled serious financial losses for the company and probably their jobs as well.

The boss methodically went around the room, from one person to the next, detailing each problem and articulating the consequences. After stating each point and assessing blame, he asked, or rather demanded (stentoriously fortissimo), "Am I clear?!" Perhaps the best analogy would be Mussolini admitting he had a shouting problem. Joe knew he was next and he was already melting into his exquisite leather-upholstered chair.

"Thanks to you," the CEO roared, thrusting his lit cigar directly into Joe's face, "our company has just lent nearly $4.3 million dollars to the executive vice president of that Long Island subsidiary, with less personal information about the recipient than if he'd applied for a janitorial job!

"I admit," the CEO conceded, "that this deal might end up going through, and you will have—finally—done your job, but the risk that you have assumed here is so enormous that I need not warn you," and there was that lit cigar again, sending billowing noxious fumes right up Joe's nose, "who will be absorbing the loss if this Long Island genius doesn't deliver!"

Joe attempted to resume breathing, but the problem was no longer the petrochemical-carcinogenic cloud layer and olfactory offense that the CEO had deposited in his face, but the realization that his boss was undeniably correct. He had indeed authorized a loan with far too few guarantees, and if the deal went bust he didn't have the $4.3 million to cover the loss.

Such morbid thoughts were a signal that Joe's mental fan belt was loose, which in turn was a sign of other mechanical trouble; his eyelids began to flutter as if they were stammering; his speech became especially garbled, as if his words were randomly plucked from a Scrabble board; and his head started bobbing like a Smurf on a dashboard. And this was not to mention his acute upper-respiratory distress as a reaction to the cigar smoke.

All of this resulted in his boss sending him a demeaning, flat "Are-you-stupid-or-something?" look.

Suddenly Joe had an idea, and he glanced at his watch. The borrower had told him that he would be leaving his office at 4 o'clock to fly overseas. It was now 2:23, and he knew that there was a 2:47 train from Penn Station that went right to the Long Island office. If he ran like a demon, he might just make it.

Joe bolted from the conference room without so much as an "Excuse me," and made a beeline for Penn Station. He had sixteen long blocks to run, complicated by a steady rain beating down. In this weather, the chance of hailing a cab was probably less than nil.

When Joe got outside, the anguished bedlam of Manhattan greeted him: the junkies, the panhandlers, the New York throngs so dense that people appeared to be standing in queues just to walk down the sidewalks; the staccato clamor of the jackhammers; the steam shooting upward from the sewers, as if the world underneath were an inferno; and the tall ominous facades of countless office buildings.

He had exactly twenty minutes to catch the train. A sprinter on a varsity track team might be up to the task, but he wouldn't have had nearly as much incentive as Joe did that afternoon. Racing precisely because his future depended on it, Joe dodged pedestrians, bicyclists, cars, and trucks in his mad dash to the train station. Half a block into his marathon, he realized he didn't have a chance to make it crosstown in time. He doubled back to Union Square, praying that he would spot someone getting out of a taxi and he could then jump in. If this plan failed, he would board a subway at Union Square that, hopefully, would make the three blocks in time.

As he figured, hailing a taxi in New York City on a rainy day was a project that should only be undertaken by someone who had half a day to devote to the cause. With not even half a minute to spare, Joe abandoned plan A and proceeded to plan B.

Joe descended beneath the asphalt into the steely entrails of the earth, to board the subway. But even underground, there was no escaping the razorbladers, the lowlifes, the bums, and the shopping bag ladies of both genders who crowded the station. With seven minutes left and no time to spare, his briefcase mowed down anyone not astute enough to see a madman running for the train. Joe took the turn for the uptown N & R lines, but directly in his path was one of the subway's denizens, peddling his wares.

"Pencils for a quarter, pencils for a quarter!" he hawked, his voice clangorously meshing with the deafening din of the station. The man wasn't moving out of the way, but this was an easy tollgate to clear: Joe fished a coin out of his pocket, tossed it into the protruding can, and took off for the subway platform at breakneck speed.

It wasn't far now, just one more staircase and he would be there. But the erstwhile beggar was on his heels. "Mister! Yo, Mister!" he kept on shouting, following right behind Joe. This was not Joe's day to play Big Brother or to be Mr. Philanthropy. He had paid his dues and just wished the bum would leave him alone so that he could catch his train and be on his way. Bouncing up the steps like a mountain goat, the beggar was right on his heels and kept calling after him. Exasperated, Joe turned to see how he could shake the fellow loose.

Out of breath and clutching his chest, the man waved a pencil, "Your pencil, mister! Here's your pencil. You paid for it, now take it!"

It took Joe a second to realize what the man wanted, and when he finally comprehended, he apologized meekly, "I'm sorry. I didn't realize that you were a merchant." Joe grabbed the pencil and lunged for the train just as the doors were closing.

Four years later, Joe again found himself in that same subway station. Thinking back to that fateful rainy afternoon, he shuddered at the dimensions of that crisis. Fortunately, the Long Island deal had been salvaged, and it had not only turned a handsome profit, but it had redeemed him in the eyes of his CEO. Since then, several other lucrative projects had also been chalked up to his impressive account.

Today, Joe had a meeting on Roosevelt Island, and it didn't make sense to fight the traffic in a taxi when the subway could take him right there. This time, however, he wasn't in a rush.

He entered the subway station and strolled over to a newsstand to purchase a newspaper. It had been a hectic day for Joe, and he hadn't had a chance to find out what was happening outside his corporate agenda. The man in the stall looked at Joe long and hard and then, pointing a finger, he announced, "I know who you are."

Joe immediately regretted that he had ever approached the booth. He started backing away, but he didn't get very far.

The newsstand proprietor stood up and declared, "You're the guy who once said to me, 'I didn't realize you were a merchant.' Now years ago I didn't know I was a *merchant* either. I had never thought of myself in those terms. But I started thinking … if you could say that—a Wall Street–looking guy like yourself—then maybe there's really something to it. And, hey, look what's become of me! See this little place? I got a whole bunch of these. Nine here in the city, three out in Queens, a couple on Pelham Parkway—all together fourteen. All thanks to you!

"So, help yourself. What would you like? The *Post*, *Newsday*, the *Times?* Hey, I know what you want: The *Journal*. Take whatever you want —it's on the house. And … thanks a lot, buddy!"

Rabbi Hanoch Teller

For the Sake of a Beard

How important is it for a rabbi to have a beard?

The fact is, I was almost refused even the possibility of taking the test for a city rabbinate in Israel because I didn't have a beard—and to this day I am the only city rabbi in Israel who doesn't have a beard.

Indeed, the biblical portion this week commands, "You shall not destroy the corners of your beard" (Leviticus 19:27), and—although our talmudic sages interpret this to mean that it is forbidden to shave with a razor blade on the skin from which a beard usually sprouts—rabbinic interpretation notwithstanding, even in our modern times most rabbis do sport at least a goatee.

Nevertheless, for personal reasons, I have chosen not to wear a beard, being mindful of a Yiddish vignette in which the Keeper of the gates to Eden asks one would-be entrant, "Jew, where is the beard you shall have?," and the other would-be entrant says, "Beard, where is the Jew you should be?" But one day a year I do appear in public with a beard—on Purim (the Jewish festival of merrymaking). And therein lies a tale that occurred this Purim and that can prove that even a Purim beard can teach a powerful lesson!

Some twenty years ago my wife presented me with a Purim gift of a remarkably realistic-looking beard, one that seemed to be "made for my face" and provided me with an instant Purim costume. Initially in Lincoln Square, Manhattan, and for the last seventeen years in Efrat, I would proudly appear at all Purim celebrations—from the various readings of the biblical Book of Esther to the sundry Purim "shpiels" (humorous plays) and *l'chaims* (toast with schnapps)—with my special

Purim beard. "At least once a year we have a real rabbi," my cooperative congregants would remark.

And at the conclusion of Purim I would lovingly place my beard together with my precious, scribe-written Megillat Esther (Esther scroll) and specially crafted wooden grogger (noisemaker) for the next year's Purim festivities.

This past Purim, no different from the previous ones, found me as a "bearded" rabbi. After the traditional Purim "shpiel" which generally made fun of my nonhirsute appearances during the other 364 days of the year, I went on to a Bar Mitzvah celebration rather far from Efrat on the coastal plain of Israel. One of the teenage waiters, Lior by name, was bedecked with purple hair in honor of Purim and seemed fascinated by my beard. He asked to borrow it, to which I gladly acquiesced.

When I was about to leave, he asked if he might keep it; "After all," he explained, "I used to go to day school (yeshiva) and I still have religious feelings." I spontaneously responded that I would gladly give him the beard if he would agree to pray each morning with phylacteries (*tefillin*). "I can't make such a commitment," he said. I (perhaps lamely) told him of my sentimental attachment to this particular beard, but promised that I would make every effort to send him a similar specimen. He returned the beard and we exchanged telephone numbers. From the Bar Mitzvah I went on to Bikur Holim Hospital, where I had a patient (the administrative secretary of one of our high schools) to visit.

Obviously, I entered the hospital with my beard, because I especially wanted to cheer up the patient. During the course of my stay at Bikur Holim I used the public telephone, and at length returned home to rest. That evening I was scheduled to appear at a fiftieth birthday celebration Purim party in Tel Aviv—and when I set out, I discovered that I had misplaced my beard at some point during the hospital visit. I checked on the way to Tel Aviv, but neither the patient nor the public telephone could give a clue as to the whereabouts of my missing beard....

The next morning, while sitting in my office, I received a telephone call from someone whose voice seemed unfamiliar. "Rabbi, this is the waiter, Lior. Remember me? Well, you don't have to bring me a beard.

"An amazing coincidence happened. You see, my grandfather is recovering from surgery in Bikur Holim Hospital in Jerusalem. I went to see him yesterday afternoon after work. On my way out I stopped off to call my girlfriend, and right next to the public telephone was a fake beard that is a dead ringer for the one you lent me. I kind of see it as a sign from God. I put on *tefillin* this morning, and I plan to continue to do so every day of my life."

I put down the phone with tears in my eyes. I have come to believe that coincidence is God's way of telling us that he is still anonymously in charge. My wife has already started to track down another beard for next Purim.

Rabbi Shlomo Riskin

Letter to a Mensch-in-Training

From the time of the birth of his son, Caleb, Boston
Globe columnist Jeff Jacoby has written a letter to his son
on his birthday. This letter was written to Caleb on his
ninth birthday.

My beloved Caleb,

There was an awful story in the paper a few days ago.

"A 16-year-old Brighton High School student," it began, "has been charged with slashing a 14-year-old girl's face with a razor blade in a Dorchester park, leaving a gash that required more than 100 stitches to close." The story was on the front page of the Metro section, along with a large photograph of the fourteen-year-old. Her face is now disfigured by an angry red scar stretching from her forehead to her lip. She said that she and some of her friends had been challenged to a fight by another group of girls, and had been told that if they didn't show up, the other girls would find them and beat them on the street.

I made a point of showing you that story so we could talk about it. I asked you to imagine what it must be like to attend the schools these girls go to, or to have to worry about the things that must constantly be on their minds. The story quoted the fourteen-year-old as saying she "believes girls in the city these days must assemble a cadre of friends at a young age to back them up or risk getting more seriously injured or even killed. And she fears being labeled a snitch for identifying the girl who slashed her face."

Such violence and intimidation are far removed from anything you've ever experienced, Caleb. But you are no longer too young to know that many other children are not so fortunate—including some in your own backyard. When we talked about that news story, I told you that safety is one of the reasons Mama and I send you to the Hebrew Academy—a religious day school—instead of public school. You've never seen a fistfight, never mind a gang brawl with razor blades. When you first read the story, you weren't even sure what a razor blade *was*.

But it isn't metal detectors or security guards that makes your school safe. It isn't a zero-tolerance policy on weapons, or penalties for fighting. It's an emphasis on values and character that began on the first day of school, and that your teachers and parents treat as no less important than academics. As a three-year-old, you would come home from nursery school singing songs based on the Bible stories you were learning—Abraham's hospitality, Rebecca's kindness to strangers. Now as a nine-year-old, you come home with monthly "*midos* sheets" meant to reinforce good character—*midos* (or *midot*) is Hebrew for character traits—by having one of your parents initial the page each time you demonstrate the particular virtue being emphasized that month: cheerfulness, gratitude, kindness to others.

Does emphasizing character in this way ensure that you'll never be involved in violent or criminal deeds? Will it guarantee that you never treat another person with cruelty or malice? Can your teachers or your parents know for a fact that *you'll* never slash anyone's face with a razor? Unfortunately, there are no guarantees. How you turn out will depend, ultimately, on how you choose to live. The most your parents and teachers can do is equip you to make the right choice.

So we work at it, always keeping an eye out for ways to reinforce the better angels of your nature. When you brought home your report card in December, I wasn't thrilled with the grades you had gotten in behavior, self-control, and respect for teachers and peers. Which is why I offered you an incentive: If on your next report card all your behavior marks went up, you would be rewarded with one of the *I Spy* books you like so much. Three weeks ago your second report card came home, and what do you know? Your conduct and character had improved across the board. Way to go!

Of course, Mama and I care about your progress in English and science and religious studies, too. Sure, we want you to grow up to be good at math. But it's even more important that you grow up to be a mensch.

It's a message I try to reinforce whenever I can. After every meal, I tell you constantly, make sure to thank the person who prepared it—and that includes the "kitchen ladies" at school. When you play with your brother, you're not allowed to torment him—kindness and courtesy aren't only for outsiders. "Make us proud of you," I say each morning when I drop you off at school—a daily reminder that while your parents' love is automatic, their admiration is something you must earn.

At nine, you're off to a great start, Caleb—bright, energetic, inquisitive, articulate. Who knows what great things await you? Just remember: Whatever else you grow up to be, make sure to be a mensch.

All my love,
Papa

Jeff Jacoby

A Special Moment

Ihave two fifteen-year-old twins—Jacob and Shira—both of them wonderful, extraordinary children, in my opinion, and both of them, in their own way, very devoted to Jewish life. Very distinct ways, but devoted nonetheless. Jacob wrestles with having autism, and as a result of his autism, he has had to give up certain dreams. How ironic that the child who most loves Torah study, who most loves daily Tefillot (prayers), has not been able to participate in formal Jewish education, or Jewish camping because nobody creates a program that he is able to be part of. And Jacob has watched his sister go off to Camp Ramah summer after summer with sorrow because he misses her, and with envy. Every other kid goes to Camp Ramah despite the *Tefillot,* and despite the *Limmud* (learning). And Jacob, the first time he was told that there were non-Jewish camps, asked:

"Do they have Torah studies?"

"No."

"Do they do Shacharit?"

"No."

"Then why bother going to camp?"

And I, of course, as the Abba (father), made my peace eventually with the particular strengths and challenges of each of my children, and one of those uniquenesses meant that at Camp Ramah, the summer camp that I most love, there was no place for my son who loves Torah— until this summer. This summer, for the first time, the Amitzim Program (for children with special needs) allowed a child to attend with an aide, thus making the inclusion inclusive, and allowing Jacob to participate. Jacob says that this summer was the greatest summer of his life, and that the greatest week of the greatest summer of his life was his time at Camp Ramah, because he got to spend a week with his sister at Camp Ramah, which was, he said, "The dream of a lifetime!"

It was indeed the dream of a lifetime, not only his, but mine as well. So I want to share with you the exact moment that was for me, *dayenu* ("enough").

After serving as camp rabbi for one week each summer for as long as my kids have been alive, my daughter, Shira, last year, banished me from camp. I was not allowed to be camp rabbi because, for God's sake, she is a fourteen-year-old teenage girl, and who wants her dad hanging around at camp? But this summer she is a mature fifteen-year-old girl, which makes all the difference, and she decided that since this was her last summer as a camper, that I would be allowed to come back as camp rabbi for the final week of the session (in part because she did not want to take the bus home. Those of you who are parents know that tainted love is good enough!).

So I am there as camp rabbi for a week, and Jacob and Elana were invited to join me for Shabbat. Jacob had already enjoyed his week up at camp with *Amitzim*, but he came back with Elana, his mom, my wife. Part of the last transitional celebration for the Machon Edah, the final year of Ramah, is a very, very raucous Minchah (afternoon) service. Those of you who have never seen a Far West USY (or a Camp Ramah in California) Minchah service are missing extraordinary worship. Teens jump over tables, literally. Their singing is nonstop, their creativity and humor are amazing, and the energy level is astonishing. Camp Ramah in Ojai has a Beit Knesset (House of Worship) in the round. When you shut all the doors and windows, the noise level reverberates in your sternum. You don't have to rely on your outer ears; your inner ear can hear each and every shout and stomp, and your inner ear wants to be covered just as much as your outer ones.

As the Minchah service is about to start, Shira is sitting in the middle of the Beit Knesset with her friends on one of their iron-hard benches. She stands and emerges from the Beit Knesset and says to me, "Where's Jacob?" I point out where he is on a nearby path, and she walks over to him and takes him by the hand, saying "Come with me." Then she leads her brother into the Beit Knesset which is just a complete noisy *balagan*.

I will point out to those of you who do not know, that autistic kids have trouble with loud noise.

So Jacob walks in, Shira holding his hand—he doesn't really have a choice in this—and she continues to pull him through the crowd. Shira uses her other hand to move the dancing, singing, shouting teens out of the way. Jacob uses his spare hand to try to cover both ears, but he makes himself walk with his sister through the room. When Shira reaches her bench in the middle of the noise and the chaos and the jumping and the shouting, she asks one of her friends to move over, and they make room for her and her brother. Shira sits Jacob down and she sits next to him with her arms around him, causing Jacob to get so excited that he leaps up and tries to bolt.

I am standing next to the bench beside the twins, and Elana is on the far side of the room, against a wall. Every time Jacob leaps up, Shira helps calm him down and brings him back. Occasionally I have to go and smile at him and help him come back. The entire time that Jacob is there, he has a smile on his face so big, you could see it from the *chadar ochel* (cafeteria), which is a long way away.

And at that moment, if I had dropped dead—*dayenu*, it would have been sufficient.

To see my twins in the Minchah service of Camp Ramah, Machon year, sitting together; to watch the other Machonies smiling at Jacob, encouraging him with their warmth, telling him sometimes, "It's good that you're here," and even when they were not telling him verbally, smiling to let him know how welcome he was, to see Jacob mustering superhuman strength to stay in that noise—despite his intense feelings already—because his sister had given him the greatest *kavod* in the world; to see my girl so loving and sweet that she is able to transcend most teenagers' self-absorption; to know that she could contribute something that no other person on the planet could do at that moment; and then to look across the room to see Elana with a smile as big as Jacob's, and to know that our family was complete, that we were all there together, and that our complete family included Camp Ramah, included all of the Jewish people—that was *dayenu!*

In an instant, a dream that I had abandoned and a prayer that I had stopped saying was granted me. *Dayenu.* It's enough. If I never have another *dayenu* moment, I will look back on that one and say, whatever else life brings, it was worth it—for that shimmering moment of pure bliss.

Rabbi Bradley Shavit Artson

Epilogue

While I was writing *And God Created Hope*, I moved to Stroudsburg, Pennsylvania, to become rabbi at Temple Israel of the Poconos. I needed to find new doctors, so I made an appointment with one of the local specialists. He suggested that I have my lungs checked as part of a thorough physical exam.

He scheduled me for a CAT scan, expecting to find nothing out of the ordinary. Well, surprise, surprise! When I returned to the doctor for the results, he told me that there was a spot on my lung, and he couldn't rule out lung cancer.

Next, he scheduled me to have a PET scan, which would show if anything was going on in my throat. Three days later, I went to the surgery center, and through an IV, they inserted some dye, which flowed through my entire upper body, so I could be scanned. I lay still for sixty-five minutes, trying to "zone out," actually counting the seconds (one thousand one, one thousand two, one thousand three …) and trying to act like the macho man that I did *not* feel like.

My doctor had scheduled the next appointment for a week later. I asked him for an earlier date, but he said that it took that long for the results and the evaluation of the scan. It turned out that the results and the evaluation were all done two hours after the test, but I didn't know that then.

So I had a whole week to think about the possibility that I might be dying of lung cancer.

What made it really scary was that my mother had died of lung cancer. She was a heavy smoker. I've never smoked, but I had already presumed that this might be genetic and that my life was over.

And so I began to plan.

What would I do with the time I had left? First, would I take chemo and radiation for the cancer? I decided absolutely not, since I didn't want to spend the next year suffering through mind-and-body-torturing treatments that would, at best, give me maybe another month or two of life, life that wasn't really life at all. I've seen too many of my congregants and friends go through that, and I knew it was not for me.

Would I quit my job as rabbi? Yes, I would do that immediately upon receiving the test results and cancer diagnosis, and I even began working on my final sermon. I would tell my new congregation that there are places in this world that I want to visit with my wife, Ellen, and that I especially need to return to Israel for a final visit, so I'd be resigning from the pulpit. I would thank them for the lessons they'd already taught me even in the short time we'd had together, and I'd ask their forgiveness for any pain I'd caused them.

I would complete my relationship with them before I left.

After seeing other parts of the world, I'd return home and begin to travel all across the country, giving a lecture to anyone who might be interested, titled: "Final Life-Thoughts of a Grateful Rabbi." During the lecture, I'd talk about how gratitude was the first feeling I'd had after learning of my impending death. Above all, I'd say I'm grateful for the life I've been granted, and I consider my life a precious gift to me from God.

After gratitude would come everything else, all my other feelings and thoughts. I would talk about how the world can only be repaired when gratitude replaces entitlement, when we move outside ourselves toward others in our lives.

When I thought about dying, I realized that I wasn't angry, just sad that I wouldn't live to see my kids' life-cycle events or share in the lives of my grandchildren.

I felt like my hopes, dreams, and aspirations had been reached, and that I'd die happy and fulfilled. If my time had come, I'd be ready, unafraid, and pleased with what I'd accomplished in my life. I knew that I'd mattered to a lot of folks, and my teachings and memories would be my final gift to them and to the Universe.

I believe that when our mission on this earth is accomplished, we can be ready and prepared to leave this world for whatever comes next. The problem is: Who among us knows when our missions have been accomplished? We don't. So, if God has decided that my earthly purpose has been fulfilled, who am I to argue?

I've known too many people who have "lived too long." They spent their final years in pain or totally unable to communicate with those they loved. I would, indeed, be fortunate, because I would leave this life on my own terms, proud and grateful.

Smart guy that I am, I was sure I had it all figured out.

Needless to say, thank God, the results came back showing that the spot on my lung was some benign scar tissue left over from who-knows-what and who-knows-when.

I was elated. I really was. But, to tell the deep, dark, honest-to-God truth, I was just a wee bit disappointed at the same time. I was actually looking forward to the last year of my life. I was going to be able to fill the closing chapter of my existence with passion! Between seeing the world, teaching people across the country the truths I'd learned, and finishing my book on grief and hope, my days would be filled with joy and creativity. They would be filled with *life*, not death, and when the end came, I'd feel that my life had been well worth my fifty-nine years of effort.

That's my story, and it has a happy ending. Sort of.

The gnawing-in-my-*kishkas* question I continue to ask myself ever since this happened is: *What's stopping me from doing all those things I was going to do if I was going to die?*

How many of them can I still do right now, even *without* a death sentence hanging over me? Why do I have to wait until the Angel of Death comes calling for me, *for real?*

These are the real questions, not thoughts of dying one day, that continue to haunt me.

Rabbi Melvin Glazer

Yiddish as Therapy

It's no pleasure to be required to spend three days flat on your back, the TV set showing four lousy stations (one of which broadcasts nothing but evangelical messages), and the food lousy (in small portions, too). But when you have had a heart attack, that is the extent of permissible hospital activities. You lie there and hope not to be attacked by your heart a second time, at least not now. Next week, maybe. But not now. The recognition of your mortality is nowhere more pronounced than under such circumstances.

Finally, they let you get up. You smell like a goat, you need a shave, and you feel regret at having eaten all the garbage that put you in the hospital in the first place. *Kishka* and *schmaltz:* peasant foods. They cost nothing to make but cause blood to behave like glue as it sludges through veins and arteries. No wonder your heart can't get oxygen.

So with needles in my arm, and by my side a vertical pole holding intravenous drips, I was permitted to walk up and down the central corridor of the hospital a little after midnight. Why not? They feed you at 5 a.m., so it's not illogical that you should go for a walk at midnight.

It was while taking this walk that I saw her, a well-tailored, fortyish woman standing in the corridor. She was crying—genuine, uncontrolled sobbing—a woman in the grip of terror.

I stopped and asked what was wrong. (You may inquire, "What business was it of yours to make such an inquiry of a stranger on the verge of hysterics?" But when you have just suffered a heart attack, you look for ways to be nice. Some strange logic allows you to conclude that mitzvot count for more when you're close to going down the tubes of eternity in half an eyeblink.) The crying woman told me that her mother was in the room just down the hall, she could barely breathe, it was a terrible strain on her heart, and she did not know if her mother could survive such a situation. I asked her mother's name.

"Estelle Cohen," she replied.

I asked, "How old is your mother and, by any chance, does she speak Yiddish?"

"My mother is eighty-two, and yes, she does speak Yiddish," the daughter said, "but living in Milpitas doesn't give her much of a chance to practice."

"Let me see what I can do," I said as I waddled off to visit Mrs. Cohen, the back of my hospital gown flapping in the wind and permitting the entire Western world a view of my posterior. It wasn't a pretty sight. "It's no skin off my nose if people stare," I thought. "It's not a state secret that has to be kept under wraps, you know. Besides, there isn't much I can do about it."

Mrs. Cohen was sitting up in her bed, almost convulsed with her inability to get a full breath. She held a tube attached to a machine that made humidity and she was trying to breathe some of that moisture into her clogged lungs by periodically putting the end of the tube in her mouth and breathing in, but she was not very successful. She coughed a great deal. And when she did, they were large, dry, spasmodic coughs. It was clear she was in some distress, though by no means in extremis.

She looked up at me as I entered her room, pulled a chair up next to her bed, sat down, and began to speak to her, quietly and calmly, in Yiddish.

"Hello, Mrs. Cohen. I just met your daughter outside. She told me you have not been well. I wish you a speedy recovery. Tell me, how are you feeling?"

She looked at me between coughs and wheezes as if I asked her about a size 19 bustle frame.

"You speak Yiddish?!," she asked in a rich Litvak accent.

"Do you hear me speaking Yiddish? Of course I am speaking Yiddish. But tell me how are you feeling?"

"Lousy, thanks," she said, followed by more gasping, coughing, and holding her chest. I became more calm in the midst of her terrible anguish. She looked frightened. I took her hand in mine.

"Where were you born? Tell me about your mother. Did you have a pleasant childhood?"

She began to talk. I think she needed a little sympathetic companionship. And each time she paused, I asked another question.

"How old were you when you met your first boyfriend? Tell me about your husband. What was it about him that you found worthy?" I was running a risk here. Maybe the husband was a drunk who beat her. But I figured she was a widow and that she would speak of her husband in a golden glow. I was right, and lucky.

As she began to speak of her husband, it became obvious that she was coughing less now, and she was speaking more calmly. The light of terror had gone from her eyes.

"And then what happened?" I asked as she came to another pause. "Did your mother have many brothers and sisters? Tell me about your uncles and aunts."

And the more she talked, the better her breathing became. She put down the tube and told me how her mother made cholent. She waxed poetic about her uncle Mottke, who was a numbers runner in the 1920s and who may have been a paid functionary for Murder, Inc. She spoke eloquently of her youth in Red Bank, New Jersey, where her parents had a boardinghouse.

And each time she paused, I asked the same question: "And then what happened?"

Now she was speaking with no breathing discomfort at all. The humidity tube was discarded. She talked and talked and talked. A rich Yiddish. An abundant Yiddish. A real Litvak Yiddish, what is often called the most elegant kind. I reveled in her picturesque vocabulary.

"And then what happened?" I asked. She talked. I listened.

After twenty minutes, a physician came in, more out of breath than Mrs. Cohen had been twenty minutes earlier. He had been sum-moned to help alleviate her crisis, but by the time he got there, I had already done that. Mrs. Cohen was telling me about how many unborn eggs her mother would put into chicken soup. Do you, dear reader, have any idea what an unborn egg is and the quantity of them I must have eaten as a child to give me a heart attack sixty years later?

The doctor looked at Mrs. Cohen, hale and chipper now, talking a mile a minute. And he looked at me listening to her, waiting for the opportunity to say, "And then what happened?"

"What are you doing here?" he said to me, not particularly pleasantly.

My hackles went up at once. "Doctor," I said, in a not predomi-nantly friendly manner, "I don't take kindly to such a hostile approach." Then I realized that, because Mrs. Cohen and I had been speaking Yiddish, I had spoken to the doctor in Yiddish, too. He looked very con-fused. It turned out that he was from Colby, Kansas, and he would not have known what an unborn egg was if it had been shoved up his nose.

"I just cured your patient," I continued, switching to English. "And I want a consultant's fee."

Instead, Dr. Kansas asked me to leave so that he could examine Mrs. Cohen. She and I said good-bye and, like the view available to the rest of the world, she saw my posterior on the way out. There wasn't much I could do to prevent it. As I said, it wasn't a pretty sight.

I was proud of that moment and wondered if, by accident, I had discovered some unknown therapeutic value for Yiddish.

Daniel N. Leeson

Tikkun Olam

Ialmost didn't go. Fresh out of medical school, I had spent the last several months working in the impoverished village of El Valle, deep in the central highlands of the Dominican Republic. In a modest clinic made of cinderblocks, four of us—a Dominican doctor, a medical student from Puerto Rico, a nurse, and I—provided the only medical care for the entire region. We would see up to seventy patients a day with every conceivable ailment.

Many of the patients were Haitian migrant workers, who came seasonally to harvest crops. They lived in abysmal conditions in huts made of grass and palm leaves with dirt floors. There is a deep sense of mistrust that exists between the Dominicans and the Haitians, fostered by centuries of hostility between the two countries.

So slowly, little by little, the Haitians who came to the clinic began to gravitate toward me. I tried to help them as best I could, given my own limited knowledge and the clinic's meager resources. I visited the sick in their squalid homes, brought medicines they could not afford, and tried to treat them with dignity and respect. People began to refer to me as the "Haitian Gringo." I became friendly with the local witch doctor, a large imposing Haitian who, I gradually realized, worked as hard as I did to try and bring hope to the lives of these desperate people. While I mostly spoke to the Haitians in Spanish, I tried to learn some of their Creole-French dialect, and they would grin with delight at my primitive attempts to speak it.

On one of the last few days of my stay in El Valle the witch doctor came to see me. "You have treated us well," he said, "we wish to give you a present before you leave." Knowing the poverty of these people, I shook my head and said I could not take something from people who had so little. The witch doctor smiled. "No, not that kind of gift," he said. "We have seen you are a man of God," he continued, "we would like to take you to meet him." My jaw dropped. "Be here tonight at sunset," he said as he turned on his heel and left.

When I told Fernando, the Dominican doctor, what had happened, he violently objected to the idea of my going with them. "They'll take you to one of the Voodoo ceremonies and then cook you for dinner!" Surprised by the force of his outburst, I had decided that going was probably not a good idea. Yet as sunset came, I felt a near-irresistible urge to discover what they had meant.

As darkness fell, I found myself standing at the appointed meeting place. The witch doctor appeared with five other men and silently motioned for me to follow. Two of the men carried large flaming torches to light our way. We headed into the deep woods and followed a trail that inclined upward. As we walked, I became aware of the presence of more and more people who had joined the procession. After walking for what seemed to be a very long time we finally came to a clearing at the top of a large hill. A large semicircular pavilion had been built of connecting tree trunks with a thatched roof over it. Silently, the witch doctor pointed to a small woven mat, indicating that I should sit. The other members of the party filed into the pavilion and surrounded a huge pile of wood in its center.

Voodoo is difficult to explain. More a collection of ancient beliefs and rituals than a religion, it nonetheless permeates the lives of its adherents. The assembled multitude began a slow dirgelike chant in a language I could not understand. A woman in a bright red bandanna brought me an earthenware cup containing a steaming black liquid that looked like coffee. I hesitated for a moment. "Do not be afraid," she whispered. I drank it. Almost immediately the sound of drums began, huge drums pounding out a primal, pulsating beat. Suddenly the large pile of wood seemed to burst into flame, creating a massive bonfire that surged skyward. One by one, people began exuberantly dancing around the fire in rhythm to the intoxicatingly throbbing beat.

Something odd began to occur. The drums sounded as if they were speaking, calling me to the flames. The flames began to twist and turn, then seemed to form shapes and figures that danced within the fire itself. I arose, summoned by the calling drums, and made my way to the inferno. I began to dance, whirling and twisting to the pulsating rhythm of the drums. I became the dance and felt the fire was dancing with me. The intense beat grew faster and faster, the dancers throwing themselves into frenzied gyrations. Then it happened …

Despite the noise and motion, I felt a sudden stillness, and it seemed that somehow my consciousness lay suspended outside of my body. In one transcendent moment I sensed the sheer wonder and beauty of the entire universe. I felt an indescribable sense of oneness with all of creation and with it a tremendous sense of peace (a moment referred to by Zen masters as *saturi*, or enlightenment). In the fire I felt the warmth of a million suns that glowed with a near-perfect light. A sense of holiness and divinity filled me. Then suddenly the fire seemed to break into pieces that fell everywhere. I screamed; helplessly watching the wondrous light scatter. A sense of profound sorrow came over me, then utter darkness …

I awoke on the steps of the clinic. The morning dew covered me and I was stiff in every joint. To this day I have no idea how I got back. Fernando was furious, but said nothing. The next day with little fanfare, I left.

The images of that night have never left me. I have heard that the Haitians often prepare hallucinogenic mixtures of mushrooms and herbs for such occasions, but I know in the deepest part of me that the experience was much more than just a psychedelic vision. The image of that perfect light that broke into pieces has haunted my dreams ever since. Years later, in an old book, I came across the ancient kabbalistic legend that tells of a time when the universe was filled with a divine light. This light was shattered and fell to the imperfect earth in the form of sparks or shards that found their way into each and every living thing. It is, the legend continues, humankind's mission to seek out these sparks, release them, and once again restore them to a level of divinity. This process (called *tikkun olam*, or repairing the world) is accomplished by individual conscious acts of compassion, mercy, justice, and kindness.

Upon reading this story for the first time, I experienced that which can only be referred to as a "flashback." The entire event began playing back, yet now with a different sense of understanding and new meaning. For this is the challenge that faces each of us (in particular those of us who seek to heal the minds, bodies, and souls of those who suffer from illness): How do we reach beyond day-to-day human pettiness and greed to discover a deeper value in the midst of a flawed and suffering world? These poor, simple people had shown me that, through each of our efforts (no matter how small and seemingly inconsequential) and our acts of compassion and kindness, these sparks can be released.

Thus freed, the flames may return once again to a level of divinity, where their rekindled fires can perhaps help to repair an imperfect and fractured cosmos. The vision of the light is always with me; a constant reminder that our work here on earth can be sacred and just, whatever that work may be. The task is to neither hide from nor reject the world, but to both embrace it and strive to restore it, all of it, exactly as it is....

Blair P. Grubb, MD

Aviva's Hair

Aviva stood in front of the full-length mirror in the hall combing her hair. She turned halfway around to look at it. Her hair almost fell to her waist, it was so long. Her mother walked in. "Oh Mom, my hair is so long—I love it that way," said Aviva. Her mother took the brush out of her hand and lovingly brushed the hair back. "Now get me the ponytail holder and I'll pin it up for school," she said.

Avi came back in a minute with the ponytail holder. "That keeps it out of my eyes," she said. "Thanks, Mom."

Her mom walked her out of the house, helping with her backpack as they waited for the school bus. When it came, her mom gave her a kiss. She hopped on and waved as it pulled away.

Aviva went to a Jewish day school and loved it. One of the things she was learning about was *derech eretz*—good manners, respect for others, the elderly, the handicapped, and the ill. Just before the bell rang, she walked into her classroom and went up to her teacher. "Mrs. Weil, can you please tell me what happened to Nathan? He hasn't been in school for a month or more and I miss him."

Mrs. Weil turned to Aviva. "The bell will ring in a minute, honey, but if you remind me at the break we'll talk about Nathan, okay?"

Aviva nodded and went to her seat. At the break the other kids scampered out to the playground, but Aviva went to Mrs. Weil. "Okay, now please tell me about Nathan," she said.

Mrs. Weil looked at the little eight-year-old. "Nathan has been very sick. The doctors discovered he had cancer and they operated on him and then gave him chemo."

"What's chemo?" asked Aviva.

"Chemo helps cure cancer. Usually the doctors put an intravenous line into your arm—that's like a needle with a bag on it—and drip the chemo into your body. Sometimes it makes the patient very weak and sometimes they throw up. And they lose their hair." Aviva was getting more and more upset. "So they get better? Does the hair ever grow back?"

"Yes," said Mrs. Weil, "it does grow back and sometimes while the patient is bald they wear a wig—you know, a kind of tight-fitting cap you put on your head with hair on it—usually hair that looks like your original hair. You know, Nathan had light brown hair—sort of like yours. Well, he'll be back at school tomorrow and we must show him *derech eretz*—remember."

Aviva had tears in her eyes. She liked Nathan, and hoped the other kids would be kind. That evening, Aviva told her mother and father about Nathan. Her mother said, "I knew about it and have been in touch with Nathan's mother. I took food over there a few times, because they spent so much time in the hospital with Nathan, Naomi didn't have time to cook for the family. But I didn't want to tell you and upset you. I'm glad he's coming back to school—that means he's feeling better."

"But, Mom, he won't have any hair. I hope the kids won't make fun of him. "I hope not," answered her mom, "but you have all learned about *derech eretz*—maybe that will help."

The next day Nathan came to class wearing an Indians baseball cap. "Hey, man," said Jonathan, one of the classmates, "what's with the cap?"

"I ... have to wear it," muttered Nathan.

"I think he looks nice in it," said Aviva. "Well, I think he looks dumb, especially in school," said Jonathan, as he leaped out of his chair and grabbed the hat. The other kids gasped. Nathan was completely bald. By this time he had tears in his eyes. Aviva ran over to Jonathan, grabbed the hat, and pushed Jonathan into his chair. "Leave him alone, you bully," she shouted. "You haven't learned anything about *derech eretz*, have you?"

Mrs. Weil came in, "What happened?" she asked.

Jonathan leaped up. "She pushed me," he shouted.

"He grabbed Nathan's cap," said Aviva, "and that wasn't very *derech eretz*, was it?"

"I want everyone to leave Nathan alone," said Mrs. Weil. "He's been through a very bad experience and we're glad to have him back with us. Remember what we learned about *derech eretz* and being kind to others who are not as fortunate as we are. Now let's get started with our lesson."

Aviva sat down next to Nathan. He looked pale and tired. She straightened the hat on his head.

Nathan's mother was there after class to pick him up. He got up from his desk and turned to Aviva. "Thanks, Avi, I won't forget what you did."

"It was nothing," murmured the young girl.

Avi came home from school and said to her mother, "I know what I want to do." She went upstairs and brought down a scissors. "Please cut my hair up to my shoulders," she said.

Her mother was shocked. "But you love your long hair so much."

"Mom, I want to give my hair to the hairpiece lady to make a hairpiece for Nathan until his hair grows back."

Her mother began to cry. "Avi, I never heard of anything so kind in my life. Are you sure you want to do this?"

Avi nodded. "I like Nathan and I don't want people making fun of him and feeling sorry for him. We didn't learn about *derech eretz* for nothing."

"Okay, let's get a cloth and collect the hair," said Mom, as she began cutting. "There's one good thing—it will grow back soon." Avi nodded.

When the hair was cut they took it to Nathan's house. Mrs. Goldberg opened the door and Avi's mom said, "Naomi, Aviva has something for Nathan, please take it."

"Miriam, what is it?" asked Naomi, opening the bag. "Oh, my God, it's hair." She looked at Aviva. "It's your hair."

"It's for a hairpiece for Nathan," said Aviva, "until his own hair grows back."

Mrs. Goldberg kneeled down and hugged Aviva. "And you did that on your own for Nathan? You cut your gorgeous hair, so he would have a hairpiece? You are some wonderful little girl." She began to cry.

Just then Nathan came in. "Hi, Mom. Hi, Mrs. Rosenbaum—hi, Aviva. You cut your hair! Wow, it's so much shorter now! And you did that just for me." He put his arm around Aviva. "This is some kid—you should have seen her smash Jonathan this morning."

"Well, he insulted you and I didn't want to let him get away with it," said Aviva.

"Aviva cut her hair and we'll have a temporary hairpiece made for you with her hair—it's almost your color," said Nathan's mother.

"Aviva, did you really do that?" Nathan began to cry. "That's the nicest thing anyone ever did for me. You really learned the lesson about *derech eretz*. I'll never ever forget you."

"And neither will I," added Mrs. Goldberg.

"See you in school tomorrow with my hair on," said Nathan, giggling.

Aviva blew him a kiss.

Bea Stadtler

Tradition of Charity

A young woman's gift to honor her grandmother inspired an act of generosity no one anticipated. Maxine Weinstein was so tired, she could barely move. At the front of the West Hartford synagogue, her thirteen-year-old granddaughter, Jillian Deitch, was reading a Hebrew passage about the importance of charity. Five hundred other guests at Jillian's Bat Mitzvah listened intently, but Mrs. Weinstein struggled to hear. Many months of dialysis were taking their toll.

"I was at my lowest point of energy," she recalls. "I was getting dialysis three days a week, and I almost didn't make it. But I came and basically spent the whole night in that one chair."

The ceremony, which signified Jillian's passage into adulthood, also provided her first chance to perform a truly generous act. Forgoing the usual bounty of Bat Mitzvah gifts, Jillian asked guests to donate money to the Yale–New Haven Transplantation Center, where her grandmother was receiving treatment. She collected $25,000 for the hospital and ten boxes of food for a woman's shelter in Hartford.

"Mostly kids will ask for presents or money," Jillian Deitch says. "I feel like I have a lot in life, so I wanted to help others. My grandmother was really happy with care at the hospital, so it was the perfect opportunity." Remarkably, the ceremony spurred another gift, which no one saw coming. Kellyanne Jones, who catered the event, approached Mrs. Weinstein's daughter, Jaime Weinstein, the following day and asked her mother's blood type. A few days later, Ms. Jones, a thirty-four-year-old mother of three, decided to contact Maxine Weinstein. "She sent me flowers out of the blue with a note that said, 'We're a match. Love, Kellyanne,'" Mrs. Weinstein recalled.

Although relatives had offered to donate a kidney to Mrs. Weinstein, they all shared a condition that prevented it. But Ms. Jones stepped forward, giving Mrs. Weinstein new hope. "Now we speak every day. She was incredibly generous," says Mrs. Weinstein. "Such an unexpected gift fits in the context of the Jewish community," says Jaime Weinstein. "In our community you give back, and it can take many forms," she says.

But it also reflects the cycle of generosity returning to a family. Mrs. Weinstein's parents made a practice of philanthropy. Like other traditions, the spirit of giving passed to Mrs. Weinstein, who in turn passed it down the family tree.

"It's in my soul and I want it to be in my children's and grandchildren's souls," she says. "When you're blessed in life it's the right thing to do."

Light Out of the Holocaust

Elie Wiesel once wrote of the Holocaust (Shoah): "How does one commemorate the death of an entire community? What must one say? How many candles should one light, how many prayers should one recite, and how many times? Perhaps someone knows the answer. I don't. I am still searching."

Countless are the diaries, histories, chronicles, films, and other media that remind us of the horrors of the Holocaust. The blackest night in history of the Jewish People will never cease to be retold, yet never be fully understood. Nevertheless, there were sparks of light in that blackest of nights—the taste of a mother's kugel, the Passover seder in a Nazi concentration camp, the people who found ways to brighten their day, if even for a few moments. We must not let these stories become the sole basis of Jewish life, but on the other hand, we must never forget the torture our people endured, and the tiny flickers of light that occasionally illuminated the shadow and the gloom.

A Mother's Kugel

*This is a story that was written down by a victim of the
concentration camps who survived and now lives in Israel.*

In 1943 he, his brothers, and his mother were imprisoned in the
ghetto of Kovno. One of the things that kept them alive was the
Sabbath, which they clung to with all their strength. Each week when
the Sabbath came and the lights were kindled, the songs sung, and the
prayers recited, new life entered the souls of the Jews. The Nazis understood the power of the Sabbath among the Jews and set out to destroy
it in a typically clever way. They gave the Jews their week's supply of
food on Sunday, figuring that they would surely devour the small portion of bread in the first few days of the week so they would have nothing to eat by the time the Sabbath came. But the Nazis did not reckon
on the power and the piety of the Jewish woman. Now read the story as
the son tells what happened:

The older members of our family learned to discipline themselves
and to divide their bread into a portion for each day, but the under-
nourished, famished children would cling to the mother pleading,
"Mother, we are not able to break this bread into pieces, one for each
day. Mother, you do it for us!"

And so my mother, that most unfortunate of all creatures, bore
with what courage and strength she had the burden of the family, and
she divided the bread into pieces, one for each day. It was not easy
work. She divided the bread into the smallest pieces possible, trying to
make the portions as alike as she could and worrying in the moment of

decision how she might be able to set aside something—no matter how little—for the coming of the Sabbath.

"Remember, children, the days pass swiftly. The holy Sabbath approaches and knocks upon the door! Remember, for the sake of God's name."

But the mother's heart—a merciful heart—knew what a trial it would be for the children to put aside their bread and not eat it all up until the end of the week. So she also took upon herself the task of keeping the bread.

"Listen, children! The pieces of that are for the Sabbath I shall keep for you. Let each of you give me as much as you like *l'kovod Shabbos* [in honor of the Sabbath] and I shall keep it!"

"Yes, yes. This is best, Mother!" Many voices spoke at once.

But one of the children, who lay on a sickbed, hesitated and called out in a shy voice: "If we all give bread for Shabbos, Mother, will you make a good kugel for this Shabbos for us like you did last Shabbos?"

"If God wills it! If God wills it!" answered the mother in a whispered prayer.

"That was wonderful kugel. How was it prepared? Tell us, Mother!" said one of the children, who remembered its taste from the week before.

"Secrets like that cannot be told, children!" the mother smiled.

She knew only too well the hidden secret of the kugel's preparation, and it filled her with shame now. She did not reveal her secret. What was there to reveal? Should she tell them that from her own portion of that cursed bread she had taken a bit each day and that from these bits came the wonderful kugel—but that now her youngest child was sick and each day she gave him part of her own bread, so she could no longer set aside anything for a pie?

"This Shabbos too, dear children, you will eat good kugel, if God wills it!" she said, taking the pieces of bread from the children, and placing them with trembling hands onto the white Shabbos tablecloth.

"I promise you that this will be a good pie, an especially good one, children!"

She had made a promise—and she fulfilled it.

Indeed, a Sabbath kugel the likes of this one had never yet been made. She gathered together potato peelings and carefully hid them away. When no one was looking, she soaked them in water and cleansed them so that no dirt remained upon them. After they had dried, she ground them in her bare hands. Into this flour she put salt, pepper, a little bit of bran and grass. And to this strange mixture there was added for spice—a mother's hot tears....

"May it be His will"—she whispered in her heart a prayer as she worked—"May it be His will that this food will be sweet to my dear children, and that they may find in it the taste of the manna from heaven, just as our fathers did in the wilderness. And may it by Thy will, O Master of the world, that I should not bring disgrace, God forbid, by the work of my hands to Your holy Sabbath ..."

All the while this humble creature labored preparing the pie, a single thought pursued her like a bee!

"Who knows? Perhaps—God forbid—this is a profanation of the Sabbath, a pie made of such refuse, of potato peelings.... Perhaps, "she thought in her heart," I should add to this strange mixture some drops of oil? They will surely give it a flavor!"

But if she were to take the few remaining drops of oil for the pie what would she use to kindle her lights for Shabbos? For she had no candles: only wicks and oil.

A struggle went on within her soul. Food or lights? Both of them for the honor of the Sabbath: Which was more important? For a moment she thought: "Surely the Sabbath lights take precedence, for must we not say the blessing to kindle the Sabbath lights? It is a mitzvah [religious commandment] for which there is a special blessing."

A moment later she repented, saying to herself: "What good will this light do for my sick boy who lies upon his bed? His very life hangs in the balance. A pie mixed with a little oil may give him strength; it will be good medicine for him."

Then her heart trembled within her:

"But the mitzvah of kindling the light may also be beneficial for my sick boy. For the child is dependent on Heaven's mercies, and there is no more favorable time for a Jewish woman to offer a prayer before the throne of glory than at the time of candlelighting."

Food or lights—what should she do?

At that moment a thought came to her mind, a daring thought: "I will bless the Sabbath lights—without oil! And He Who dwells in the heavens and Who knows all the thoughts of man will look into my heart and He will understand. He will know that I have used the last drops of oil for the honor of the Sabbath, and to save a human life. He will forgive."

And so it happened that at the sunset of that Sabbath eve in the Kovno ghetto she stood in front of her "lights"—singed wicks without a drop of oil—put her hands over her eyes, and recited the blessing and whispered a prayer:

"Master of all worlds! Accept my Sabbath lights which have no light. May You in Your great mercy kindle them with Your heavenly flame. Our Father in Heaven, forgive a sinful, shamed woman for having stolen the oil for the wicks in order to kindle the joy of the Sabbath in the hearts of my children, who are wasting away before my eyes. And if I am not worthy and my prayer returns empty before You, then turn Your ear, O merciful Father, to the songs of the holy Sabbath which my children—among them even my sick one—will sing in my humble dwelling when I put on the table the Sabbath kugel which I have made."

The kugel was brought to the table. The children tasted in it the taste of paradise, and they sang in a joyous chorus:

"*Mizmor shir leyom haShabbos!!*—A song for the Sabbath day!"

And my mother? She swallowed her tears, and did not even notice that in that dingy ghetto room the Sabbath Queen in all her glory and in all her beauty was spreading her white, radiant wings over the singing Sabbath children, and was herself singing a song to the same melody:

"*Mizmor shir leyshes hayil!*—A song of glory to the Jewish mother!"

Rabbi Samuel H. Dresner and Rabbi Byron L. Sherwin

Seder in a Nazi Concentration Camp

Pesach fell early in 1945. I don't know how we knew. Obviously no one had a calendar in camp. I am not even sure that the event I am about to describe did take place on the fifteenth of Nissan. I don't think it really mattered. Thirty years have passed since then, a lifetime.

It might have had something to do with feelings of national pride. The camp was a microcosm, a mix of people from almost every European country. There were Polish women, hostile toward us, their Jewish compatriots; there were the Russian girls captured on the front as soldiers, courageous and brave; the Greek girls, dark-skinned and beautiful, who would form a circle and dance gracefully on their holidays; the French women who sang *La Marseillaise* at roll call on the day Paris was freed. Then at the very bottom were we, the Jewish girls and women who for years had been driven from ghetto to ghetto, from camp to camp, each time losing someone we loved; the only ones who did not receive letters, who had no country to go back to.

The camp itself was a "good" one. I, by then an alumna of two others, could appreciate it. We were housed in a former industrial plant, a solid brick building; the work was not too hard, and, at least in the beginning, we were not hungry. As the front moved closer, people from other camps were brought in. The place became crowded and food scarce. The women on the Jewish block, a huge hall with close to one thousand inmates, grew haggard and irritable. Morale was at its lowest. But the winter had passed and the first signs of spring were there.

I looked back to the springs of my childhood, remembering the excitement of the approaching holiday, the hectic preparations, the house smelling of cleanliness, the new clothes, and above all the seder. It was the only night when a little girl was allowed to stay up late, sip real wine, put a ransom on the *afikomen*, so that her father, leaning back, could finish the story of the Exodus in a singsong cadence.

And as I remembered all that, the highlights of the *Haggadah* came back to me in Hebrew, the language I had mastered. And suddenly, something hit me. The story could have been written about us. I think it was then that I decided we were going to have a seder. I spoke to my closest friends, who became as enthusiastic about the idea as I was.

How does a person arrange a seder in a German concentration camp with no matzah, no wine, no *Haggadot?* But by then we had learned to be resourceful. Someone with connections in the kitchen "organized" a huge white sugar beet. Another got hold of empty bottles. White paper had been smuggled from the factory to the camp.

The night of the seder we pushed all the tables together in the middle of the room, and covered them with the white paper. We cut the beet diagonally into thin slices that resembled white matzah, filled up the bottles with "coffee" that could pass for wine. There was even a Passover plate with a bone, some grass, and an egg-shaped white stone.

There were some angry voices and murmurs of discontent. But eventually they complied. Then we appealed to them to save their rations for the next day and at least that night not eat bread. The voices grew even angrier, and I, over those angry voices, intoned in Hebrew, "Blessed be You, God of the Universe, who kept us alive to see this day." A translation recited by my former classmate followed.

Suddenly it was very quiet. I picked up a slice of beet and held it high for everyone to see. "This is the bread of our suffering ..." I began. "We are slaves in the land of Germany, but God will deliver us from here with an outstretched arm and with a strong hand. In every generation they rise to destroy us and the Blessed Holy One saves us from their hands."

The ten plagues, each one beginning with blood and ending with the death of the firstborn, applied to us. As I implored God to "turn the Divine's wrath upon those who did not know God and who did not invoke the Divine Name," I noticed a figure, a greenish cape thrown over the shoulder, standing by the open door. It was a young SS woman. I don't know how long she had been standing there, or how much she heard and I will never know why she turned around and left and did nothing.

We ended the seder with a promise that should we survive there would always be a slice of white beet on our seder table. The promise, like many other bargains one makes with God in times of stress, was seldom kept. White sugar beets are hard to come by in the city of New York. But the mitzvah of "You shall tell your children" was observed and I would tell my children the story of the seder in camp until it became another legend, one of those tales that started with "Once upon a time, long, long ago ..."

Thirty years have passed since then, a lifetime, but those who were there did not forget.

Shortly after my novel was published, I was sent on a tour to promote it. It was in Cleveland that I faced my largest audience. A woman seated in the first row, sensing my stage fright, smiled at me reassuringly. When I finished my talk, she got up, turned to the audience, and said, pointing at me, "I know her." I was with her ..." Then, looking back at me she choked, "Tell them about the seder."

"Tell us, tell us," the audience chanted. And I did, the way I am telling it to you now. What I could not understand was, why were the people crying? I still look back on that evening as one of the highlights of my life.

Henia Karmel-Wolfe

My Father, My Hero

"I want to *do* something with my life," I told my father. "I want to accomplish something. What have *you* ever accomplished?" It was an awful thing to say, cruel and smug and snotty. The only plea I can enter in my defense is that I was fourteen at the time and, like every adolescent, the one thing in this world I could see with crystal clarity was my father's clay feet.

No man is a hero to his valet, the aphorism runs. Perhaps no father is a hero to his adolescent son. But even at fourteen, I should have known better than to ask what my father had ever accomplished. He had made a good marriage to a good woman, with whom he was raising five children in a home filled with love, laughter, and integrity. Pedestrian achievements? In my father's case, they were nothing short of heroic.

On the day after Passover in 1944, my father and his family were rounded up by the Nazis. Along with other Jewish families from their region of eastern Slovakia, they were taken from their homes and transported to a ghetto in the nearby Hungarian city of Satoraljaujhely. For six weeks they were kept in the ghetto, which grew increasingly crowded as more and more Jews were brought in. Then it began to empty, as Jews were taken out.

They left on a Thursday. With only the belongings they could carry by hand, they were marched to the waiting train. As each boxcar filled, its doors were chained and locked. There were no seats inside, no windows, no water. The only toilet was a bucket on the floor. For three days of suffocation, thirst, and stench, the train moved. When it stopped, David and Leah Jakubovic and their five youngest children—Franceska, Markus, Zoltan, Yrvin, and Alice—were at Auschwitz.

The doors opened. There were blinding floodlights, shouting SS guards, snarling dogs. The Jews were forced off the train and onto the platform; men and women were made to line up separately. *"Raus! Raus!"* they heard. "Out! Out!" In the noise and the confusion, they made their way along the platform at the end of which Dr. Mengele waited, performing the "selection." Some Jews he waved to the right, some to the left. My father, a strong eighteen-year-old, was sent to the left. His clothes were removed, his head was shaved, and a number—A-10502—was tattooed on his arm. My father's mother and father and his youngest brother and sister went the other way. Later he learned that they had been taken immediately to the gas. Yrvin was ten years old. Alice was eight.

Within a day or two, my father's other brother, Zoltan, was also killed. His sister Franceska lasted a few months longer. Of the seven members of the Jakubovic family who were rounded up by the Germans in the spring of 1944, only one—my father—was still alive in the spring of 1945. By then, he had been through four concentration camps. At the end he was in Ebensee, a satellite of the grim Mauthausen camp near Salzburg, Austria. He was nineteen years old, he weighed sixty-five pounds, and he was dying of typhus and starvation. When the Allies arrived at Ebensee, my father was nearly a corpse. He would spend the next month in a delirious fever in a field hospital. Later he would learn that he had also contracted a form of tuberculosis.

His trials didn't end when the war did. He made his way back to his native village in Slovakia, only to discover that strangers had helped themselves to his family's small house. He struggled to support himself—buying this, selling that, smuggling something else. Making a living would have been a daunting prospect for anyone in war-blighted Eastern Europe in 1945. What must it have been like for a young death camp survivor with no family, no property, and no home?

In 1948, the communists seized control in Czechoslovakia. My father, desperate not to be trapped again in a totalitarian dictatorship, got out. He managed to procure an American student visa and to raise the price of an ocean crossing. He got off the boat in New York on May 14, 1948—and was robbed on his first night in America. It is almost literally true to say that my father started out in the New World with only the shirt on his back.

He went to work as a manual laborer, nailing window sashes in a carpenter's shop. After a while he tried his hand at sales: mattresses first, then appliances, then furniture. In time he opened a furniture and appliance store of his own. His initial visa authorized him to stay in America for no more than one year. He has been here, so far, for fifty-two.

In all my years growing up in my father's house, when money was often very short and luxuries were few, I cannot recall ever hearing him complain about his circumstances. It is as if he decided that, after Auschwitz, no setback or misfortune was worth even a moment's self-pity. Nor can I ever recall hearing him boast—about anything. Perhaps he was never one to blow his own horn. Or perhaps he lost the urge to brag once he saw the utter degradation to which human beings can be reduced.

My father makes a point of giving some money to charity every day. I asked him one time, after watching him slip a few dollars to a panhandler who clearly had no good excuse to be scrounging for handouts, why he gave money to somebody so patently undeserving. "It's not my job to decide if he deserves," he told me. "A man came up to me with an empty hand. When somebody asks for help and holds out his hand, you don't turn him away."

That was, for him, a pretty long speech. He is not an especially eloquent man and to my knowledge he has never spoken before an audience. He still talks with an accent and sometimes garbles his syntax. But actions speak louder than words, and those who know my father have always known what kind of man he is.

His store was never a great success. He is not a born salesman, and never learned the art of talking uncertain customers into buying something they weren't sure they wanted. Nor was he much good at leaning on customers who had taken delivery of some furniture or an appliance, but couldn't be bothered to keep up their payments. Nevertheless, he earned a name for himself, as he learned during the "long, hot summer" of 1968.

When race riots erupted in Cleveland that year, my father's furniture store stood at Ground Zero—at St. Clair and 103rd, in the heart of the city's Glenville neighborhood. For days, the area was wracked by pillaging and arson; the violence was made worse by the mayor's order that all white police officers stay out. To deter looters, signs reading "Soul Brother" appeared in the windows of black-owned establishments, but there was no such sign in my father's window, and by the time it was safe enough for him to venture back into the city, he expected to find his store reduced to a burnt-out shell.

He found it untouched. The pawn shop next door had been gutted and the rioters had ransacked the A&P supermarket across the street, but Mark's Furniture & Appliance Co. hadn't suffered so much as a broken window. At the height of the riots, my dad later found out, a group of tenants who lived in the apartment units above the store had come down to the street and formed a human chain in front of the entrance. "Stay away from this place," they told the looters. "It belongs to a good man."

Once I asked my father if there was anything that had been uppermost in his mind when he was in the camps. Was there something he always concentrated on, some purpose he always clung to, a goal he always kept in mind?

No doubt I was hoping to hear something lapidary. Something like the exhortation of Simon Dubnov, the renowned Jewish historian whose last words before being murdered in the Riga Ghetto were,

"*Yiddin, schreibt und farschreibt*—Jews, write it down, write it all down." Perhaps my father would tell me that he tried to remember everything so he could one day bear witness to what he had seen. Perhaps he would say that he always looked for ways to sabotage the Nazi operations. Or that he never stopped dreaming of revenge. Or that every morning and every night he recited the *Shema*, the Jewish credo: "Hear, O Israel, the Lord is our God, the Lord is One."

This is what my father told me: He was always careful to watch his shoes. He slept at night with his shoes beneath his head, he said, because if you lost your shoes you wouldn't survive for long.

It was hardly the answer I had imagined. I had expected something inspiring, something courageous. Shoes? In the middle of the most evil hell ever created on earth, my father was thinking about his shoes?

But I have come to understand that my father was right. If shoes were essential to his survival—and when you are force-marched from Poland to Austria in the open in January, they are—then shoes were precisely the thing he had to think about. The Jakubovic family, awash in blood, was nearly extinct. My father had to survive. The Jews had to survive. Somehow, despite everything, they had to go on, and if shoes could keep this Jew alive, then nothing was more important than shoes.

Some Holocaust survivors emerged from their ordeal embittered and angry. Some came out cynical and untrusting. Some survivors, furious with God for not stopping the slaughter, turned their backs on faith and became enemies of religion. Some sank into black depression. Some slowly lost their minds.

If my father had done nothing but survive the Holocaust, his life would be worthy of note. That he survived as a decent man and a believing Jew, that he can still laugh and love and look on life's bright side, is nothing short of magnificent.

My father turned seventy-five this year. He has five children and—so far—fifteen grandchildren. He keeps the Sabbath and fasts on

Yom Kippur and eats matzah on Passover. Every morning and every evening, he says the *Shema*. He is a Jew who survived and who survived as a Jew. His life is a continuing defeat for Hitler, who had hoped to rid the world forever of men such as my father. In an age thin in heroes, my father is mine.

What did he ever accomplish? I never again asked such an insulting question.

Jeff Jacoby

A Priest Embraces His Jewish Roots

One night last week, as thousands of Montrealers gathered in a West End synagogue to commemorate the Holocaust, an enigmatic and dark-featured man in a priest's collar sat quietly in the audience.

He looked like one of the many dignitaries in attendance, there to pay homage to the millions who perished. But at one point in the ceremony, a request came from the stage: Would all the Holocaust survivors in the audience please stand up?

Amazingly, the priest rose, and started to cry.

Father Romuald-Jakub Weksler-Waszkinel is a living embodiment of an apparent contradiction: He is a Catholic priest and, as he discovered as an adult, also a Jew.

"I cried and cried," he recalled of the emotional gathering last week. "I thought of all the people who were exterminated. Of my mother, my father, my brother, and all my ancestors. I am alone."

Father Weksler-Waszkinel, a professor at Lublin Catholic University in Poland, was in Canada to promote Christian-Jewish dialogue at the invitation of the Canadian Jewish Congress.

He also came to visit an elderly Canadian woman in Toronto in the hopes of finding clues to his long-hidden past.

But mostly he came to tell his remarkable story of survival, at a time when the world's gaze turns back to the end of a horrible conflict sixty years ago. Born Jewish, Father Weksler-Waszkinel survived the war by being hidden in a Catholic home. He only learned the startling truth many decades later.

He was born in 1943 in the Jewish ghetto of the small town of Swieciany, then part of Poland and now in Lithuania. His parents,

Jakub and Batia Weksler, knew their baby risked death at the hands of the Nazis. Desperate, Batia managed to make contact with a gentile couple, Piotr and Emilia Waszkinel, and begged them to take her infant son.

To accept was to risk death. So Batia Weksler made an appeal that would prove prophetic: "You are a Christian, and Jesus was Jewish," she told the fearful Emilia. "Save my child, a Jewish child, and in the name of Jesus whom you believe in, he will grow up and become a priest."

The Catholic couple sheltered the little boy and raised him as their own. And one day, as if driven by blind destiny, their son announced that he would enter the priesthood. He couldn't understand why his parents weren't happy. His father scoffed, his mother cried into her handkerchief.

He stuck with it, even while doubts about his identity gnawed at him. As a little boy, town drunks taunted him by calling him a Jewish bastard. He searched in vain for a resemblance to his parents and their Slavic features. He himself was afraid of the truth. The church had taught that the Jews killed Jesus: "It's not possible I was one of the killers," he thought.

It wasn't until he had already been a priest for twelve years that Father Weksler-Waszkinel confronted his mother, who was ailing. They met for supper one night.

"I took her hands, and covered them in kisses. I said, 'Mother, you must tell me. It's just one part of the story of your life, but it's my entire life. It's my roots.'" Sobbing, his mother confided the truth.

"You had wonderful parents," she told the thirty-five-year-old, "and they were killed. I saved your life."

Stunned, he felt the need to confide in someone, and wrote to another Polish priest. Karol Wojtyla had been Father Weksler-Waszkinel's professor in Lublin. Now he was Pope John Paul II. The pontiff responded: "My Beloved Brother. I pray so that you can rediscover your roots."

The priest combined the names of his two families. Eventually, he traveled to Israel and met his father's brother. He was shown a photo of his mother, in whom he finally saw the light of self-recognition. His uncle embraced him as a long-lost relative, but also confronted him: How could he choose to embody two thousand years of hatred toward Jews?

"I'm not two thousand years old," he replied, "I'm just forty-nine. I can only change the attitudes of others. To really belong to Jesus means to love Jews. You can't be observant and anti-Semitic at the same time. I believe my destiny is to purify the house I live in."

While in Israel, he also brought up a name that his father had often mentioned to him: Niusia, a young Jewish girl from his home-town. In another stroke of fate, one of his hosts knew her, and she lived in Toronto.

Now in Canada, Father Weksler-Waszkinel disembarked from a bus in Toronto, and an eighty-year-old woman recognized him immediately. She had never seen Father Weksler-Waszkinel, but instinctively knew it was him.

Niusia Nodel grew up across the street from Father Weksler-Waszkinel's Jewish family. She also remembers his Catholic parents, and the kind Polish woman who took him in. "She was very brave. Because she was in danger for doing what she did."

"As a mother, I know what it is to raise a child," said Mrs. Nodel, who also survived the war in hiding and saw her family wiped out. "I held back tears for his mother, who wasn't alive to see him grow up."

Now Father Weksler-Waszkinel struggles to reconcile his two faiths. He wears a Star of David overlaid with a cross, which he glued together himself. Since arriving in Montreal, he finds that everywhere he looks, he sees people who resemble him.

"When I'm with Jews, I feel I'm with my family. It's irrational. I live in Poland, where I'm a bit like an orphan."

Lublin, whose population was one-third Jewish during the war, doesn't have a single Jewish family left, he says.

Mainly, the sixty-two-year-old priest says he is in Canada because he wants to bear witness to history, and his personal tale, which he describes as "miraculous."

"I am here as a Catholic priest who is Jewish, and who discovered his roots. And now that I discovered them, I love them."

Ingrid Peritz

Beyond Kindness

It was March 13, 1938. Hitler marched into Vienna, Austria. He was greeted by ecstatic crowds, frenzied in their applause. His parade of swastikas swam in the air like birds bringing unknown fruits of deliverance. Everyone was out except the Jews. We were hiding in our apartments, trembling with fear, aware that his entrance meant possible extermination for *not* wearing the swastika and thus being recognized as what Hitler had described as "the enemy, the crud of the earth who had betrayed all that Germany and its allies stood for." He proclaimed, "Only total removal could re-create the world as it was meant to be." My family and I, in our soon-to-be-destroyed apartment, were living among both Christians and Jews. There were five of us: mother and father, I and a younger brother in our mid-teens, and our eighteen-year-old brother. Our building superintendent, Fritz, was Christian. How would we be dealt with? Who would be allowed to live, or destined to perish? Fritz was key. He would be asked the crucial question, "Where are the Jews?"

That day arrived. "Are there Jews living in this building?" asked the Nazi youth in their impeccable uniforms and emotionless voices, as though they were asking if there were mice or roaches in the basement. Looking directly at them, shoulders square, voice simple and strong, Fritz replied without mincing words. "No Jews here. Only Christians."

In the days that followed, Fritz behaved as he always had in his role as superintendent of the building. Occasionally he asked if we were well, if we needed anything. The Nazi storm troopers filled the streets, shooting at random anyone they wished—a child stealing potatoes for starving Jewish parents, a young man with a Jewish star sewn on his arm—then laughing as if they were at an amusement park shoot-ing at duck decoys. Ah, Fritz, how you must have loved humanity to take such a risk! I wonder if you knew you saved these five lives. I know that all who did not have supers like you—most of my extended fam-ily—were slaughtered in their homes or in the camps. We stayed, living as though at any moment our lives could be cut off with the snap of a finger. Finally, in August of 1939, we left. War broke out the next month. We went to America, living at first with an aunt who had migrated to the States some years earlier when she foresaw what was to come. I grew up determined to honor Fritz's love of humanity and cul-tivate it in myself. Perhaps it was part of the reason I decided to become a psychotherapist and psychoanalyst and in that small way serve others. Fritz was an ordinary human being, but he acted with pure consciousness and connection in the most exemplary of ways. He was just a super. He was also a just and superior being.

Wilhelm Weiner, PhD

Beshert

I heard this story from a fellow tourist on a recent trip to Israel. My tourist friend conveyed the story, which he heard from his Israeli family.

My friends, the Goldbergs (all the names in this story have been changed to protect the privacy of the family), are Holocaust survivors, as are their cousins. Chaim Goldberg attended the wedding of his grandson Elan, who was to marry Tzippora Segal, but had never met Tzippora's grandparents until the day of the wedding. Chaim Goldberg was introduced to Chana Segal, Tzippora's grandmother. While Chaim and his wife, Miryam, were chatting with Chana and her husband, Baruch Segal, Chaim and Chana were staring at each other, and became distracted from the conversation.

"Don't I know you?" Chaim asked Chana.

"I was just thinking the same thing," said Chana. "It was probably in one of the concentration camps during the Holocaust. There were many of us there, but we have both grown so much older now, we probably look much different than we did sixty years ago.

Suddenly Chaim got a flash of memory. "Chana," he yelled. "It can't be. You can't be that Chana?! What was your maiden name?"

"Before my marriage to Baruch Segal, my name was Chana Pincus."

At that point Chaim almost fainted. He leaned on his wife, Miryam, for support.

"Oh, my God," yelled Chana. "You are Chaim Goldberg!"

All four of the grandparents were given chairs—Chaim and Miryam Goldberg, Chana and Baruch Segal.

This is the story that unfolded

Before the Second World War, Chaim Goldberg and Chana Pincus had been married to each other for a short time. They had no children. Miraculously each had survived the Holocaust. Following their rescue from different concentration camps, each one searched and searched to find the other. Finally, each came to the sad realization that the other had not survived. Despondent, they went on with their separate lives. In time, each married again and had children, who in time had their own children.

Now, Chaim and Chana were meeting—sixty years later—never knowing that the other had survived the war. And, miracle of miracles, their grandchildren were getting married to each other—Elan Goldberg and Tzippora Segal—whose grandfather and grandmother, unbeknownst to the bride and groom, had been married to each other before the black night of the Holocaust. Now they were joining in holy matrimony, putting back together a family that was torn apart by the Nazis, and was now, in a strange way, whole again.

Cecelia Ostrov Euster

Babe Ruth and the Holocaust

A thletes usually avoid politics like the plague. Baseball diamonds and basketball courts inhabit a world where all that matters is a player's athletic skills, safely distant from the turmoil of political controversy. But every once in a while an issue is so morally compelling that an athlete feels he must cross the barrier that separates his insular neighborhood from the rest of the world.

That's what Babe Ruth did sixty-five years ago this week. The issue that moved him was the Holocaust.

Throughout the spring and summer of 1942, the Allied leadership received a steady flow of reports about German massacres of tens of thousands of Jewish civilians. Information reaching the Roosevelt administration in August revealed that the killings were not random atrocities, but part of a Nazi plan to systematically annihilate all of Europe's Jews. In late November, the State Department publicly verified this news and, on December 17, the U.S. and British governments and their allies released a statement acknowledging and condemning the mass murder.

But aside from that Allied statement, there was little indication that the Roosevelt administration intended to do anything in response to the killings. There was no talk of opening America's gates—or the gates of British-ruled Palestine—to Jewish refugees. There was no talk of taking any steps to rescue the Jews. As quickly as the mass murder had been revealed, it began to fade from the public eye.

Dorothy Thompson was determined to keep that from happening. And Babe Ruth would help her.

Thompson, the first American journalist to be kicked out of Nazi Germany, was once described by *Time* magazine as one of the two most influential women in the United States, second only to Eleanor Roosevelt.

Thompson herself was of German descent, and in the autumn of 1942, she contacted the World Jewish Congress with the idea of mobilizing German-Americans to speak out against the Nazi persecution of the Jews.

As a journalist, Thompson understood the news value of German-Americans protesting against Germany—especially in view of the well-publicized pro-Nazi sentiment in some segments of the German-American community. Just a few years earlier, more than twenty thousand supporters of the German American Bund had filled Madison Square Garden for a pro-Hitler rally.

The World Jewish Congress agreed to foot the bill for publishing Thompson's anti-Nazi statement as a newspaper advertisement. During the last week of December 1942, the "Christmas Declaration by Men and Women of German Ancestry" appeared as a full-page ad in the *New York Times* and nine other major daily newspapers.

"[W]e Americans of German descent raise our voices in denunciation of the Hitler policy of cold-blooded extermination of the Jews of Europe and against the barbarities committed by the Nazis against all other innocent peoples under their sway," the declaration began. "These horrors ... are, in particular, a challenge to those who, like ourselves are descendants of the Germany that once stood in the foremost ranks of civilization." The ad went on to "utterly repudiate every thought and deed of Hitler and his Nazis," and urged the people of Germany "to overthrow a regime which is in the infamy of German history."

The names of fifty prominent German-Americans adorned the advertisement. But the signatory who was by far the best known to the American public was George Herman "Babe" Ruth.

Widely regarded as the greatest baseball player in the history of the game, Ruth, known as the Sultan of Swat, at that time held the records for the most home runs in a season (60) and the most home runs in a career (714) as well as numerous other batting records. Having excelled as a pitcher before switching to the outfield and gaining fame as a hitter, the amazingly versatile Ruth even held the pitching record for the most shutouts in a season by a left-hander. Not surprisingly, Ruth was one of the first players elected to the Baseball Hall of Fame.

By participating in this German-American protest against the Holocaust, Ruth used his powerful name to help attract public attention to the Jews' plight. Timing is everything, both on the baseball field and beyond, and the timing of Ruth's protest was crucial: Precisely at the moment when U.S. officials were hoping to brush the Jewish refugee problem aside, Babe Ruth helped keep it front and center.

In an era when professional athletes rarely lent their names to political causes, and when most Americans—including the Roosevelt administration—took little interest in the mass murder of Europe's Jews, Babe Ruth raised his voice in protest. Home runs are not the only thing about Ruth worth remembering.

Dr. Rafael Medoff

The Amazing Actions of the Citizens of Piea

Over sixty years ago, from 1943 through 1945, my family was protected from the Nazis by the villagers of Piea. In May 2007, the entire town of Piea was recognized and honored by the Jewish community of Torino, thanks largely to the efforts of the Torino Jewish community and my sister, Michelina de Leon Treves.

The community of Piea d'Asti, in particular the DeGiorgis and Pescarmona families and Don Ambrogio Isidoro, the local priest, were recognized for having sheltered and saved Jews during the Holocaust. Now, at eighty-three, my sister recalled those years: "I was born in Torino, but if someone were to ask me where I come from, I would say, 'I am from Asti,' and it would not be a lie. It is thanks to the people of Asti that I have lived, married, raised my daughter, and watched my parents age and die. In those years, I learned that even on the darkest night, there is always a bright star in the sky. Mine was called Piea."

When we arrived in Piea, we were greeted warmly by the locals who came to know us as the DeGiorgis family. We were given food, housing, and work. We lived simply, as farmers, mingling with the other villagers. My father assisted the villagers in many ways, because he was so handy, and I became the family member who attended church every Sunday, who milked the cow we had purchased and brought her to pasture at the edge of the road, together with a couple of goats and a sheep.

I helped the farmers, our friends, in the fields and vineyards, actually enjoying the farm work and the camaraderie that developed among us.

We were embraced by those simple people, who would bring my little sister, five-year-old Emilia, back home when she ran off, who offered a helping arm to my ninety-year-old grandfather, and who helped my sister occasionally visit her fiancé Giorgio Treves, a partisan living "underground" in a nearby valley town. During our two years in Piea, we believed that our Jewish identity was unknown to the townspeople. Only after the liberation did we learn that the people of Piea had known that we were Jews and yet had kept this secret during the two years we had lived among them. They had kept this secret, jeopardizing their own lives, since Nazis regularly came through Asti villages looking for hidden arms and young men who had deserted the army during the confusing days of the short-lived armistice in July of that infamous year, 1943. Partisans were also hiding in those hills, and battles were frequent.

As we prepared to return home from Piea, my father, Giorgio de Leon, spoke to the townspeople:

Dearest Friends,

The day has arrived in which I am again free to return to my own home and especially, to my work among my old employees, my own workmen.

In this time of happiness, I want to thank all of you dear "Pieesi" for having welcomed us to this village. We found in you that warmth, that hospitality for which today I can do nothing else but thank you and express to you our eternal gratitude.

And so, we leave this town where we have spent two years with you, in the midst of you, doing all sorts of jobs. We leave here proud of your friendship, promising you that I will come to visit every now and then together with my family.

I want to express before all of you gathered here my special gratitude to the family of Giuseppe and Laurina DeGiorgis of Porta di Sotto and to Signor Venturello, who have protected us, putting yourselves at great risk and danger. To Signor Corio, the tobacconist, who gave us shelter knowing who we were and knowing what could befall all of us. And to all of you who, without exception, guarded our secret with care. Remember us as we will remember you—with affection, as we are now, here all together. I salute you and I wish you every blessing.

[Speaking to the "band" made up of an accordionist and a clarinetist]: Music, maestro!

In 1963, twenty years later, the six of us—my husband and I and our four daughters—traveled to Italy. We spent wonderful days visiting with family. We made a special pilgrimage to Piea to visit those who had hidden us during the war. What a warm and loving welcome we received. We went from house to house, where we were introduced warmly to everyone. Food and drink awaited us in every single house.

Over the past decades, I have spoken to dozens of school groups and other groups about my experiences during the Holocaust. I have spoken about the residents of Piea and their righteous deeds over and over again. But with those who had actually protected our family long deceased, I did not take formal steps to have Piea recognized as a community of "righteous gentiles." Now, thanks to the desire of the Torino Jewish community to recognize all of those who helped save Jews during the Holocaust, the people of Piea have been formally thanked and celebrated. I am so grateful that day has finally come.

Additionally, a boulevard in a villa in Torino has been dedicated to the "Giusti del Piemonte e della Valle d'Aosta—the Righteous Ones of the Region of Piedmont and of the Valley of Aosta." Signs on the trees of that avenue honor their memory. Now they truly will never be forgotten.

Giorgina Vitale

Great Escapes

While countless lives were snuffed out during the Holocaust (Shoah), a few were fortunate enough to constitute the "saving remnant." The dramatic stories of escape and ultimate reunion comprise a glorious chapter of courage and heroism even in the midst of this Kingdom of Night.

The lengths to which some people were able to go to breach the wall of death and escape into life is a chapter of Jewish history that defies logic and reason. But they did, and the events surrounding the experiences of these valiant and daring souls is another point of pride that Jews should hear about and retell and retell and retell.

Caution: Jewish Minds at Work

Berel Kasachkoff, like thousands or his brethren at the time of the Russian revolution, knew that freedom to live as a Jew *and* as a human being mandated escaping from the Soviet Union. The Russians knew this as well and accordingly stationed sentries all along their borders. A problem, Berel conceded, but nothing a *yiddishe kopf* could not overcome. One might say this was a rather flippant attitude, considering that the border guards were heavily armed and instructed to shoot on sight. Berel, however, had big plans and would not allow a technicality—no matter how formidable—to stand in his way. Thus, armed with only his wit and a prayer on his lips, Berel headed for the Polish border.

When Berel arrived at the most secluded spot he could find close to the border, he discovered that even there the border crossing was heavily guarded, and he was forced to scuttle his first plan. As he considered his options, he noticed that not only was the area well patrolled, but also the sentries were on a state of high alert.

It was only four months since the Revolution had erupted, and whereas every citizen feared his neighbor, Red Army soldiers were afraid of their own shadow. Not an especially auspicious climate for breaking the law ... until Berel concocted a way to use it to his advantage. Bravely and defiantly, he made a beeline for the guardhouse and marched off toward his destiny. He strode past the few merchants lined up at the border crossing, each of them displaying their papers and travel permits. Berel did not have a legitimate document to his name. The only identification papers he possessed had been forged to enable him to avoid the draft. The forgery was amateurish, but the papers were the best he had been able to afford; those papers were the last thing he would present to guards, who were under orders to send anyone with questionable papers directly to jail.

"Halt!" ordered one of the soldiers.

Berel kept marching.

"I said, '*Halt!*'" Berel kept right on marching.

A second soldier aimed his rifle at Berel's heart. Berel could hear the cartridge slide into the breech.

Berel continued marching toward Poland, on a collision course with the soldiers and their itchy trigger fingers.

"Papers!" the guard commanded.

Berel looked at him unbelievingly. "What did you say?" he asked.

"Papers! Let me see your identification papers!"

"My papers? You want to see *my* papers? You mean you're asking to see *my papers*? Why, I should have you all shot! Don't you know who I am?"

For a moment there was silence. Berel's eyes blazed with anger, fury, wrath, and righteous indignation. By this time he was fairly shouting. "Well?" he bellowed. "*Do you know who I am?*"

The soldiers looked at each other. Before they could answer, Berel snarled, "Let me see *your* papers!" and then screamed "*Now!*"

Stunned by the ferocity of his voice and the authority of his manner, the soldiers began rummaging through their pockets.

Berel continued shouting. "I ought to have you shot, then drawn and quartered for good measure. The absolute insolence! The ultimate impudence! The outrageous audacity! And you call yourselves soldiers?!"

"We didn't know—"

"*Silence!*" Berel ordered. The guards meekly passed him their papers. He gave them a cursory inspection, then threw them on the ground. "Fools! Idiots! You can be sure that when I return from my official mission I will have your *heads*!" he roared. Then Berel spat in disgust at their feet, and proceeded to cross the Russian checkpoint into freedom.

As he entered Poland, he couldn't resist a parting shot. When he figured he was beyond the range of their rifles, he shouted at the top of his lungs, *"Now do you know who I am?"*

"N-n-no," they shouted back.

"Berel Kasachkoff, at your service!" He tipped his hat, gave the stunned guardsmen a brief but polite bow, and then ran for his life.

Rabbi Hanoch Teller

The "Seder" of Righteous
Gentiles: A Family Liberation

The Netherlands, 1945

When Emperor Napoleon invaded Russia in the early 1800s, his military government forced all citizens to take last names. In Augustova, near Minsk, one Jewish family was called into the military office to pick a last name immediately after Tisha B'Av, the day when Jews remember the destruction of the First and Second Temples. They had just been to the synagogue where they prayed and wept as they remembered the destruction of Zion, the poetic name for the Land of Israel. So this family chose the last name *Zion*. In 1856, the Zion family left Russia and settled in Holland, in a village called Eibergen, where they opened a clothing store.

In 1940, the Germans invaded Holland. In 1941, the Jews of Holland were ordered by the German Nazis to report for "resettlement." The Zion family had three brothers and three sisters who decided to go underground. Even though Jews had little social contact with their Calvinist Protestant neighbors, they were helped by the ministers of the Calvinist church, Puritans who helped organize the underground movement.

Even before the war, one of the Dutch ministers would go across the border from Holland to Germany to try to convince the German Calvinists to oppose the Nazis. Soon, the German ministers, who wanted to prove their loyalty to the Nazis, refused to allow him to speak at their services. After the Nazis invaded Holland, this minister, who was called Fritz "de Zwerver" (Fritz the Wanderer), would go from church to church in Holland on his bicycle. Since all rubber had been confiscated by the Germans, his bike had wooden wheels.

One Sunday morning Fritz arrived in Eibergen and walked to the podium of the Protestant church (the most important part of the Calvinist service was the sermon preached from the Bible). Even though there were pro-Nazi Dutch officials sitting in the front row, he opened his Bible to Exodus 1:15–22 and read the story of the midwives in Egypt who saved the Hebrew male children from drowning. Then he said to the congregation, "Who is the pharaoh today? The Nazis! Who are the babies who have to be hidden? The Jews! Who are the midwives today? We are! It is our job to outsmart the pharaohs, to have the courage of the midwives and to protect the Jews and all those being persecuted." Then he got on his bicycle and went to the next village. The people were inspired by Fritz de Zwerver, who encouraged them to organize an underground. Many members of the church participated, and hid Jews in their houses. Dutch architecture emphasizes large roofs on houses, under which Jews and other refugees who went into hiding were placed.

During this period, Sallie Zion's family was hidden by these righteous gentiles in forty different places. When the person protecting them would say, "I can't hide you any more," he would have to find another hiding place. Sometimes the family was told ahead of time that they would have to leave in a day or a week. Then someone would come from the underground, usually at night, on a bicycle, take them to a safe house, and hide them under the roof.

The last place Sallie Zion and his brother stayed was at the home of the Wassink family, who lived in a large farmhouse on the outskirts of town. They could see people coming across the fields to the house, and so could be alerted when danger approached. Sallie and his brother were hidden under the roof, a triangular space about three feet by six feet. (Sallie Zion carved a poem he wrote on one of the beams in the roof.)

Since they were on the outskirts of the town, they did not need to hide during the day. They were able to help with the household tasks, but always stayed indoors. When necessary they would go up a rope ladder, which could be folded and pulled up. The ladder was hidden behind a large embroidered wall hanging, traditional in Calvinist homes. It was embroidered in Dutch with the biblical words: *Blessed are you when you come in and when you go out.*

Hidden with Sallie Zion and his brother were two Jewish girls, sixteen and eighteen years old, a Russian pilot, a Canadian pilot, and a British pilot who had been shot down and taken in by the family. Also hidden was the Wassink family's oldest son and a first cousin who had been called to work in a German factory and did not want to go. All were hidden in one very narrow area.

A couple of days before the liberation of northeastern Holland from the Nazis in March 1945, a lookout for the Wassinks reported that thirteen Nazis and two Dutch collaborators were approaching. Quickly, all the illegals hid under the roof. In order to remove all signs of the hidden illegals, Mrs. Wassink cleared away extra cutlery and dishes. She turned to her eldest daughter, gave her the stolen ration cards used to purchase extra food, and told her to hide them in the barn in an old stove. Then she turned to her ten-year-old son, Wim, and told him to go visit relatives, but not to run, lest he arouse suspicion. As Wim nonchalantly twirled a stick in the air, the Nazis spotted him and told him to come with them into the house. Other Nazis were coming down a path where a large log had fallen. Each German had to step over the log, but one who had a big potbelly tripped and fell. Wim wanted to laugh, but had to keep it inside. When they brought the boy into the house, it was about 11 a.m.

The Nazis searched the house. One of them came to the kitchen and saw a large, black pot on the stove. He turned to the mother and pointed to the big pot, saying "too much food." She stood up and held her two fingers forming "V" in a victory sign and said, "This big pot is enough for two days."

While the Nazis continued to search, the Wassinks sat down for lunch. In a Calvinist household, everyone sits down for the big meal at lunch, a prayer is said, and the Bible is read. The prayer Mrs. Wassink recited in Dutch was, "May the evil Nazis be struck by blindness, just as the evil people of the biblical city of Sodom were struck by blindness when they came to molest the guests taken in by Lot" (Genesis 19). The Nazis continued their search and even measured the inside and outside of the house to see if there was any unaccounted-for space. However, they measured the length and not the width. The hiding place under the attic was luckily in the width of the house. The Nazis even went up to the attic with a lantern. It shone on the hidden people, but when the Nazi held the lantern and tried to look through a crack, the light of the lantern blinded him, so in a way, Mrs. Wassink's prayer came true.

Then one of the Germans took Wim to the pigsty. "We know there are people hiding here," he said. "If you don't tell us where, we will throw you in with the pigs."

The boy thought, "Pigs are certainly better than Nazis." The soldier began beating him, and he screamed. (His older brother, one of the people in hiding, got upset and wanted to run and help Wim. The Russian pilot, Alex, took a pillow and shoved it over the brother's head until he calmed down.) Wim did not reveal anything.

After the beating, Wim's mother turned to the officer and pointed to her son. "Look how you have beaten him! Look at his bloody nose!" The officer apologized and told the German who had beaten the child to go to the yard, pump some water, and wash the child's face. Then the Nazi officer told the family they would have to leave their house. He put up a sign declaring the house off-limits. At night the underground came to extricate the people hiding "under the roof," including Sallie Zion, and several days later the Allies arrived and liberated Eibergen.

On Dutch Liberation Day, May 5, the Wassink clan and all those they helped like to get together. They pull out the old iron pot and sometimes eat carrot stew. The embroidery of "Blessed are you when you come in" (which once covered the rope ladder leading to the hide-away) hangs on the wall next to the framed yellowing Nazi poster instructing everyone that this house is off-limits. Though after the war the old house itself was razed, a scale model was constructed (like a dollhouse) showing the secret spaces. The family sits together on those occasions and the younger members ask the elders to retell the story in detail, so that it shall never be forgotten. In a way this annual get-together is their personal Passover, complete with symbolic foods and stories of courage and divine help. It is an interesting coincidence that the Torah reports that Lot served his guests in Sodom matzah, and so the rabbis say that the rescue of Lot and his endangered guests (in fact, angels) occurred on Pesach.

Noam Sachs Zion and David Dishon

The Cry of the Shofar

My grandparents evaded the Nazis during the terrible war years of 1943 and 1944 by hiding in different places in France. With them were my mother, my uncle, and a group of children whose parents had been deported to the concentration camps. My grandparents took care of them throughout the war.

In the summer of 1944 they were in the Department of Gers. But they couldn't stay there much longer. Too many people knew of their whereabouts. It was only a matter of time till the Germans would hear about them and about the Jewish school that my grandfather ran for the children. They had to leave, but where to?

An exciting rumor reached their ears, giving them hope. "The Italians are leaving Nice and going back to Italy," they were told. "The Italians like the Jewish people. They will take you with them."

My grandfather had heard about the Italians. The Italians, even though they were on Germany's side, did not allow their Jewish citizens to be deported. It sounded like a good plan. Nice, on the southern coast of France, would be their next destination.

But when they arrived at the train station of Nice, the Italians had just left and the Germans were coming. The train station was already swarming with Nazis in uniform, clicking their heels, and barking *Heil Hitler*. Nice was far from the safe haven they had hoped for.

Rosh Hashanah, the Jewish New Year, was around the corner. They would stay in Nice through Rosh Hashanah and then they would try to figure out where else they could run to. Meanwhile, they stayed in the home of a kind, gentile woman.

On Rosh Hashanah, my grandfather, his family, the children, and a few assistants of his gathered to say the Rosh Hashanah service. The service of Rosh Hashanah is always a serious one. But on the Rosh Hashanah of 1944, the darkest year of the darkest war that humankind has ever known, it was an especially serious one. The lives of the little group were in danger. All over Europe and Russia, the lives of the Jewish people were in danger. Millions had already perished.

They reached the part in the service when the shofar, the ram's horn, must be blown. The call of the ram means many things. It is the call of the Day of Judgment, when each of us must account for our deeds of the past year. It commemorates the ram which appeared to Abraham when God had told him to unbind his son Isaac and remove him from the altar. It is the reminder that one day God will gather God's flock from the four corners of the world and bring them to Israel. God would usher in the days of the Messiah when nation shall no longer war against nation. And the Messiah would build the Third Holy Temple.

My grandfather had a shofar, but how could he blow it? The sound of the shofar is very loud. The Germans were all around. Many of the French citizens were German sympathizers. They could not risk being heard.

My grandfather did not know what to do. To blow the shofar would endanger their lives. But on Rosh Hashanah you must blow the shofar. It is the mitzvah of the day. My grandfather was not one to compromise when it came to religion. (In all the years of war, despite poverty and want, he ate only strictly kosher food and made sure his group did the same.) He must blow the shofar. The question was how?

The gentile owner of the house came up with an idea. The house was close to the train tracks, she said. If they blew the shofar exactly when the train went by, the train would drown out the sound of the shofar and no one else would hear it.

It sounded like a good plan. The little congregation waited until they heard the distant rumbling of a train. My grandfather recited the blessing over the shofar. Then came the *Sheheheyanu*, a blessing thanking God for "sustaining us and enabling us to reach this occasion." Yes, after four years of running and hiding, it was a miracle that they had reached this occasion.

The rumbling grew louder. It was time! *Tekiah,* one of my grandfather's assistants announced quietly. My grandfather sounded the long, wailing sound of the shofar: too-oo-oo-oo-oot. *Shevarim,* announced the assistant. Now it was a burst of three short staccato blasts: toot-toot-toot. *Truah.* That was the broken, sobbing sound: tut-tut-tut-tut-tut-tut. And while the people in the room all heard the trumpeting of the ram's horn unmistakably, no one outside heard a thing. The plan had worked.

The age-old sound of the shofar aroused awe in the hearts of the people present. There is a God; God listens to our cries! The ram's horn seemed to express all the anguish, pain, and fear they had experienced. But it symbolized their hope and eternal trust too. Here they were, a group of Jewish fugitives led by a short man who walked with a limp, surrounded on all sides by the enemy; yet they had succeeded in fulfilling God's commandment. Despite the odds, goodness had prevailed over evil, faith over despair. Hope filled their hearts again.

They prayed again, until they heard the rumbling of the next train, at which time my grandfather blew the shofar again. And so on. And nobody outside the small, serious group of praying adults and children ever suspected anything.

Everyone was happy. The group of Jews because they had been able to fulfill the mitzvah. And the owner of the house because she had been able to help them.

Shortly after Rosh Hashanah the group left Nice. This time they headed north to Grenobles, where it was a little safer. In a year or so the war would be over. My grandparents, my mother, my uncle, and many of the children survived that terrible time, thank God.

And the Jewish nation survived. True, a third of them, six million innocent souls, had gone to their death, for no other reason than that they were Jews. But as a people they had survived. And, incredible though it sounds, so had their belief in the one God and the Divine's eternal goodness.

Sterna Citron

Whoever Saves One Life
Saves a World Entire

It's April 1938. My mother has just returned from Romania after visiting her dying mother. She passed through "Anschlussed" Austria in a sealed railway car, and is seated at the kosher table aboard the French superliner *Ile de France*. Joining her for dinner is a stranger, one Martin Lichtenstein of Breslau, Germany. As the great Art Deco ship crosses the Atlantic, conversation at the table reveals that Mr. Lichtenstein has, after much effort and interminable waiting, obtained from the U.S. Consulate in Berlin a U.S. immigration number for his family. The number will enable them to enter the United States and so escape the storm gathering over Germany's Jews. Immigration numbers alone are not sufficient. They are less than useless if the lucky possessor does not have notarized affidavits from relatives who are U.S. citizens. The affidavits affirm not only a family relationship of reasonably close degree, but that the undersigned have the means and agree to support the new immigrants for up to five years. This is to ensure that they will not become a public charge, and a drain on the United States of America. Martin has an aunt in Detroit and is headed west after docking to ask her if she will sign for him and his family. At some point in the uneventful voyage, my mother gives Martin Lichtenstein the business card of Bloom's Bargain Floor Coverings Store in West New York, New Jersey.

A month or so later, Mr. Lichtenstein shows up at the store. He is distraught and depressed. His aunt in Detroit was unable or unwilling to sign the affidavits. It was, after all, the Depression. And besides, no one would have predicted what was about to happen in the land of Bach, Goethe, and Schiller. Then began a redemptive moment. My parents, Sam and Sally, told Martin Lichtenstein that they would be his family's sponsors. They said that they were his cousins. They opened their books and Internal Revenue Service records to the Immigration authorities to demonstrate that not only were they relatives, but they possessed the wherewithal to sponsor this escaping family. They agreed to support the Lichtensteins for as long as was required.

They signed all the crucial affidavits. According to the Lichtensteins' son Kurt, "They signed whatever was put in front of them."

On Friday, March 3, 1939, as she passed the Statue of Liberty about to dock in New York, the USS *Manhattan's* manifest listed four passengers with the surname *Lichtenstein*. It was some eleven months after Sally had inadvertently met Martin Lichtenstein and barely six months before the German invasion of Poland.

Sam Bloom got in his truck, with the GO WHERE THE THRIFTY GO TO SAVE logo emblazoned on its side, crossed the Hudson, and arrived at the pier on West 18th Street to pick up the strangers he had sponsored and for whom he was now responsible. Martin and Katie and their children, Irma and Kurt, awaited their American benefactor eagerly, though with understandable trepidation. The *Manhattan* arrived late Friday at 9:30 p.m. after a stormy crossing. The Sabbath had, in its inexorable way, begun eighteen minutes before sunset. Though new refugees, the Lichtensteins were also observant Jews. They would not ride in the truck on Shabbat. Despite Sam's pleas—that this was their first day in the United States, that he had with significant effort and inconvenience come to fetch them, and that no one would question this one-time trespass of Sabbath rules—they politely, but steadfastly, refused to board the truck. Sam Bloom, ever-resourceful, escorted them to the nearest hotel. They also refused to sign the hotel register. Sam signed the register for them, and went home in his empty truck. He came back Saturday night, to fetch them after the Sabbath was safely over. They got into the truck without objection. He took them to our then-new family home in Palisades Park, New Jersey. After a Sunday's respite, he spent the next week finding and renting an apartment for them on 58th Street in West New York, New Jersey. Then he went on to obtain, using every contact he knew and with his own persistent, sometimes relentless style an Edgewater, New Jersey, peddler's license for Martin Lichtenstein, so that he might begin earning a living. These were still the days of the Great Depression. A peddler's license was no small thing.

I was a little boy back then. From my child's perspective, the Lichtensteins were the source of great bounty. They gave me a mechanical toy car. A marvel of German technology! They gave the family a Zeiss-Ikon camera, which served as the family camera for many years. There were also some little silver whiskey goblets—a few of which I still have. But the pièce de résistance was a scooter that had a floorboard with a ratchet that was attached to the rear wheel. By shifting my weight back and forth I could make it move without *ever* putting my feet on the ground. I loved it, and was heartbroken when my father inadvertently drove over it, bending the rear wheel beyond repair.

The families became and remained good friends for a long time afterward, veritable "cousins," visiting back and forth and attending each other's simchas. I remember spending an almost-too-intense-for-me Sabbath in their home. I remember Irma's marriage at the Broadway Central Hotel in New York City. And so the years passed.

In October 1961, my father, Samuel Bloom, died. At his funeral the rabbi of the synagogue where he regularly attended morning services remarked that though Sam had done this saintly act of saving a family from the Holocaust, the Lichtensteins were not present at the funeral service. Yet indeed they were there. Nonetheless, there were hurt feelings and without Sam Bloom around, and his beloved Sally, my mother, going through difficult times, and my preoccupation with my studies, my new spouse and daughters, and beginning a career, the two families lost touch.

Fifteen years later, our family was on a shopping expedition to New York's Lower East Side. We walked into Charlie's Place on Orchard Street, looking for clothes. Seated, with a yarmulke on his head, was Kurt Lichtenstein. I recognized him immediately, walked over to him and said, "Kurt, I'm Jack."

There was no sign of recognition.

"Kurt, I'm Jack Bloom."

Still no recognition.

"Kurt, I'm Sam Bloom's son."

Kurt's eyes lit up and he blurted out, "Jackie!"

Excitedly, we interrogated each other. Are you married? How many kids? Where do you live? We exchanged addresses. Having Kurt and his wife Brocha's address meant that they received our High Holy Day cards annually, each of which included a family photo.

Sometime thereafter, Kurt invited us to the Bar Mitzvah of his fourth son in Monsey, New York. My wife and daughter, Rebecca, were seated at some distance in the women's section. I was honored with an *aliyah* among the men. Afterwards for the kiddush we were seated at long tables, laden with potato and noodle kugels, nestled in their aluminum containers, large bottles of soda, bowls overflowing with chopped liver, pickles, cole slaw, and potato salad, all the accoutrements of a lavish kiddush, that paid little attention to presentation but ensured that no one would go away hungry.

I was seated across from the Lichtensteins' fifth son, who was under ten years old. He was looking around when suddenly his eyes went wide. He said to me,

"You're *the man in the picture*."

"Yes, that's right, I'm the man in the picture."

"You *saved my father from Germany*."

"No, I didn't save your father from Germany. My father saved your father from Germany."

"Your *father saved my father from Germany?*"

"That's right!"

He stood up, grabbed a full potato kugel, and pushed it toward me.

"Mister, have the WHOLE pie!!"

That Sabbath day, I reaped—in the wide eyes and plain words of a little boy—what my parents had sown. And although he didn't know it, my reward was far, far bigger than a potato kugel could ever be—even a whole one.

Long before 1938, it was written, "Whoever saves a single life saves a world entire." My parents saved a family they did not know from a destiny none could have imagined. They gave life to Kurt and Brocha's five sons, grandchildren, great-grandchildren, and all their descendants, numbering as of 2008, fifty-two, and increasing year by year.

Rabbi Jack H. Bloom

Rabbi Yehudah Arieh Leib Alter and the Soldier

Everybody usually thinks that *holy* means "far out." But the Heilige [holy] Ishbitzer says *holy* really means "right there."

What is the Ishbitzer saying? That, for example, God is called Holy because the Divine is always there when you need God.

And it's the same thing with the *tzaddikim*, the holy Jews. In former good days, what did simple Yidden do when they were in trouble? They went to the big rebbes, the Holy Masters, because the *tzaddikim* were always there for them. Yes, the rebbes taught the most exalted Torah. They encouraged people to do *teshuvah* (repentance), tried to fix their souls. But most of all, they wanted to ease the burden of suffering Yidden in this world. What they wanted most of all was to help …

At the beginning of the twentieth century, Russia and Japan went to war. And, sadly enough, the Russian authorities loved to draft young Jewish men, especially yeshivah students, into the army to fight the Japanese. These poor Yidden didn't want to interrupt their studies, or risk their lives for a country that gave them nothing but trouble. And they knew that their time in the army would be nothing but insult and pain. So what did they do? They went to the Holy Masters, like Rabbi Yehudah Arieh Leib Alter, the Heilige (holy) S'fas Emes, for help. And the rebbes would bless them that through some miracle, they would not have to go to the war.

One day the S'fas Emes noticed a young man waiting with all the others for a blessing to be saved from the army. And this Yiddele looked so gentle, so sweet, it was clear that he *mamash* (really) wasn't fit to be a soldier. When it was his turn to see the rebbe, his voice was so low the S'fas Emes could hardly hear him. And all he said, so softly and sadly, was, "Holy Master, I've been drafted."

The S'fas Emes had never seen anybody look as broken as this holy Yid. "Gevalt," he thought. "He's just a child. He's much too young for all this." Then, turning to the young man, he said, "Wait here." He went into his private room, and when he came out a few minutes later, he silently handed the boy a book.

The young man glanced at the title; it was a manual on how to do circumcisions, how to perform a *bris*. The youth looked at the S'fas Emes in surprise. "Holy Master …?" he started to ask. But the rebbe interrupted him:

"My sweetest friend, listen to me. Read this book, learn how to do a circumcision. And I bless you that even if you do have to go into the army, you should come back safe and whole and *b'shalom*, in peace."

"But, Rebbe!" the young man cried. "I don't want to go to war! Bless me that I won't be drafted at all!"

But the S'fas Emes was no longer paying attention. He was already talking to the next person in line.

In the end, the sweet young Yid did go into the Russian army, and was sent to basic training. Army life was very hard for him, especially one thing: the other soldiers—peasants, really—were *mamash* SO dirty. Their uniforms were always wrinkled and soiled, their shoes were never shined. They never cleaned their barracks. They didn't know how to stand in straight lines, and they didn't even take care of their rifles. The Jewish boy had always been very neat, very orderly, and he hated living in such sloppiness and filth. He himself was always careful to keep his own things in perfect order and so—*gevalt!*—he was the only one in his unit who looked or acted anything like a proper soldier. And whenever he had a few spare minutes, or he felt particularly sad and lonely, he thought of his strange meeting with the Holy S'fas Emes.

And, as the Rebbe had instructed, he read the little manual on circumcision from cover to cover.

One day a general came to review the new recruits. He immediately noticed the sorry state of the rooms, the clothes, and the rifles, and shouted at the commanding officer: "What's going on here? Is this how soldiers are supposed to be? It's a total disgrace!"

"Sir, I'm really so sorry," the officer said. "To tell you the truth, I'm also ashamed of these men. I've tried to get them to shape up, but.... Still there is one soldier I'm really proud of—a Jew. He's always clean and neat, he follows orders well. He's *mamash* a good soldier, despite his being Jewish."

"Is that so?" the general said. "Then bring him to me. I want to see this Jew for myself."

When the sweet Jewish soldier was ordered to report to the Russian general, he trembled in fear. What could such an important person want with him? It couldn't be anything good! Still, he had no choice, so he appeared as instructed at the door of the commanding officer's private office. The general ushered the boy into the room. Then suddenly, without saying a word, he took out a pistol and pointed it at the young soldier. The poor Yid started to shake even harder. The general looked at him coldly and demanded in his most intimidating voice, "Is it true what they say, that you only eat kosher food?"

The young man was afraid to admit it, but he knew better than to lie. He swallowed hard and answered, "Yes, sir."

The general marched up to him and held the pistol against his chest: "You are now a soldier in the army of the czar of Russia. And the czar requires that his soldiers have strong bodies. They must eat all the food they are given. I hereby order you to eat whatever is put before you, kosher or not!"

Suddenly the young Yid was more angry than afraid. Eat *treif* food? Never! So he said, in a clear, strong voice, "I'm sorry, sir, but I cannot obey that order. I'm a Jew. I serve God, not the Russian czar."

The general stared at him again. Then he asked, "Is it also true that you keep the Jewish Sabbath?"

This time the young soldier didn't even hesitate. "Yes, sir, I do."

"What?" the general cried. "A soldier of the czar wasting time, taking a day off every week, and in the middle of a war? I hereby order you to work every day!" And he pushed his pistol harder against the youth's heart.

The young Jew knew that this was *mamash* the test of his life. The general could kill him in a second. Still, he squared his shoulders, stood up a little straighter, and answered firmly, "I'm sorry, sir, but I can't do that. There is no way I will work on Shabbat. I may be in the Russian army, but the only One I serve is God in Heaven."

Suddenly the general smiled and put away his gun. "It's all right," he said to the astonished Yiddele. "I'm not going to shoot you. It's just that I had to be sure. You see, nobody knows this, but I'm also a Jew. I was drafted, just like you, and worked really hard in the army, just like you do. I kept a low profile, and after a while people forgot I was Jewish. And now, as you can see, I'm at the top.

"But my wife just had a baby—a son. And the thing is … I don't know exactly why, but I want him to have a real kosher circumcision. Now I can't go to a regular *mohel*, because I have to keep his *bris* absolutely secret. If the army remembers I'm a Yid, I won't just lose my position, I could also lose my life.

"So I've been looking all over for a Jew here in the army who can do the circumcision quietly for me. And when I heard about you, I thought you might be the one. I'm not really religious, but I do know one thing: A *mohel* has to keep Shabbos and eat kosher and generally observe the commandments. That's why I asked you those questions. I was testing you, to see if you kept the *mitzvot* (commandments).

"And now that I see what a good Yid you are, I'll make you a deal. I want you to be my *mohel*. I'll sign a pass for you, tell them I need you on my staff, and take you home with me. And after you circumcise my son, I'll give you civilian clothes and you can go on your way."

The young Jewish soldier couldn't believe his ears. *Gevalt!* Thanks to the little manual, a circumcision was something he knew how to do. And for the first time, he *mamash* appreciated Rabbi Yehudah Arieh Leib's true holiness. The rebbe had such *ruach hakodesh* (divine spirit) that he'd foreseen not only his own need, but also that of this hidden Jew.

The boy grasped both of the general's hands, lifted up his eyes to Heaven, and cried, "'*Hodu Lashem Ki Tov*—Give thanks to God, for He is good.' And give thanks to his servant and messenger, the Holy S'fas Emes!"

Rabbi Shlomo Carlebach

Words of the Wise

$\mathcal{K}$ing Solomon was famous in his day, and in our day, for his great wisdom. He is reputed to be the author of some of the great books of the Hebrew Bible (*Tanakh*), such as Proverbs, Kohelet (Ecclesiastes), and Song of Songs. This is what scholars refer to as part of the Wisdom Literature of the ancient world.

From Solomon's day to ours, great minds among the Jewish People have given birth to deep wisdom—in sermons, in stories, in life experiences. In this section we meet a chaplain's brave action during the Second World War, a sensitive physician, a writer with great psychological savvy, an aged grandmother, and a youngster who learned wisdom the hard way. All of them are part of the circle of wise people who populate the Jewish world, past and present.

Rabbi Gittelsohn's
Iwo Jima Sermon

The fight for Iwo Jima in 1945 was one of the bloodiest of World War II. A tiny island in the Pacific dominated by a volcanic mountain and pockmarked with caves, Iwo Jima was the setting for a five-week, nonstop battle between seventy thousand American Marines and an unknown number of deeply entrenched Japanese defenders. The courage and gallantry of the American forces, captured by the dramatic raising of the American flag over Mt. Suribachi, is memorialized in the Marine Corps monument in Washington, D.C. Less well remembered, however, is that the battle occasioned an eloquent eulogy by a Marine Corps rabbi that has become an American classic.

Rabbi Roland B. Gittelsohn (1910–1995), assigned to the Fifth Marine Division, was the first Jewish chaplain ever appointed to the Marine Corps. The American invading force at Iwo Jima included approximately 1,500 Jewish Marines. Rabbi Gittelsohn was in the thick of the fray, ministering to Marines of all faiths in the combat zone. He shared the fear, horror, and despair of the fighting men, each of whom knew that each day might be his last. Roland Gittelsohn's tireless efforts to comfort the wounded and encourage the fearful won him three service ribbons.

When the fighting was over, Division Chaplain Warren Cuthriell, a Protestant minister, asked Rabbi Gittelsohn to deliver the memorial sermon at a combined religious service dedicating the Marine cemetery. Cuthriell wanted all the fallen Marines—black and white, Protestant, Catholic, and Jewish—honored in a single, nondenominational ceremony. Unfortunately, racial and religious prejudice was strong in the Marine Corps, as it was then throughout America. According to Rabbi Gittelsohn, the majority of Christian chaplains objected to having a rabbi preach over predominantly Christian graves. The Catholic chaplains, in keeping with church doctrine, opposed any form of joint religious service.

To his credit, Cuthriell refused to alter his plans. Gittelsohn, on the other hand, wanted to save his friend Cuthriell further embarrassment and so decided it was best not to deliver his sermon. Instead, three separate religious services were held. At the Jewish service, to a congregation of seventy or so who attended, Rabbi Gittelsohn delivered the powerful eulogy he originally wrote for the combined service:

> Here lie men who loved America because their ancestors generations ago helped in her founding, and other men who loved her with equal passion because they themselves or their own fathers escaped from oppression to her blessed shores. Here lie officers and men, Negroes and whites, rich men and poor ... together. Here are Protestants, Catholics, and Jews together. Here no man prefers another because of his faith or despises him because of his color. Here there are no quotas of how many from each group are admitted or allowed. Among these men, there is no discrimination. No prejudices. No hatred. Theirs is the highest and purest democracy ...
>
> Whosoever of us lifts his hand in hate against a brother, or who thinks himself superior to those who happen to be in the minority, makes of this ceremony and the bloody sacrifice it commemorates, an empty, hollow mockery. To this, then, as our solemn duty, sacred duty, do we the living now dedicate ourselves: to the right of Protestants, Catholics, and Jews, of white men and Negroes alike, to enjoy the democracy for which all of them have here paid the price ...

We here solemnly swear that this shall not be in vain. Out of this and from the suffering and sorrow of those who mourn this will come, we promise, the birth of a new freedom for the sons of men everywhere.

Among Gittelsohn's listeners were three Protestant chaplains so incensed by the prejudice voiced by their colleagues that they had boycotted their own service to attend Gittelsohn's. One of them borrowed the manuscript and, unbeknownst to Gittelsohn, circulated several thousand copies of it to his regiment. Some Marines enclosed the copies in letters to their families. An avalanche of coverage resulted. *Time* magazine published excerpts, which wire services spread even further. The entire sermon was inserted into the *Congressional Record*, the Army released the eulogy for short-wave broadcast to American troops throughout the world, and radio commentator Robert St. John read it on his program and on many succeeding Memorial Days.

In 1995, in his last major public appearance before his death, Gittelsohn reread a portion of the eulogy at the fiftieth commemoration ceremony at the Iwo Jima statue in Washington, D.C. In his autobiography, Gittelsohn reflected, "I have often wondered whether anyone would ever have heard of my Iwo Jima sermon had it not been for the bigoted attempt to ban it."

Michael Feldberg, PhD

Franz Joseph and Anshel's
Secret Room

Everyone has heard of the famous, wealthy banking family, the Rothschilds. The founding father of the Rothschild clan, which exists to this day, was Anshel Rothschild, an Orthodox Jew who lived in the middle of the nineteenth century in Austria. Anshel amassed a huge fortune and established a close relationship with the emperor of Austria, Franz Joseph.

From time to time the emperor would send visitors to the luxurious and famous palace of Anshel Rothschild. It was the most lavish, luxurious, and well-appointed palace in all of Austria, and everyone wanted to see its beauty and wealth.

During one visit, Anshel took his guest on a tour of the palace. He showed this important government official, whose position was just under Emperor Franz Joseph, room after room, and the guest was awed by the beauty of the gold, the silver, the furnishings, the chandeliers, the imported fabrics. Everything was a sight to behold. There existed nothing like it in all of Austria.

When Anshel passed a certain door, he continued walking, but the guest asked to be shown the room behind the door.

"I am sorry," said Anshel. "This is the one room in the palace that I cannot show you."

"Why not?" asked the guest. "I would love to see every nook and cranny of your remarkable palace."

"I simply cannot," answered Anshel, and continued walking.

The tour concluded, and the official returned to his master and reported everything he had seen. The palace was even greater than one could imagine. "However," said the official to the emperor, "there was one room that Anshel refused to show me."

"Why not?" asked the emperor.

"I do not know. But I can guess. You know how wealthy those Jews are. My theory is that in that room there is a magic moneymaking machine. That is why he is so wealthy. Behind that door must be a machine that creates the wealth of Anshel Rothschild." The emperor did not know whether to believe his official, so he sent a second government official to see the palace of Anshel Rothschild. The second official came back with the same story. And a third, and a fourth.

By now the curiosity of Emperor Franz Joseph was greatly aroused, so he decided to go himself and visit the palace. Anshel took the emperor for the same tour as he did all the other visitors from Franz Joseph's government. And when they reached the "forbidden room," the emperor asked to go inside and see what was there.

Anshel explained that that was the one place he could not show anyone. After the emperor insisted, Anshel gave in, and agreed to show the emperor the secret room. He took out his keys, opened the door, and invited the emperor to enter. Franz Joseph looked around, and was amazed at what he saw. There, in a small room, was a simple pine box, and some plain white cloth on a table. That was all there was!

"What is this all about?" asked the emperor.

"We Jews have strict rules about burial customs," explained Anshel. "When a person dies, he must be buried in a very simple coffin, a plain pine box. And his body must be enveloped in a plain white shroud. This is to maintain the equality of all God's creatures. No one is permitted to be buried in a fancy, expensive coffin, or in luxurious clothing. Though some may live affluent lives, and others may suffer dire, abject poverty, in death all are equal."

"But why is this here in this room?" asked the emperor, impressed but still confused.

"At the end of each day I come to this room, and view the coffin and the shrouds, and I am reminded that even though I have great wealth and power, and I have important influence in the highest echelons of the Austrian empire, I am still one of God's simple creatures, and at the end of my life, this is the end I will come to, like all of God's other children. I do this lest, after a day filled with high finance and major financial transactions, I think too highly of myself, and develop a bloated sense of myself."

Franz Joseph was amazed, and in fact, he was speechless. His respect for Anshel Rothschild grew even greater than before. He never questioned the sincerity, honesty, or integrity of Anshel again.

Rabbi Yitzchak Cohen, as told to Rabbi Dov Peretz Elkins

In Memory of a Gangster's Mother

I grew up in Chicago, where my father and grandfather were both rabbis. One Sabbath afternoon when I was a young boy at my grandfather's home, a big Cadillac pulled up. Three burly guards stepped out with a well-known Jewish gangster. The man walked in and laid an envelope on my grandfather's table filled with cash. "This is for my mother's *yahrzeit*." (*Yahrzeit* is the anniversary of one's death. It is a special Jewish religious obligation to give charity on a *yahrzeit* in memory of a beloved parent or others.) Then he left.

I was surprised at my grandfather. "How can you accept money from that man, on the Sabbath of all times?" (Religious Jews may not touch money on the Sabbath.) My grandfather said softly, "Don't you understand what happened? This man is a criminal who lives an ugly life. But for one brief moment he looked on a calendar and saw that it was his mother's *yahrzeit*. He remembered his mother's dreams for him, that he grow up to be a Jew, that he grow up to be a *mensch*. For one brief moment, he wants her memory to live within. That was a sacred moment, and I do not want to take away from it."

That story says it all. Even from beyond the grave, our loved ones can reach out and touch us, and change us.

Rabbi Eli J. Schochet

Washing the Body

The ring of the telephone jolted me from sleep. After a somewhat hectic night on call I had tried to retire early. In a half-dazed state, I answered the phone. I recognized the voice on the other end instantly. He said, "It is time. Meet us there in half an hour." I put down the phone, dressed quickly, and began to reflect on what I was about to do …

He had been a good man, generous, kind, and well liked. A pillar of the community, what is often referred to in Yiddish as a *mensch*. He had been my patient for a long time, one of the first patients in whom I had placed an implantable defibrillator. Slowly, over the years, he changed from patient to good friend. We had faced many crises together over the years, and somehow his failing heart always managed to pull through. When he was diagnosed with lung cancer, both of us knew he would not last long. On the last clinic visit prior to his death he looked at me and said, "You have been a good friend over these years. I have only a little time left. Would you be part of the Chevra Kaddisha after I die?" I froze, speechless. The Chevra Kaddisha, or Holy Society, is a voluntary group in the Jewish community whose sole purpose is to prepare the body of the deceased prior to burial. It is the greatest of honors to be asked to do such a thing, and almost before realizing it I said, "Of course."

Over the following months the other members of the group prepared me. Tradition dictates that the funeral take place as soon as possible after death; thus, there is often little notice. We meet in the parking lot of the funeral home. We greet each other and converse quietly until the other members of the group arrive. Together as we enter the funeral home the mood is restrained, as each of us has a set responsibility to attend to.

The dead must be treated with the greatest of respect at all times and our duties must be performed quietly and meticulously. We gather together, wash hands, and recite a blessing. Then, with the greatest of care, we wash the dead. Ever so gently, careful to avoid any sudden or jarring movements, his body is sponged clean. Odd, to see the man I had known in life in the stillness of death. Even though my mind often drifts back to memories of him in life, I try to focus on washing the same torso where the implantable defibrillator I once placed still lies. When the cleansing is complete, his body is carefully and gently given a ritual bath (*mikvah*) for symbolic purification. Then after he has been fully dried, we dress him only in a plain white linen shroud. As we do this, I recall a passage from the Talmud that says, "When a child is born his fists are clenched as if to say, 'All this will be mine.' Yet when a man dies his hands are open, as if to say, 'I bequeath this all to you for I can take nothing.'" Finally his body is placed into a plain wooden casket and a prayer shawl is wrapped around him. During this entire time my heart has been pounding and beads of sweat have covered my forehead. Somehow this has been more stressful than performing a procedure on a living patient. Now finished, we gather and ask for forgiveness from the soul of the departed (for each of us realizes that our minds have not been totally focused during the process of preparation). On occasion, one of the group will stay behind, sitting at the side of the casket reciting verses from Psalms until the burial is complete, making sure the body of the departed one is not disturbed. On the drive home I cannot help but wonder why I was so nervous beforehand, and why I now feel such a feeling of satisfaction (as well as relief). I sense that I have fulfilled a sacred obligation, a debt that the deceased can never repay.

Perhaps my anxiety was because of the distinct contrast between this and the attitudes I have witnessed toward the dead during my medical career. While in my residency the attending physicians would often utter phrases like "death with dignity," their actions all too frequently fell short of that ideal. We have tended to see death as some kind of failure on our part as physicians, rather than the natural or inevitable process it is. We retreat from the dead (and their families) as soon as possible, unsure of what to say or do. Death seems to be one of the few subjects that remain forbidden in American society, and physicians, for the most part, seem little prepared to deal with it.

Several weeks later another patient (of a different ethnic and religious tradition), whom I had known for years, died after a prolonged illness. This time, instead of leaving the family after they were informed, I stayed as they mourned and then escorted them to the patient's bedside. After a moment of silence I turned to leave, but one of the family members said, "Please, don't go yet, doctor." She took my hand in hers, as the rest of the family gathered around the bed. Then, in the clearest and most beautiful voice she began to sing "Amazing Grace" (interspersed with frequent interjections of "Amen" by the others present).

I noticed that the usual noise of the ward had stopped, as everyone present, physicians, nurses, and visitors patiently stopped everything for a moment, just to listen.

Blair P. Grubb, MD

Red Ribbon—Blue Ribbon

The Daughters of Miriam home for the aged sits on a high bluff overlooking New Jersey's Garden State Parkway as it races through Passaic County on its way to New York State or, in the opposite direction, to the ocean at the tip of Cape May. The contrast between the frenzied movement on the Parkway and the torpid tempo of life in the home is compelling.

I have been visiting that home for the aged since the early 1940s. One of my two grandmothers was there then because her physically deteriorating condition caused her to fall frequently. She died there in 1948. When I first visited the facility, it was small, with only a single brick building. Today it is large and sprawling with multiple additions to the original residence as well as several new and freestanding buildings.

On one hand, it is good that places like the Daughters of Miriam home exist to care for the aged. The supervision is good, the care affectionate and responsible. But underneath the surface pleasantness, there is an unspoken understanding that all recognize: This is a place where a person goes to die. Here, women who were once beautiful young brides and men who were once handsome young suitors spend their final days. The residents of the facility are almost always unprepared for and resistant to their entry into this world, often unable to comprehend what has happened to them, frequently unhappy, and sometimes suicidal. The children of the aged suffer, too. Good intentions notwithstanding, it is a difficult and guilt-filled decision to place any family member in such a facility, no matter how good the care.

The population at the Daughters of Miriam home for the aged is predominantly Jewish, though non-Jewish residents live there, too. For almost sixty years I have seen the occupants of the home receive good care from considerate people.

In 1982, it became my mother's turn. Who knows? Someday it may be mine. Her Alzheimer's-induced deterioration had begun some years before and, at first, not recognizing the symptoms of her condition, my family was amused by her actions. They appeared eccentric and even comical, not menacing. But we were fooled. The eccentricity was a harbinger of a severe and radical change in personality that eventually led to a complete inability to function.

When the full truth of her physical condition and deteriorating mental state became known, my brother and I took the necessary steps to institutionalize her, the greater burden being placed on my brother and sister-in-law; he lived nearby while I live on the other side of the continent.

Whenever business travel brought me to the area, I expanded my schedule so I could visit my mother. And so it was that I presented myself on a number of occasions, far too few in retrospect, at the Daughters of Miriam home during the years of her confinement.

A large and well-lit social hall, comfortably holding fifty to seventy-five people, was the place to which we would invariably gravitate during my visits. Sometimes, I would meet Mom in her room and sometimes we would stroll in the gardens, hand in hand, to sit on a bench under the trees. There, she would tell me stories about her childhood, anecdotes that I already knew, though was anxious to rehear. But inevitably she would seek out the company of her peers, perhaps to display me (to show that she was not alone and abandoned), other times because she felt most comfortable being in the company of her contemporaries. It was not that she was uncomfortable with me, but it multiplied her pleasure to be simultaneously with both me and her peers.

The room had chairs arranged haphazardly, but the men and women subconsciously seated themselves in a great ellipse, moving the chairs to create the geometry. As residents came into the social hall from their own rooms—everyone in this section of the home was able to walk or capable of negotiating a wheelchair—they would seat themselves at some point on the ellipse's perimeter and then fade away.

Fade away? Now that's a peculiar term. I need to explain myself.

Though there are exceptions, at some point in the lives of the aged—that point being determined by an unknown interaction of age and genes—the old stop living and fade away. While their basic bodily functions of breathing and eating continue during the decline, they languish nonetheless. And how does this condition manifest itself? Somewhere in the cycle they develop a thousand-yard stare, their smiles wither, they communicate less frequently, and moments of human contact become more infrequent. Suddenly, one day, they are gone—alive, but ... elsewhere.

So as I would sit in the recreation hall with my mother, surrounded by these fading people, I frequently wondered what I could do about it. But thinking like that was living in a fantasy world. Smarter, better-trained people than I couldn't fix this inexorable march, so what could I do? Should I shout, "Wake up, all of you. Live again! Don't fade on me"? That's an easy thing to say, but is little more than Hollywood bravado.

On the other hand, might these people be motivated to shake off their lethargy by the simple expedient of asking them for advice? All of us like to be asked for our opinion, so why not the aged, in fact, particularly the aged? When was the last time that anyone had asked them for help? It is a basic human need to give, and no one was making that demand of them. Let me try.

However, the inquiry could not be fatuous or obvious. A worthless inquiry, such as "Do you think we will have good weather today?" was not the right approach. A distinctive, uniquely engineered question, one geared to the base of knowledge that only the elderly are likely to have, might be successful. In effect, the question had to be substantive.

"Ahem … Ladies and gentlemen!!" I said with a voice guaranteed to get their attention and speaking in Yiddish so as to assure maximum communication. "I am sorry to trouble you, but I am desperate for advice. A terrible but highly specialized problem has me at my wit's end and I need your counsel."

Hardly anyone looked up. Most did not react. The thousand-yard stare was in full force with that group of about thirty people.

I continued, "The matter has to do with keeping an evil eye away from a child," the exact word used being the Yiddish, *ahora*. I was sure that most would know it.

Six women reacted immediately. Their heads popped up as if on a string. I had gotten their attention. Well, that worked. The subject was certainly kooky enough.

"My mother, who is seated here," I continued with an unsmiling face, "has told me how to prevent an *ahora* from becoming attached to a beautiful child, an event that is natural to the evil eye. She suggests that it is necessary to pin a ribbon of a distinctive color on the child's undergarment. The specific difficulty that I face deals with the color of the ribbon. My mother no longer remembers so I have selected a blue one. Is this the correct choice? I don't know what to do. What do you think?"

A woman of at least ninety-five slowly stood up, extricating herself from her wheelchair, and, casually swiping a neighbor's walker, came over to where I was seated. She was about four and a half feet tall. With every eye in the room now attached to her, she stopped in front of me, her face level with mine, and peered at me as if to assure herself that the person to whom she was about to speak was capable of understanding her. Her eyes squinted. Her lips pursed.

In all the visits I had paid to my mother at the Daughters of Miriam facility, I had never known this woman to speak, to react in any way, or even to walk. In fact, I had never seen her out of her wheelchair.

She chicken-necked to bring her face even closer to mine. Our noses were almost touching. She looked at me from the left; then the right. Finally she spoke.

"Vos has du gezukt? A blaue bandl fur an ahora?? S'iz ganz meshiga. Nur a rote bandl. Farshtest du kind? A rote bandl!" she said as if speaking to someone with a need to wear a football helmet to avoid hurting himself.

A free-form, contemporary translation of her remarks to me might be summed up as follows: "Moron!! Are you for real? What kind of an idiot would use a blue ribbon against the evil eye? That's ridiculous! It is an absolutely mandatory requirement to use ribbons that are red. Have you any idea what I am talking about, putz?! Only a fool would even conceive of a blue ribbon to ward off the evil eye."

She then went back to her chair, sat down, and farted, the final constituent being a statement of her disdain for my suggestion. I was afraid to move. Something very weird was going on here.

Then, twenty-three women (I counted them) all began to talk at once. Their response was instantaneous and bordered on violent. They all began arguing mightily as to the proper ribbon color required to counteract the evil eye's fascination with an infant. While there was absolute agreement that the ribbon had to be red (except for one Mizrachi Jew from North Africa who suggested that pink was the custom in her village until 1910, when red had been adopted as a more effective and trustworthy way to keep the evil eye at bay), the discussion suddenly took on a new and unanticipated direction. The women were, without any prompting from me and by common but unspoken agreement, now posing alternative techniques that were supposed to be even more helpful to stay the offending hand of a powerful but negative force. In effect, having demolished my original suggestion, they had branched out to the realm of greater efficiency in evil-eye-management techniques. It was like the Harvard Business School's approach to inventory or slumping sales.

"Frankly," said a lady from upstate New York, "my mother said that spitting three times between extended index and middle fingers of the left hand will completely eliminate the presence of the evil eye and will dissipate its influence. And if my mother said it, you can be assured that the information is accurate."

"That's absurd," said another, a Holocaust survivor born in Kovno, Lithuania. "The technique you describe is only to get rid of unwanted guests."

"A pot! You need a clay pot!!" said a second-generation American woman whose Yiddish was no longer accurate. But she had gotten the general drift of the discussion. "You must use a pot in which you have kept dirt gathered at night and by a full moon. Then you take the dirt, cast it over your left shoulder with your right hand, and make an incantation to drive out the evil eye."

Then, with less certainty, she scratched her head and continued. "Or is the it right shoulder with the left hand? And the incantation? Let me think a moment ... Oh, me. I've forgotten it. No! No!! I have it. You say the blessing for miraculous events; and the evil eye is finished, let me tell you, sweetheart."

She paused, a puzzled expression on her face, and concluded her contribution with, "Maybe I have gotten the rules for an evil eye mixed up with those for exorcising a dybbuk."

An African American nurse whose duties included observing the residents in the social room (and whose Yiddish had gotten to be fairly good after five years of employment there) chimed in with her Southern folk wisdom. "My mother said that when bad spirits were out walking, and could snatch a child like *that*," snapping her fingers for emphasis, "you put a piece of camphor in a little bag and tied it around the child's neck. The stink keeps away all bad spirits and you can always find the child in the dark."

"You have that mixed up with polio," said my mother, now getting into the conversation. "You put a piece of camphor in a cotton bag, fix a silk drawstring on it, tie it around the child's neck, but not too tight. That child will never spend a minute in an iron lung; and some even say that garlic is better than camphor."

I just sat back and listened. In all my visits to this home for the aged, I had never seen such a vocal display as this. Such life! Such animation!! And all from a throwaway line about the color of a ribbon.

The fact is that no one had asked these elderly men and women for an opinion on anything for a very long time. They needed to be asked. They wanted to give. And like Willy Loman in Arthur Miller's *Death of a Salesman,* they needed to have someone pay attention to them. What they missed was being listened to. If this experiment carried any meaning at all, it was that the march ever closer to mindlessness was being accelerated because they weren't contributing to anyone else's life. Life is a process that requires several orders of magnitude of giving and only a little taking.

For the next year, until my mother's condition caused her to be sent to a separate wing where she was bedridden for the rest of her life, whenever I went to the Daughters of Miriam home, the men and women would become excited when I walked into the room with Mom. They waited expectantly for me to ask them for their help. And I never disappointed them.

"Friends of my mother. A few days ago I sneezed while a dead person was spoken of. My mother said that something on my head should be pulled to ward off evil, but she did not know what it was. Is it the nose? The chin? What?"

Daniel N. Leeson

Check Out My Room

A prominent rabbi of Newton, Massachusettes, attended a house-warming party at a large, beautiful home in this wealthy suburb of Boston.

Guests oohed and ahed, checking out every unusual piece of furniture, every exotic light fixture, every imported piece of handcrafted art, the thick azure carpets, the golden hand-carved door handles both inside and outside, and on and on and on.

During the course of the evening, the homeowners related to their guests that they had paid the highest fee for their interior decorator, but it was worth every penny. The results were astonishing. Every decision, down to the last window treatment, was just impeccable. They could not have been more pleased.

"This," they declared, in contrast to what most people thought was how a home should be furnished, "was interior decorating."

About an hour passed and the elderly mother of the hostess, who lived with her daughter and son-in-law, asked her rabbi friend to come upstairs and take a look at her room.

Having left the posh living room and dining room of this large, magnificently appointed, and lavish home, the elderly woman opened the door of her upstairs bedroom and pointed her finger toward the windowsill. When the rabbi looked, he was astounded at what he saw.

The woman did not point, as her daughter did, to any of the furniture or decorations in the room. She pointed only to the windowsill, toward a row of charity boxes, what are called in Yiddish *pushkes*—one for every worthwhile cause imaginable. There were boxes for hospitals, *yeshivot* (religious schools), orphanages, battered women's shelters, homes for children who were blind or deaf, funds for the handi-capped—you name it! One for every single Jewish institution she could find that distributed charity boxes for people to drop coins in and return when full.

Before modern methods of fund-raising took hold, these small charity boxes "decorated" kitchen windows in every traditional Jewish home. "Now, Rabbi," said the elderly woman, gazing proudly at her windowsill filled with charity boxes—"*this* is interior decorating!"

Rabbi Dov Peretz Elkins

True Love

How easy it is to confuse love with passion! One father said of his teenaged son, "I don't know if he's in love or in heat!" Feelings of attraction can change more quickly than the seasons, but love, in its truest form, is steadfast and unchanging.

Love is what Mr. and Mrs. Strauss shared. Mrs. Isadore Strauss was one of the few first-class women passengers to go down with the *Titanic* in 1912, and she drowned because she could not bear to leave her husband.

They remained calm throughout the excitement of the sinking vessel. They both helped frightened women and children to find places aboard lifeboats. Finally, Mr. Strauss, who had repeatedly urged his wife to claim a spot safely aboard a lifeboat, forced her to board one.

She was seated for only a moment, however, when she sprang up and climbed back on deck before he could stop her. There, she caught his arm, snuggling it familiarly against her side, and exclaimed, "We have been together for a great many years. We are old now. Where you go, I will go."

For them, true love was about commitment. And it was about faithfulness. And sacrifice. Not everyone finds such love in another person—though it is a beautiful thing when it occurs. But a committed and faithful love can always be found in another realm. It exists at the very core of authentic spirituality. This is a fact that whole and happy people build their lives around.

Steve Goodier

Providence

*A*truism about life is that we never know what tomorrow will bring. An old Yiddish proverb informs us, "People plan and God laughs." (In Yiddish it is an untranslatable rhyme: *Man tracht und Got lacht*). The fascinating thing about serendipity is that many good things are born by accident, at the right time, the right place, and in the right circumstances. Often, as in the case of the famous Four Chaplains, we push fate and something good comes out of something bad. And sometimes serious illness teaches us lessons that we never dreamed we would learn. All these events prove the old saw that there is no experience in life from which we cannot learn something important and valuable.

The Accident

It was, after all, a mistake. It had been one of the worse nights of my residency. There had been so many admissions that I had virtually lost count, and I barely was able to keep up with the needs of my own patients, much less all the other ones I was cross-covering. I was desperately rushing to finish checking labs and ordering tests before hurrying off to morning report. Later that day I was struggling to fight back fatigue and finish attending rounds when I received a page to report to radiology immediately.

"Oh great," I thought. "Now what's wrong?" However, upon my arrival I was the sudden focus of congratulations and pats on the back.

"Great pickup!" they said. "Look at that," one of the radiologists said, pointing to films and an upper GI series hanging on the viewbox.

"A small bowel tumor, classic appearance!"

I stood there dumbfounded. I had no idea what they were talking about. I picked up the chart and leafed through it. Then I realized what had happened. In my haste to keep up with everything the evening before, I had ordered an upper GI on the wrong patient!

Looking more closely at the chart, I learned that the patient was a priest and the director of a local Catholic college. He had been complaining of cough and fever, as well as nonspecific malaise and therefore (as was common in those bygone days) was admitted to the hospital for an evaluation. The upper GI showed a leiomyosarcoma of the bowel that luckily had not spread, and he was operated on the next day. The surgeon paged me in the operating room to show me, saying, "You really saved this guy's butt. I've never caught one before." I was too embarrassed to say anything, so

I nodded my head politely and walked out. I didn't tell a soul what had happened.

The hectic pace of residency quickly resumed and the incident was soon forgotten. About a week later I was paged to the surgical floor. When I returned the call, one of the nurses informed me that one of the patients wanted to speak with me. I told her that I didn't have any patients there. She replied, "It's a priest, and he's quite insistent on speaking with you." I froze and felt a deep, sinking feeling in the pit of my stomach. In a near trancelike state, I slowly made my way to his room. As I entered, I had a sudden urge to throw myself at his feet while saying, "Forgive me, Father, for I have sinned," but instead I quietly introduced myself and took a seat by his bed. A distinguished-looking man in his late fifties, his piercing eyes seemed to stare directly into my soul.

"Were you the one who ordered the test on me?"

I nodded my head and said nothing.

"Why?" he asked.

"It was … an accident," I stammered. I told him everything, the words almost pouring out of me, a relief to finally tell someone. He appeared pale and said nothing for a long time, the two of us sitting in utter silence. After a while he finally spoke.

"The last several months have been something of a spiritual crisis for me. I had begun to question how I had spent my life, and the very core of my beliefs. I was offered a new and important position, but I didn't feel capable or worthy of it. Then, I began to feel ill and I was going to turn the offer down." He paused. "Since the surgery my symptoms seem to have disappeared. I now know what I should do. You see, my son, I believe there are no accidents. When they came to take me for the test, I knew that something was amiss, yet at the very same time I felt deeply that I had to go."

He seemed to sit more erect in bed and his voice gathered force. "The day before I had prayed for some sort of sign to guide me, and now

I understand that you were chosen to be its instrument." As he spoke I felt the hairs on the back of my neck rise and a strange sensation came over me. The noted theologian Rudolph Otto used the term *numinous* to describe such events. To him *numinosity* described the feeling that somehow we are undeniably, irresistibly, and unforgettably in the presence of the Divine. It is our experience, even for a moment, of something that transcends our human limitations. Carl Jung called such events "synchronistic," defining *synchronicity* as a coincidence that holds a subjective meaning for the person involved. However, like all subjective experiences, what one person may find as meaningful or significant another might see as meaningless or due to chance.

I sat there stunned, not knowing what to say or think. The priest smiled. "Such talk troubles you, doesn't it?" he said. I told him of my own inner struggles, trying to reconcile reason and faith in the context of my own religious tradition.

"Ah," he replied, "one of your people grappled with such questions long ago. I will introduce you to him."

My beeper summoned me. As I rose to leave, he asked that I wait for a moment and sit on his bed. He placed his hand upon my head and said, "I offer you my thanks in the words your people once taught us. 'May the Lord bless you and keep you, may his face shine upon you and be gracious unto you, may he lift up his countenance upon you and give you peace …'"

Several months later I was called to the hospital's mailroom to sign for a package that had just arrived for me from Europe. I was shocked to see that it had come from the Vatican. Opening it, I found it was from the same priest, except instead of father his title was now monsignor (a "knight" of the church) and a special assistant to the pope! Inside was a short note that said, "As you once helped me through my spiritual turmoil, may this aid you through yours." Enclosed was a beautiful bound English translation of the great physician/philosopher Moses Maimonides's monumental work on the struggle between faith and reason, *The Guide for the Perplexed* (complete with commentaries). I walked to the small patient garden next to the hospital entrance, sat, and heard the soft songs of the birds and caught the smell of the spring blossoms in the clean air.

I sat holding the book and was lost in thought for a long time. It was, after all, just a mistake … wasn't it?

Blair P. Grubb, MD

Driving Elijah

He has told you, O man
What is good, and what the Lord
Requires of you: Only to do justice,
To love goodness,
and to walk humbly with your God.

Micah 6:8

It had been a bad week. While trying to recover from surgery, I received news that, because of an unexpected huge increase in the cost of labor and supplies, the grant that I had worked so hard to get would run out before my research project could be completed. Simultaneously, several faculty members announced that they would be leaving, making a difficult work schedule even worse. I was in a bitter mood when I drove to the community center to pick up my son after his basketball practice. As we scurried out the door to get to his piano lesson, a small white-haired old man, hunched over a walker, approached us and said, "Could you please give me a ride home?" He had apparently missed the last seniors' bus of the day and was stranded. Before I could utter a word, my son (who was eight at the time) virtually shouted, "Sure we can!" I sighed. We were on a tight schedule and this was the last thing I needed. But he looked so frail and pitiful that I reluctantly agreed. As I pulled the car around, my son carefully helped him off the curb, and then together we eased him and his walker into the backseat. I was somewhat surprised when he mentioned where he wanted to go, as it was a fairly nice part of town. When the man asked what my son's name was, my son (in his usual exuberant manner) proceeded to tell him not only his name but also his school, where we lived, his favorite sports, and that my wife and I were physicians!

Before the man had a chance to say a word, he quickly added, "Daddy's upset 'cause his grant money's gone."

"Really?" the man replied, after which he asked what kind of research I did. In the course of my attempts at explanation he asked several surprisingly insightful questions. I asked if he had been involved in research in the past. "No," he replied somewhat wistfully, stroking his beard, "I worked for a bank." I was about to ask another question when he suddenly announced, "Ah, we're here."

I pulled over and my son and I helped him out of the car. He no longer seemed quite as old or as frail as he had at first. Indeed, his white beard seemed to glisten and his blue eyes seemed to twinkle. He expressed his thanks and shook my hand firmly, saying, "Don't give up, things always seem to turn out alright." I did not feel comforted.

As we whisked off to my son's piano lesson, he looked at me and in his youthful innocence asked, "Could that have been Elijah?" I laughed. In his Sunday school class he had listened to the many folktales about the biblical prophet Elijah. Legend has it that he perpetually wanders the earth, each time in a different guise or form (usually of someone helpless or in need), to test the goodness of men and women and reward those he deems worthy. "Those are just stories," I said, and fell silent, putting the incident out of my mind.

Several weeks later, the office of the college's foundation called to say that they had received an anonymous grant of $10,000 to be used for my research. I was shocked and asked if he knew who had given it. He replied that the lawyer from the bank handling the donation had said he was under strict orders not to reveal its source. I put down the phone with a feeling of elation when I suddenly remembered the old man. A strange sensation came over me and I sat in silence. "No," I said to myself, "it couldn't be."

Nonetheless, I called the community center to see if anyone knew who the old man was. No one could remember anyone like that. I left work and drove to the center and looked and asked around about the man, but to no avail.

With the anonymous grant we were able to complete the project. To this day I have no idea if the old man and my sudden deliverance from failure were in any way connected. The rational part of me keeps saying they aren't, but somehow I can't help wondering.

When I told my son what had happened, he jumped up and down and smiled from ear to ear. "See, Dad," he exclaimed, "we were driving Elijah!"

Blair P. Grubb, MD

Running Out of Gas

Running out of gas is not one of my favorite pastimes. Especially, when it's late on a Friday afternoon. Particularly, in an unfamiliar neighborhood. The kind of neighborhood where you just don't take a leisurely walk, even in the daytime. I was scared.

It started out innocently enough. I was taking my wife to a doctor's appointment in a distant location. Since my car wasn't working properly, I had rented another vehicle for a few days. I printed out directions from my computer. It seemed that we would be able to get to and from our destination easily enough.

Of course, the appointment took longer than anticipated, but as we left the office it looked like we would have no trouble in making it home in time for Shabbat. We located the car, exited the lot, drove a block, and kaput, the car stopped dead in its tracks.

One look at the gas gauge was enough for even a mechanical greenhorn like me to figure out that we were out of gas. I was pretty sure that, earlier in the day, the tank was not that close to empty. Was the gas gauge on this rental car faulty, or had someone helped themselves to the remainder of our precious petrol while we were delayed in the doctor's office?

Not to worry, I sighted one of "Chicago's Finest" just a block away. I told my wife to keep the doors locked as I reached out for help. As I approached the policeman, I straightened up and presented my case.

"Officer. I am a rabbi, the Jewish Sabbath begins at sundown, I'm stuck and out of gas. It could take the motor club a few hours to get here. Could you please drive me to the closest service station?"

"No," was his quick, to-the-point response. "You can walk. It's only six or seven blocks."

Those were the longest seven blocks I had ever walked. Trying to focus on a few words of Torah to calm my fright and to turn my excursion into a mitzvah project, I finally reached my destination, safely.

The gas station attendant was holed up in a little booth with three panes of thick glass that separated him from the outside world. The microphone in the booth projected his booming voice to those standing in line as he took their money through a thin sliding drawer. Another reminder of life in this tough neighborhood.

I peered through the bulky security glass and focused on the goods offered for sale. Drinks and snacks abounded but I couldn't spot even one empty gas can. Sure enough, when I asked the attendant if he had something I could transport the gas in, his one-word reply—"Nope"—started to put me in a real panic.

"Where is the closest service station?" I inquired. "Six blocks that way," he motioned with his thumb.

At this point, I did the only thing I could think of: I started searching the garbage cans. It must have been a real scene for those filling up their cars, watching a man with a long beard and black hat rummaging through the trash.

But someone was looking out for me that day. The sight of the large gallon-sized plastic orange juice container that I finally spotted was a dream come true. I pulled it out, emptied the remaining contents and proceeded to fill it with gas.

I hardly noticed the person in the car at the next gas pump who was trying to get my attention. "Do you need a ride someplace?" he asked.

I tried to make a quick calculation: Is it more dangerous to walk back alone, or to accept a ride from a total stranger?

I said a silent prayer and finally answered, "Sure do. That would be so kind of you. It's just a couple of blocks away."

After giving my newfound chauffeur the directions to my stranded car, I thought it best to try and make some friendly conversation until we reached our destination.

"You know—what you are doing is a real good deed," I said.

"You mean a mitzvah," he replied. "Aren't you from Chabad?" he continued—pronouncing it "tchabad."

Shocked, I looked at him again and finally asked, "Are you Jewish?"

"No way," he answered. "Do I look Jewish?"

"So how do you know what a mitzvah is? And that I'm from Chabad?" I asked.

This is the story he told me:

"I used to go to a college out East. My roommate was Jewish, but didn't really practice it very much. On Saturday mornings there was this rabbi from the Chabad House with a long beard—something like yours—who would come to our room and try to get my friend to go to services. The rabbi would always say that he needed my friend for the services, for the *minyan* (quorum of ten).

"My friend never wanted to go. He would rather sleep. I felt bad for the rabbi and even offered to help out. The rabbi was very nice, but explained that I couldn't help with his *minyan* problem. Instead, we would talk about the world and how acts of goodness are needed. You know—more mitzvot.

"So when I saw you standing at the gas pump with that container, I thought of that rabbi and that maybe it was time to do a mitzvah."

A moment later my car was in sight. "Thanks so much," I said, about to leave the car.

"One second, rabbi, not so fast," he replied. "How are you going to get the gas in the tank without a spout?"

"I hadn't thought of that."

Sure enough, this kind soul didn't leave until he figured out a way to get the gas in the car, and made sure that it started and was ready to go.

I thanked him profusely, offered a token gift that he very politely refused, and soon we were on our way.

As we drove home and I told my wife all about the "Mitzvah Man," I realized that I had been witness to more than a random act of kindness. In fact, a heavenly window had opened just a bit, so that I could catch a small glimpse of the really big picture.

The Lubavitcher rebbe taught us that we should reach out to our fellow Jews of every background and affiliation and give them the opportunity to do even one more mitzvah. Oftentimes we are successful in persuading a stranger on the street to put on *tefillin*—even just one time. Sometimes a friendly conversation with our fellow airline traveler could lead to a commitment to light Shabbat candles that coming Friday evening.

That nagging thought often haunts us. Is it worthwhile? It's only one mitzvah. It's only one time.

Truth be told, those are really not the most difficult questions. We could definitely make the case that the value of even one good deed is infinite, it's godly, it's eternal. Especially since mitzvot are infectious— one always leads to the next.

What's worse, though, is rejection. You try your best, reach out, and make a significant pitch for a chance to connect with something holy; and you are turned down flat. "I'm not interested." "I'm not that religious." "I'm not into practicing Judaism now." Or a flat, blank look that says, "Just bug off."

It takes the wind out of your sails. You feel like you have run out of gas. You wonder whether it is really worth it.

And then the window of destiny opens for a glimpse of the eternal. Our "Mitzvah Man" reminded us that there is a much bigger picture out there.

No effort, big or small, is ever for naught. It might take a while for the words to sink in and take effect. It might necessitate a few more steps until everything clicks. Our sages taught, "Sincere words from the heart always touch the other's heart." It's just that you don't know exactly when, precisely how, or even which heart.

We made it home in time for Shabbat. That night, as my wife lit the Shabbat candles, we thanked the One Above for all his kindnesses that day. We stood in awe of our improbable rescuer, and we prayed for that Chabad rabbi on that East Coast college campus never to give up searching for his *minyan*.

Rabbi Daniel Moscowitz

Chaplain Alexander Goode

Alexander David Goode was ten years old when he witnessed a unique event in American history ... the dedication of the Tomb of the Unknown Soldier in Washington, D.C. All alone, he walked the long way to Arlington National Cemetery and stood in the long line with the others filing past ... young and old, black and white, mothers holding little children by the hands, veterans still in uniform. The unknown's identity was a mystery; no one knew his race or religion, but they all wanted to show their respect.

There were flowers, too, a huge sheaf of red English roses, crowned with the insignias of every commonwealth in the Dominion—a spray of lilies from France, a floral shield emblazoned with the words FOR VALOR from the British War Veterans, white carnations from the Gold Star Mothers of America, a laurel wreath from the Jewish War Veterans, and finally a bouquet of white roses gently laid in place by Mrs. Warren G. Harding, wife of the president.

Services began early with an honor guard marching behind the caisson bearing the coffin along Pennsylvania Avenue. At that point, generals, member of Congress, Supreme Court justices, and the president himself joined the procession to the cemetery. As the cold November sun peered through the lacework of barren trees, Alex listened as the dignitaries conferred decorations—the Congressional Medal of Honor, the British Victoria Cross, the Italian Medal for Bravery, the Croix de Guerre, and many others. There were many prayers for peace, accompanied by hymns of praise that echoed across the acres of the dead. Then President Harding stepped to the microphone and for the first time in history, the nation heard a leader's tribute over the latest media invention—the radio. "No greater sacrifice can a man make than to give his life for his brother." That message and the sound of "Taps" were lifelong echoes in the boy's mind and heart.

Alexander was born in Brooklyn on May 10, 1911, the son of a rabbi. He grew up in a traditional home where his gentle parents taught him a deep love for his own traditions and for those of others. While he was still very young, the family moved to Washington, where his father had accepted a pulpit. The new neighborhood was not friendly to Jewish youngsters, and Alex and his brother often fought their way to school. Perhaps these experiences gave Alex his later interest in boxing and wrestling, two sports in which he excelled and which earned him the respect of his peers. Through high school, he studied hard and worked at a paper route. He also joined the National Guard. Scholarships took him to the University of Cincinnati and to the Hebrew University. During that same period, he married his childhood sweetheart, Theresa Flax, a niece of Al Jolson.

Ordained in 1937, he accepted a pulpit in York, Pennsylvania, amazing his new congregation with his dedication and concern for the community. He gave time and energy to service organizations and interfaith groups. He organized a children's library, selecting books that taught the ideals of patriotism and tolerance. Then as Hitler's troops overran Europe, Goode began to devote himself to efforts to help his people, describing the terror designed to "demoralize and degrade and crush Jewish self-respect and dignity. But no nation can be enslaved, much less a religion. Those who seek to degrade us, degrade themselves."

When Pearl Harbor was attacked on December 7, 1941, he applied for a chaplaincy in the U.S. Army and was assigned to a post in the States. He pleaded for duty on the war front, but instead was sent to Greenland. With a thousand men and four other chaplains, Goode was assigned to the USS *Dorchester*. This ship was an old freighter, part of a convoy making its way through waters infested with German U-boats.

Just fifteen miles from their destination, shortly after midnight, they were torpedoed.

The hit knocked out the power and radio contact with the escort vessels, and the captain gave the order to abandon ship. In the darkness, there was complete panic as men jumped into lifeboats, crowding them to a point of capsizing. Others threw rafts overboard that drifted away before anyone could get to them. In the midst of this chaos, the four chaplains helped in distributing life jackets. When there were no more in the storage lockers, the chaplains removed their own and gave them to four frightened young men. "It was the finest thing I have ever seen or hope to see this side of Heaven," recalled one survivor. He commented on the fact that Rabbi Goode did not call out for a Jew; Father Washington did not seek out a Catholic; Reverend Fox and Reverend Poling did not ask for Protestants. They simply acted with the purest of intentions.

As the ship went down, soldiers in the nearby rafts could see the four men with their arms linked together and could hear the voices offering up prayers ... enduring examples of heroism and selflessness.

In 1951, an interfaith chapel with three altars—one Catholic, one Protestant, and one Jewish—were dedicated to the memory of these four men. Among the many speakers offering tributes, one said, "There they stood—a great light do I see at sea, the light of hope, the light of service, kindled by sacrifice supreme, to the end that the world might become a better place to live."

Miriam Newell Biskin

Thursdays with Chaim

Which is harder: Saying good-bye or saying hello?

The first time I saw him he was taking out his garbage.

It was a small bag, I recall; certainly small in comparison with my Olympic-size, industrial-strength parcel, bulging and leaking and tearing at the seams. Calling them Glad bags was clearly a cruel joke or an oxymoron, I thought.

Neither of us said, "Good morning." I guess we each thought the other one would. We both just sort of nodded politely and reentered our respective neighboring homes. I was busy.

Having just moved in, I spent much of my first couple of weeks repeating the garbage removal scene—mostly boxes, pizza and otherwise—but I rarely caught more than a fleeting glimpse of him. I concluded that he must be the reclusive type, but truthfully, I hardly gave it much thought at all. I was busy, you know.

Years passed. The kids grew up, new kids were born, and the garbage was setting new records. Every once in a while I'd see Chaim (really Hyman, but everyone called him Chaim) trimming his hedges (I knew his name because occasionally I received his mail by mistake), but he was "older," probably retired, I mused, and we seemed to have nothing at all in common. By this time we had graduated to the "Good morning" and "Snow coming" stages of communication, but that was pretty much it. And I can't really say that our nonrelationship bothered me very much. I had plenty of friends on the block and my family, religion, and career dominated my every waking moment. You guessed it—I was busy.

I don't remember when things changed. It may have been after I invited him to one of my children's weddings. Or it may have been after we stood outside one day discussing the parking regulations on our block. I'm not sure. But something did change. He wasn't reclusive— he was shy, I discovered, almost timid, and we did have things in common, after all, like a really dry sense of humor. Out of nowhere, Chaim would say the funniest and most unexpected things with a face as straight as a cookie sheet and I would double over and roar out loud. And every time I did that, the corners of his mouth would lift ever so slightly, as if to say, "Finally, someone understands me."

One year, after refusing dozens of invitations to join our family at our Shabbat table, he stunned me with his acceptance to "stop in" to our Sukkah—"just to take a look." Exceedingly bashful, he was in and out in about four minutes, and spent more time apologizing about "intruding" than he did shaking my lulav and etrog awkwardly. Chaim was born and bred in Brooklyn, but received very little Jewish education or exposure to his religion in his formative years. As such, his familiarity with law and tradition was quite minimal.

Early one morning, not long after that, I nearly tripped over a small brown paper bag on my doorstep. It was in the pre-9/11 era, so I simply bent down and opened it. Inside were three small tomatoes. I searched for a note, in the bag or on it. There wasn't any. It was several days later when Chaim, his face redder than the tomatoes, inquired how I liked his little homegrown gift. "I'm not sure how ripe they were and ... er ... and ... usually they're a little more firm," he said, in typical self-deprecating Chaim style.

"Oh, they were great," I reassured him.

"Thanks." The poets were right. A tree really did grow in Brooklyn. And on it, a relationship had begun to blossom.

But relationships, we know, are never static. Like any good tomato, if they are not watered and nurtured, they can falter and wilt, even die. And so, I decided to ask Chaim to become my Torah study partner. Mindful of his social reticence and near-total inability to take anything from anybody, I knew this was not going to be easy. But I really thought we both had a great deal to gain by it, so I began planning my approach.

I was certain that the timing and wording of the invitation were crucial and that I also needed a potent and convincing argument to counter his certain dismissal of this unexpected and perhaps outlandish proposal. And it took many weeks of mental scripting and rehearsal until the day finally arrived. We were standing outside, of course (he had never, ever trespassed over my hallowed threshold ... nor I, his), chatting about nothing, when I realized the time was now. I remember feeling foolish as I pondered my exaggerated angst. And so, I plowed ahead. "I was thinking, Chaim. What do you say ... you and I ... study Torah together—maybe once a week, for an hour or so?"

I had done it. I felt the mysterious anxiety wash away in an instant as I braced for his reaction. Predictably, it was totally unpredictable.

"Of course! That's a wonderful idea," he said. "When shall we start?"

Well, you could have knocked me over with a Glad bag.

"When shall we start?" I bumbled.

Now there was something I hadn't prepared for. "Um ... well ... I suppose ... er ... we could start ... eh ... Thursday."

Noon Thursday came, and sure enough the doorbell rang. His steps were very short and his gait saturated with trepidation. I had never seen him wearing a yarmulke before, except that one time in my Sukkah, but somehow, amid all the discomfort, he looked proud.

I directed him to my dining room table and invited him to sit and relax for a moment while I fetched some drinks for us. When I returned, seltzer and cups in hand, he was still standing, erect, as if he were awaiting roll call at Fort Dix.

"Because I'm waiting for you to sit first," he explained matter-of-factly.

Given his penchant for formality, I suppose I should not have been surprised that he also declined the seltzer.

We divided our hour in half, studying, in English, the laws of proper speech by the Chafetz Chaim (early twentieth-century sage and scholar) and *The Book of Our Heritage* by Eliyahu Kitov. His background was limited, but his grasp, curiosity, and inquisitiveness were off the charts. He commented on every passage we read, and asked questions that appeared to have been lying dormant for fifty years or more. Sixty minutes seemed like fifteen.

Chaim rose to leave at a minute before one o'clock, announcing that his time was up.

"Thank you," he recited.

"It was very nice."

I was surprised that he didn't salute me as he marched out, closing the door behind him. I quickly reopened it.

"Chaim," I called out, "same time next week?"

He seemed genuinely startled by the proposition.

"Oh … are you sure you're not too busy? I mean … er … you don't have to do this if you don't want to. You probably have your own studying to do and who knows what else, you certainly don't need me to …"

"I'll see you next week," I interrupted.

Next Thursday, noon arrived, bringing Chaim with it. And so went the next Thursday, and the next, and every week thereafter. The menu hardly changed. The syllabus shifted as we completed various texts through the years (he even brought an old book on parables of the Dubno Maggid, which we learned from), but he had to be forced to sit down before I did and the seltzer never did wet his lonely glass.

I marveled at Chaim's insight into complex principles. I often imagined that had he studied Torah when he was younger he might have scaled great scholastic heights. And those questions he asked, never-ending, revealed the incredible sensitivity that belied his reserved and proud manner. His obsession with fairness—to every single Jew, gentile, man, woman, and child, animal and plant, and even to objects that were inanimate ("They're all God's creations, aren't they?")—became a constant theme that permeated our weekly, hourly journey into some of life's most beautiful places.

Sometimes our trip included rest stops, where we ventured, ever so gingerly, into forbidden personal waters—childhood memories, minor medical concerns, and questions of faith. Those detours were brief, however, as Chaim preferred not to stray into regions where the waves were choppy and unpredictable. As we got closer, I kidded with him about it and every so often those mouth corners of his would leap, not curl, and his hearty laugh would fill the dining room. I laughed with him and treasured those moments of bonding and true friendship. Neither of us would dare say it, but we both knew it. Thursdays had become our favorite day of the week.

It was a Tuesday. I got word that Chaim had been taken to Beth Israel. He had experienced some chest pains and had possibly suffered a small heart attack. He was alert and stable, I was assured, and would return home after some routine tests. For some reason he had no phone in the hospital and could not use a cell phone there. I hesitated about visiting him, not sure if he would be entirely comfortable with an invasion of that magnitude. But then Thursday arrived. Books in hand, I trekked to Manhattan.

"Chaim," I kibitzed as I entered his room, "what on earth are you doing here?"

He popped up in his bed like a second-grade kid at the ice cream store. I wish I had brought a camera. His bushy eyebrows seemed to jump through his head. He appeared to be stuck halfway between bewilderment and bemusement.

"Me?" he blurted out. "What are you doing here?"

"Chaim … it's Thursday."

On the wall directly opposite the bed was a large clock. It read exactly twelve noon. He looked at it. I looked at him. I thought I detected momentary and very minute eye irrigation, but it just as easily could have been my own.

Chaim looked fine—better than ever. He excused the mess in the room (as if I noticed or cared) and practically scolded me for bothering to come.

"They want to run one more test on me," he said, "but I think I'll skip it. I'll probably come home tomorrow."

I pulled over one of those ridiculously oversized visitor's chairs and began reading from our usual text. Chaim instinctively reached into the top drawer of the nightstand and fumbled for something. I was surprised that he had brought a yarmulke to the hospital. It seems he had begun wearing one in order to recite a blessing whenever he ate something. I hadn't known. He offered me a leftover yogurt and some apple juice from a sealed plastic container, but this time it was my turn to refuse.

The hour sailed by. Worried that my meter had already expired, Chaim scooted me out the door. I turned around for a final glance. He was waving good-bye while motioning for me to hurry out. The next night, Shabbat arrived peacefully. A neighbor mentioned that he had seen Chaim return home an hour before. I didn't stop in.

For some reason, my sleep was fitful that night. At one point, while turning in bed, I noticed some very bright lights slicing through my broken Venetian slats. I looked at my clock. It was 4:36 a.m.

I leaped from my bed to look outside. Parked in front were two fire engines, a police car, and an ambulance. In seconds, my heart surged and my stomach swirled.

"*Chaim!*" I screamed inside.

Throwing on some pants, I dashed down the steps and out the door. His door was wide open. I gulped. I brushed past some formless and silent faces and squeezed through the narrow corridor that led to his room. I had never seen it before.

The setting was surreal, yet strangely unremarkable—like so many typical scenes in the movies. There was Chaim on the floor, surrounded by four exhausted paramedics. They had been taking turns for over an hour—trying to resuscitate a heart already departed. I anxiously peered into the eyes of the valiant hero, but they would not return my hopeful pleas. It was just not to be. It seems Chaim came home for Shabbat and began his eternal rest.

Minutes later, I dutifully covered him with a plain white sheet and wept.

At the funeral, I spoke about the privilege I had to befriend such a gentle, sensitive, and unassuming soul. I also asked Chaim's forgiveness for having ignored him for so many years and for my inability to answer all his determined questions. I pictured him wondering what all the fuss was about.

I returned home after the burial. It was simple and dignified. The January gusts sent shivers that pierced my sadness. I tightened my scarf. The block seemed very quiet. I paused as I passed Chaim's bare hedges. I lingered in the cold for a moment. So many scenes flashed through my mind. But there could have been so many more.

You know, we never really said "Good-bye." I guess we each thought the other one would.

Rabbi Yaakov Salomon

"They Shall Bear Fruit
Even in Old Age"

My mother always found comfort by being "planted" in the House of the Lord. She and my father would be found in their same seats every Shabbat and holiday at their shul. After the death of my father, my mother attended the daily morning service religiously. She became one of the "minyanaires."

My mother, all throughout her life, was blessed with a "green thumb." She could nurture the feeblest of plants, revive them, and make them verdant.

After several years of widowhood, in her eighties, she chose to leave her hometown and move to south Florida to be near me and my husband. She lived in a beautiful independent-living facility. And, yes, her apartment was full of plants.

Even though her eyesight and hearing were failing, she cared for and loved her plants. She spoke to them, and they responded by growing big and healthy and producing magnificent flowers. My mother had her special watering can; she provided the right amount of moisture and love to her plants. I visited her frequently and marveled at her plants. She lovingly showed them to me.

On several occasions, my mother said that a toad was living in one of her plants. Each morning, she would see soil and tracks of dirt near the plant pot. She would clean it and replace the soil in the container.

I remarked that since she lived on the third floor of her building, perhaps she had a lizard. Florida has plenty of lizards! "No!" she declared, "It is a toad." I humored her. After all, she was almost ninety years old. This pattern continued daily for many months.

In the final month of her life, my mother spent most of the time in the hospital. She kept reminding me to water her plants with her special watering can, and to talk to her plants. I did that often. Whenever I did go to my mother's apartment, I noticed tracks of soil near the plant pot. I never saw what was causing them.

My mother died just before her ninetieth birthday. After sitting shiva, I went to her apartment to close it up. Movers took care of large items. I, however, hand-carried her plants to my home. I placed them outside on my patio. The very next day, I took my mother's special watering can and went outside to water her plants. As soon as the moisture hit the soil, out jumped a tiny toad to greet me. Startled, I called out, "Mom, you are right. It is a toad." How happy I was to see this toad. I felt that it was sending me a message from my mother, reminding me to nurture her plants and never to doubt her. I silently promised to my mother to tend to her plants.

Now I understand more clearly the verse in Psalms, "They shall bear fruit even in old age." I keep wondering if this toad was sending me my mother's final "I love you."

Carole Orenstein Goldstein

Israel: Land of Miracles

*P*rime Minister David Ben-Gurion once said that in Israel the difficult we do immediately, the impossible takes a little longer. He is also known for another oft-quoted proverb: "In Israel, in order to be a realist you must believe in miracles."

Both of these statements are borne out by those who know Israel well. Even in the death of a promising young zionistic and idealistic youth, one family is able to find some comfort and consolation. Just to visit Israel is to learn that God has not stopped creating miracles. For new immigrants, for soldiers, for ordinary citizens, miracles happen all the time. Even amid the uncertainty, the tension, the danger, and the struggle of creating a new country, Israel's people are able to find the stamina and the idealism to bring forth new miracles in a land in which many such miracles occurred over the last four thousand years.

The Spirit of Alisa

When my daughter was murdered by terrorists in Gaza, her influence grew stronger still.

At age eleven, our eldest daughter, Alisa, had the opportunity to visit Israel for two weeks with my sister (her aunt). Alisa had the time of her life, and she came back with her first Israeli tan.

Then the real breakthrough came on Alisa's third trip to Israel, as a senior in high school. She went on the March of the Living, where they visited the concentration camps in Europe and then on to Israel. It rattled her. It made her decide who she was and what she was going to be. She was going to be an activist, working on behalf of Israel and the Jewish people.

In New Jersey we had a school set up for immigrant children who were just coming out of the former Soviet Union. Alisa announced one day that she wanted to volunteer at the school, and I asked, "What are you going to do?" Alisa was cocaptain of her high school softball team, and she answered, "Well, if they're in America, we have to make them Americans. I'll take afternoons off and teach them how to play baseball." And that's what she did.

That fall, she went to Brandeis University. She worked very hard, taking extra courses plus summer school. But she loved Israel so much that she still found time to travel those summers to Israel. In the summer of 1994, she went with Aish (an international network of Jewish learning centers) as an outreach activist and then became a campus representative.

Israeli-Palestinian violence intensified during those years, but that didn't deter Alisa, who wanted a college experience abroad. In 1995, as a junior, she was granted a leave of absence by Brandeis and she went to study for six months at Nishmat, a women's seminary in Jerusalem. She found an apartment in Jerusalem and pursued an "education in life."

Alisa was thrilled that after two years of sociology at Brandeis, she was now studying Judaism all day long. She went to the *shuk* (the marketplace) whenever she wanted, and visited people's houses for lunch. One of her favorite activities was to go to the Western Wall and just watch the people. She wrote of being inspired by the initiation of the paratroopers at the Wall, seeing them presented with the two Jewish weapons—a rifle and a Bible.

Trip to Gaza

That spring, Alisa was to stay in Israel a few weeks after Passover to finish the semester, so she looked around for a pre-Passover trip. She wanted to go to Petra, to see the archeological sites in Jordan, but it was a very expensive trip. So she e-mailed that instead she'd be going with girlfriends to Gush Katif on the Mediterranean, to get some sun.

I wasn't familiar with the geography of Israel, so on the morning she was leaving on this minivacation, we spoke on the phone and I asked Alisa where Gush Katif was.

"It's in Gaza," she said.

I think another parent might have screamed into the phone, "You're not going to the Gaza Strip! End of discussion. Cancel your trip." But I had always given Alisa the latitude to make her own informed decisions. So instead of yelling, I asked how she was planning to get there.

She explained, as only a young college kid can, the reason she was up at 5 a.m. to catch a bus from Jerusalem to Ashkelon, and from there to Gaza: It was to fulfill our three agreed-upon rules: (1) travel only by public transportation; (2) not to travel alone—she going with two other American girls; and (3) travel only to a recognized destination—a popular Israeli beach resort.

So I agreed to let her go.

On my way to shul in the morning, I turned on the radio to hear there had been a terrorist attack in Gaza. A suicide bomber drove a van loaded with explosives into a public bus near the Israeli settlement of Kfar Darom. The blast peeled away the side of the bus and seven Israeli soldiers were killed. And I knew right then in the pit of my stomach that Alisa was involved. But rather than go back home and scare everyone, I continued to shul. When the phone rang at the shul about twenty minutes later, I knew it was for me.

It was my wife, Roz. She had just gotten a phone call from one of the mothers of Alisa's traveling companions. Both girlfriends were back in Jerusalem already, but they'd gotten separated and didn't know about Alisa.

I immediately went home and tried calling the Israeli Consulate in New York City, but the phone was busy. So I called the State Department in Washington, which has an office to handle crises of Americans overseas. I gave the consumer officer Alisa's passport number, her address in Jerusalem, and the phone number of the girls she was traveling with. He said he'd call me back.

At that point, because I had run out of shul so quickly, people called the house to see what was going on. And like Jews everywhere, everyone's connected someplace with someone. So I had friends calling insurance companies in Israel to check their hospitals and HMOs to see if Alisa had been brought there. And they found that Alisa was at Soroka Medical Center in Beersheva.

No one was able to tell us her condition immediately because she was in surgery. About an hour later, the hospital called to tell us she was in intensive care.

I said, "Can you tell me where she's injured?" I wanted him to say that it was her arm or leg. He said, "She was hit in the head with shrapnel and is unconscious. You should get on a plane and come right now."

I arrived in Israel in the morning, and was met on the runway by representatives of the U.S. Embassy in Tel Aviv. They stamped my passport on the tarmac of the airport, put me in a van, and drove to Beersheva.

I was met in the parking lot by the head of the hospital, and I had to push my way through a crowd of people at the ICU. Alisa was in a bed in the corner, with a ventilator tube in her mouth.

I grew up in the 1950s and '60s, and I remember vividly on *Ben Casey* how the father would hold his daughter's hand, and she would open her eyes, mumble something and squeeze the hand back, and you knew by the time the show was over at 11 o'clock that everything was going to be okay.

But when I let go of Alisa's hand, it just fell down onto the side of her bed.

The doctor took me into a little room to talk. There was no air-conditioning, just a fan blowing hot air. He gave me a cup of orange soda, and sat me down.

I asked, "What's her condition?"

He said, "Her brain is punctured. A small piece of shrapnel about the size of your thumbnail hit her in the back of her head."

They had operated the day before, and gave her a medication to reduce brain swelling. But the damage was too great. She was brain dead.

He let that piece of information sink in for a minute or two. Then the doctor looked me and said, "We have a question."

Just as I had sensed the day before what had happened, I knew what was coming again. I looked up and said, "You want her organs, don't you?"

It turns out that over the previous year or so, I had heard lectures in Jewish law on the permissibility of organ donations under certain conditions. I also knew the talmudic dictum, "One who saves a life is as if he had saved an entire world." And I knew that we have a responsibility to be a light unto the nations.

I thought of all the soldiers in Israel on the borders, and those patrolling the streets, making Israel safe for us. And I thought of stories I'd heard about Holocaust survivors who arrived in 1948 in the midst of war, and they were given a shovel or a broomstick to fight with because there weren't enough guns. And I also thought of all those in Israel who study Torah, casting a wall of spiritual protection over us. And I thought about the bus drivers, and the guys at the *shuk* who argue over two cents …

So I called my wife and said, "Every time Alisa came back from Israel, she wasn't just a better Jew, she was a better person. It made her into who she was."

I continued: "This is our way to say 'thank you' to everyone who was putting themselves on the line for Israel, and everyone who had opened their homes to Alisa and her friends. This is our time. This is the way we can save a Jewish life."

So we donated Alisa's organs—heart, pancreas, liver, lungs, and two kidneys—to six people. Three, unfortunately, barely got off the operating table when they died. The other three survived.

Moving Forward

After a few hours, when it came time to leave Israel, they brought me to the VIP lounge at Ben-Gurion Airport. The room was crowded with reporters, and I was sitting next to one of the Israeli Army chaplains. I said, "I don't understand all the fuss." One of the reporters turned to me and said, "You have no idea what you've done for us." He was telling me, "You did something that we don't do for ourselves. You haven't blamed us for what happened to your daughter. Instead, you gave us the gift of life."

You have to remember that in those days, in 1995, the government was pushing the Oslo process at full speed. Alisa had become another "sacrifice for peace." But I didn't have negative thoughts about the government or the situation. I know the government didn't kill her. I haven't read of a single parent of a terror victim accusing the government for what's happening, even at the height of Oslo. You know who to blame. You blame the Palestinians, not a fellow Israeli, a fellow Jew.

We came out of the VIP room and the casket was there, surrounded by a color guard, draped in an Israeli flag. She was twenty years old.

When we arrived at Kennedy Airport at 6 a.m., they brought me out to speak to the press. And at that point a switch clicked in my head. All I know is that when I opened my mouth, things made sense. And suddenly, unexpectedly, I had become an activist—for the Jewish people and for Israel, and against the scourge of terrorism. It was either Alisa's *neshama* (soul) pushing her way through, or God saying, "I got you to this point. Now we're moving forward."

You have to react to a loss of a child, especially in a terrorist attack. If you don't react, it's just going to stay inside you and eat away at your psyche and your physical being. Every parent has to deal with the loss in a different way. I can go out publicly and talk about Alisa twice a day. But Roz has a difficult time even mentioning her name.

So I began flying to different cities—Waco, Texas; San Diego; Denver; and Erie, Pennsylvania—speaking about Alisa to senior citizens, high school kids, whoever invited me. And in the process I'd like to think that I helped knock down some of the "bugaboo" that had developed about the Orthodox in this country.

My message is that there's more to life than just walking around. We're all put on earth for a purpose, and out of the simplest acts of kindness, we can transform ourselves and our world. I was doing something constructive, as opposed to destructive. The work can be exhausting, but the adrenaline keeps pumping because to an extent I am keeping Alisa alive—talking about her and working on her behalf.

Childhood Education

Let me try to add some context. Growing up in Queens, New York, my family wasn't observant; we ate "kosher in" and "Chinese out." I went to Hebrew school and it was torture. I remember vividly an Israeli teacher. It was exciting to hear him talk about the Israeli wars and the struggles, but he didn't teach much. And then after my Bar Mitzvah, my formal Jewish education came to an end. The most "religious" thing I did was when my father died and I decided to say *Kaddish* for the full year. I went to shul at least once a day to say *Kaddish*. If I couldn't make it during the day, when I got back home at night I'd run out to a neighboring town. But I made sure I said *Kaddish*.

We had moved to West Orange, New Jersey, and when Alisa was ready for nursery school we enrolled her in an Orthodox school. This is just how it worked out. Alisa was doing great, learning Hebrew songs, serving as the "Shabbat *ima*," and the designated *chazzan*, too.

Then when she was almost five, it was time to go to public school. One day I came home, and my wife said that Alisa was driving her crazy. When Alisa heard that she'd be going to a public school, she put her foot down and said, "No, I'm not. I'm going to the Jewish school with my friend Becky. And Mommy has to call up Becky's mommy and find out about it, because I'm not going to public school." And then this four-year-old girl walked out of the room.

Two days later, we were looking at the Orthodox day school. We took a tour of the facility with the principal, who was extolling the virtues of day school education. And I was thinking, We have a problem here because, sure, we say *Kiddush* when I get home Friday night, and the Shabbat candles are lit before sunset. But after dinner the TV goes on in the den, and on Saturday we take the girls out shopping. So when the principal asked if I had any questions, the second question I asked (after: "How much is this going to cost?") was, "If I send Alisa to this school, will my lifestyle change?" He looked me right in the eyes and said: "No."

Technically, he was correct. The school would not change my lifestyle; it's just a building, an institution. But the principal knew that the education Alisa would get would one day make us realize that we're going to have to change our lifestyle to accommodate a five-year-old, or drive everyone crazy in the process.

So we slowly changed. We realized that if our child is going to school five days a week to learn about Shabbat and kashrut and the weekly Torah portion, then how can we say to her on Saturday morning, "Let's go to the hardware store"? We didn't become observant for several years after that. But we tried to move along as Alisa grew in her own observance.

Teaching by Example

When Alisa finished her first few weeks in school, we had parent-teacher conferences. We went in, not knowing what to expect, because Alisa had a mouth that could talk without interruption. So my wife and I sat down and the two teachers said, "We want to thank you for sending Alisa to our classroom."

Roz and I looked at each other, figuring there must be some mistake. We looked at the teachers and said, "We're Alisa Flatow's parents." They said, "Oh, yes, we know. And she's an absolute joy to have in class. She volunteers, raises her hand, asks questions, has answers, is very helpful, outgoing, and gets along with everyone!"

This continued throughout her school years. She'd always get A's, though more important for her was developing a wide network of friends, who depended on her to keep their spirits going. Alisa was what you would call a people person. In high school, the bus would pick her up at 6:50 a.m. She'd arrive early to school and would wait in the hallway for her friends, on duty to cheer them up if they were feeling down.

When she first started high school, the phone in her room used to ring on Friday nights, and her friends would leave messages on the answering machine. I said, "Alisa, since we're keeping Shabbat it's not appropriate for your friends to call." So she said, "Okay," and the phones stopped.

I found out after she died that she didn't want to tell her friends not to call if they felt they needed to. So she shut off the ringer and turned the sound off the answering machine.

She needed to teach them in her own way, which was: Don't lecture, do by example. And it went hand-in-hand with her wanting to show young people that there's more to being Jewish than restrictions on behavior and eating habits, and that you could be Jewishly observant and still be in touch with the world.

Alisa had friends on both ends of the spectrum—those who were more observant than her, and those who were less observant. She wanted to learn from those who knew more, and teach those who knew less. But she taught and learned only by action. Never a pointing finger, never a click of the tongue.

It was always that way. I recall one day when she was in elementary school, and she said to me, "We have a problem with a girl in class. She brings in nonkosher food snacks." So I asked, "What do you do when she offers it?" Alisa answered: "Oh, we pretend we're taking it, but we put it in our pocket. We don't eat it. But we don't want to make her feel bad."

Message to the Terrorists

It's always tragic to lose a child. But Alisa was so much more. She was a role model for me, a guiding light for how to conduct oneself on a daily basis. She made me a better person.

After my press conference at the airport, I arrived home in New Jersey to find my house under siege—media, neighbors, friends. It was two hours till the funeral and I couldn't focus with all the commotion. My rabbi put up his hand like a policeman, and said, "Alisa died *al kiddush Hashem*, sanctifying the Name of God. That's all you need to know."

What he said clicked. Because of that remark, I've gotten the strength to respond as a Jew is supposed to respond in such a situation.

And that is: *Do what you can to live like a Kiddush Hashem. Not just through death, but through life as well.*

Alisa never saw herself in harm's way being in Israel. She felt comfortable there; I was more comfortable with her there than when she was visiting certain parts of Manhattan. We're Jews and this is our home. And that's why we've not hesitated to send Alisa's younger siblings for extended stays in Israel.

I am always alerted to terror attacks in Israel by persistent phone calls from reporters. They ask, "Having lost a daughter, what do you think about sending kids to Israel?" That's the opportunity I'm waiting for, for them to walk into my trap. I say, "Go, because it's the right thing."

We have to send a message to terrorists who want to scare us away from Israel. We're still going to go. We're not going to become victims. If we allow fear to rule our lives, then the terrorists will have won.

Suit Against Iran

That idea motivated me to get involved politically. As a lawyer, I thought we could create a legal disincentive for those who sponsor terrorism. In 1996, Congress passed the Anti-Terrorism Act, which stripped away the "sovereign immunity" foreign countries enjoyed from prosecution by Americans.

The law was important because it empowered the victims. I'm not a country and I can't wage war against Iran or Islamic Jihad, so I rely on the tools we have at hand—the legal system. As a father, when you know the resources of your government are committed to right the wrong committed against your daughter, you can't ask for anything more.

Unfortunately, once we looked deep into the statute, we realized that it was impractical. It didn't define where the jurisdiction was going to be; what law was going to be applied; how you obtained service; how you went through a judgment; or a myriad of procedural matters. That's when we realized we were in for a fight.

So I set about working with Congress to get the bill structured in such a way that it actually had teeth. To get those changes took a lot of work, a lot of trips to Washington, and a lot of convincing that this would be good for America. I testified before both the Senate and the House Judiciary Committees in support of legislation that would allow the victims of terror who prevail in court to recover the frozen assets of the countries that sponsored the terrorism.

I met personally with President Clinton three times, and things finally came together in October 1999 with the signing of the Justice for Victims of Terrorism Act. This led to my filing a lawsuit for the purpose of embarrassing the Iranian government. We wanted to expose the underbelly of Iran, to show that no country should be permitted to sponsor terrorist attacks against innocent civilians. And personally, we were looking for closure in seeking justice against those who had murdered our daughter. The wound never heals, but we felt this would be a step in the healing process, in allowing us to get on with our lives.

In the two-day trial before a District Court judge, we demonstrated that Islamic Jihad took responsibility for the bomb that killed Alisa, and that their financial support came directly from the Iranian government. The judge awarded us $247 million, a default judgment because Iran did not appear to contest the lawsuit. So although we won, in terms of going head to head to defeat them, a lot of the wind was knocked out of our sails.

The award money was to come from $400 million in Iranian assets held in America, a down payment years earlier by the shah of Iran for the purchase of U.S. military equipment. After the shah was overthrown by Islamic fundamentalists, the United States froze the money.

But then we hit an unexpected roadblock. The U.S. government, for diplomatic reasons, opposed our efforts to collect. Clinton signed a directive overriding the law on grounds of national security. The administration argued that frozen assets give U.S. diplomats leverage in negotiating with terrorist states. And it claimed that permitting such assets to be seized would endanger U.S. properties overseas. So, unbelievably, I found myself up against U.S. Justice Department lawyers in a federal court!

But we kept fighting, and in the end, ninety-five senators voted to release the funds, and Clinton signed it into law on a Shabbat afternoon. Roz had been putting our name into the search engine on the AP wire each afternoon and evening, and that Saturday night when she put it in, up came our name in a story about the signing. Right there we said *Shehecheyanu*, the prayer for thanksgiving.

Then on January 4, 2001, the Treasury Department transferred to us about 10 percent of our award—$26 million, representing the compensatory damages. I'm still determined to find a way to collect the $200 million in punitive damages, because that's the portion intended to deter Iran's future conduct. If someone hits you up for all those millions, you're going to think twice about spending $75 million on terrorism. It's not a very good return on your investment.

Of course, we've used the money to perpetuate Alisa's memory. We have the Alisa Scholarship Fund, which in its eight years of existence received two thousand applications from college-age kids to study in Israel. We've endowed a program at Nishmat for overseas students. We're doing some work with Israeli hospitals, including Soroka Medical Center. And there will be other projects down the road, all in the merit of a little four-year-old girl who insisted on being given a Jewish education.

And I've continued to be an activist. I testified at the House Judiciary Committee, speaking about associates of Islamic Jihad who were freely operating in Tampa, Florida. We want to put terrorists out of business, wherever they may be found, so that no other father, mother, brother, or sister should have to experience what my family and many others have gone through these past years.

Why?

When Alisa was five, she got into a bicycle accident. As I drove her to the hospital, she cried in the backseat, asking why these things always happen to her. It was her third trip to the emergency room in three years.

I tried to explain that things happen that we don't understand. She didn't expect her friend to ride over her foot. She shouldn't let it bother her, because she was in the wrong place at the wrong time.

Now, when I travel around the country speaking about Alisa, I sometimes hear her saying, "Daddy, why did this happen to me?"

I gave a speech last night at a synagogue and somebody said, "I lost a child in similar circumstances. Do you believe in God?"

I said, "Yes, very much so."

"So why are there babies dying?"

"I have no idea. All I know is that our question is not to ask 'Why?' Our question is: What can I do to make life better?"

While I believe there will be a redemption and a resurrection, at the same time, we have to fix the world here and now. "As Jews, it is our responsibility to help Jews less fortunate than we are," Alisa once wrote.

That's where Alisa was heading. She'd probably have become a physical therapist or an occupational therapist. Or she'd have gone into Jewish education. But most importantly, she would have been the mother of a strong Jewish family.

Alisa loved Israel and was very proud of being Jewish. She stood up with the seven soldiers who were killed along with her, as if to say: "I am a Jew. I am here with you." So I came to realize that at that time, she was not in the wrong place. She was in the right place.

Father and Child

The last time Alisa and I were together was for a family dinner in Jerusalem. In January 1995, we took the whole family to Israel on a ten-day trip. We all enjoyed the time together, especially walking around the Old City of Jerusalem. We took one final picture of the whole family together, smiling and windblown, from the promenade in Talpiot, with the Old City in the background.

Before snapping the picture, the guide asked us, "Who do you think stood on this very same spot?" We were looking and thinking, and nothing was registering. Then I raised my hand and said, "Abraham." At the *Akeidah* (the binding of Isaac), father and child had walked for three days, and came to a point where they saw the Temple Mount. And we were standing at what could have been that very spot.

In retrospect, I think of the similarity of me standing there with my daughter. And in fact I think all Jewish parents are like Abraham. We encourage our children to be Jews; we encourage them to go to Israel. At the same time we recognize that they might wind up as a *korbon*, a modern-day sacrifice.

As hard as it's been, you put one foot in front of the other. And I'm many, many steps beyond April 9, 1995. I knew at the end of the first year that things were getting better, because I stopped crying every day.

The hardest time of the week is still Friday afternoon. It can be difficult to start Shabbat, because Alisa introduced it to us. Sometimes it's difficult for me to complete the *Kiddush* without crying, because I know that I'm supposed to bless the day, to sanctify God's Name. And I have sanctified the Divine Name with my firstborn child. She taught me so much about how to live. May her memory be forever a blessing.

Stephen Flatow

The Voluntary Tattoo

A few weeks ago a friend of mine told me a rather startling story. I started to wonder whether it was a "This could only happen in Israel" kind of story (of which I have heard and experienced many), or whether it reflected some kind of new movement of which I am unaware. I haven't been able to get it out of my mind since, and so I thought you all might want to hear it, too. I am still trying to formulate my own thoughts about it, so I welcome your insights and opinions as well.

So this friend of mine was hanging out at a pub in downtown Beersheva with some other friends. As he approached the counter to order his drink, he noticed that the young bartender, a student dressed in jeans and a T-shirt, had a short row of numbers tattooed on his arm. Given that the guy was a good fifty years too young to be a Holocaust survivor, my friend's curiosity got the better of him and he asked what the tattoo was. The young man answered, "Exactly what you think it is." My friend couldn't stop there, and pressed him further. The man replied that his grandmother survived Hitler's camps and was now nearing her end. She had given her grandson her blessing to tattoo onto his arm a likeness of the very same numbers she had on her own. My friend, in recounting this story to me, remarked that he was quite moved by the gesture.

I must admit that at first I was quite taken aback. Quickly, however, my shock turned into appreciation and not a small amount of admiration. I have spent most of my academic life studying the Holocaust from political, psychological, and personal perspectives, and this is the first time I can remember that I have come across a truly original idea in the domain of Holocaust memorialization. With what

239

amounts to probably twenty minutes in a tattoo artist's chair and the marking of a one- by three-inch area of skin, this young man has managed to both honor his grandmother and her experience, as well as send a rather striking societal message. Indeed, whether the people around him are respectful of or appalled by his choice, there is no doubt that he causes at least a hundred people a day to think about the Holocaust, if only for a moment.

My friend was most impressed by how the young man's action represents a kind of "taking back" of the image of the tattoo and the victim experience. In much the same way as African Americans have reclaimed and empowered the term *nigger* by using it among themselves, there is something powerful and honorable about taking a tattoo that was forced upon his grandmother without her consent and purposefully choosing to place it upon himself with her blessing.

The fact that Jews still exist in the world is proof that Hitler didn't succeed, and many say that simply living an honorable life can be our own revenge. This young bartender has taken this a step further. His existence would not have been possible without his grandmother's survival, but in thirty years when her life is a distant memory, his simply being alive won't be enough to memorialize her. Perhaps these numbers on his arm will be.

Indeed, one of my biggest fears regards the landscape of our global society in thirty or forty years. What will Holocaust education and memory be like when the last survivor has left us? I fear this period deeply, and I will weep the moment when our world will be deprived of the brilliance and strength of spirit and beauty and insight that Holocaust survivors bring to us.

When the Holocaust exists only in history textbooks and museums, this young man will have and show a personal connection that won't be attainable in any other way. In the summer, when he rolls up his sleeves and has no choice but to show his tattoo, he will make people think and feel and react in a way that no one else will be able to do.

So I have informally polled many people already, and received greatly mixed reviews. People over the age of sixty have tended to be enthusiastically in favor of the young man's choice, while those between the ages of thirty-five and fifty-five have generally been vehemently against it. Responses from individuals in my own generation, people in their twenties, have been fairly equally split. I'm still not totally sure how I feel about it, but I'm inclined to believe that anything that can evoke such strong emotion, on both sides of the spectrum, is worthy of deeper investigation. In any case, that young bartender in Beersheva has certainly made a lot of us think.

Alison Stern Perez

No Time for Weeping

When Israeli military forces captured the Old City of
Yerushalayim on the third day of the Six Day War, Yitzhak
Rabin was commander-in-chief of Zahal, the Israel
Defense Forces. He writes about his experiences when they
reached the most sacred shrine in Judaism, the Western
Wall, called in Hebrew, the Kotel.

Driving toward the Lions' Gate, on the eastern side of the Old City wall, we were surrounded by signs of the previous day's fighting. A smoldering tank stood by the gate itself, and the narrow alleys of the Old City, with their shuttered windows and locked doors, were totally deserted. But every now and then the eerie silence was broken by sniper fire from Jordanian soldiers who had failed to flee in time and continued to resist.

As we made our way through streets I remembered from childhood, pungent memories played on my emotions. The sheer excitement increased as we came closer to the Western Wall itself. It is still easy for me to conjure up the feelings that assaulted me then, but it's very difficult to put them into words. The Wall was and is our national memento of the glories of Jewish independence in ancient times. Its stones have a power to speak to the hearts of Jews the world over, as if the historical memory of the Jewish people dwelled in the cracks between those ancient ashlars. For years I secretly harbored the dream that I might play a part not only in gaining Israel's independence but in restoring the Western Wall to the Jewish people, making it the focal point of our hard-won independence. Now that dream had come true, and suddenly I wondered why I, of all men, should be so privileged. I knew that never again in my life would I experience quite the same peak of elation.

When we reached the Western Wall, I was breathless. It seemed as though all the tears of centuries were striving to break out of the men crowded into that narrow alley, while all the hopes of generations proclaimed: "This is no time for weeping! It is a moment of redemption, of hope...." We stood among a tangle of rugged, battle-weary men who were unable to believe their eyes or restrain their emotions. Their eyes were moist with tears, their speech incoherent. The overwhelming desire was to cling to the Wall, to hold on to that great moment as long as possible.

Yitzhak Rabin

Miracles in Jerusalem

Thisis morning as the sun rose over Jerusalem, my wife, Leah, gave birth to a beautiful baby girl at Hadassah Hospital. A few hours later I drove to the southern Israeli city of Kiryat Malachi where my wife's parents live.

After packing several personal items that my wife will need for her hospital stay, I set out to drive back to Jerusalem. As I passed the central bus station in Kiryat Malachi, I saw an Israeli soldier waiting to get a ride. I rolled down the window and asked him where he needed to go. He said his base is near Jericho, but if I could take him to Jerusalem that would be great help.

I was in a particularly upbeat mood today—after all, we were blessed with our fourth child and third daughter—but the reality around me in the holy land is down and worrisome. Israel is being attacked by its neighbors and we are fighting a war to defend ourselves.

As fighter jets from the nearby Air Force base roared overhead, we cruised down the highway, and I got acquainted with Shachaf Raviv of Beersheva. His story gives a face to and a direct association with the soldiers fighting for our land and people today.

Shachaf, twenty-one years old, is a medic in the IDF. He tells me that yesterday his senior officer sent him home for one night to spend with his family because today he and his unit will be leaving their base near Jericho and heading up north to the battlefield on the border of Lebanon to be part of a team of doctors and medics who will be giving critical first aid to the wounded soldiers and civilians.

His officer said he will not have any weekend breaks for a while and therefore sent him to bid farewell to his family. Shachaf told me of the feeling in his house last night: "No one slept. They surrounded me with love and care for hours.

"My father immigrated to Israel from Portugal in the late sixties and fought in the Yom Kippur War and my mother came from Tunisia to the promised land around the same time. They spoke of their dreams for themselves and our future.

"I am the third of four children and currently the only son in the Army. My parents named me *Shachaf,* which means seagull in Hebrew, but this morning when my mother said good-bye she held me for a long time and was crying. She kept calling me Rachamim—the Jewish name they gave me at my *brit* ceremony, which in Hebrew means 'mercy' and 'compassion.'

"She cried and said, 'Rachamim, today you will need God's compassion and protection—We all need God's *rachamim.*'"

As we continued to drive I encouraged Shachaf, and spoke to him about the great role he has in protecting the Land of Israel and the Jewish people in Israel and ultimately Jews all over the world.

At noon I turned on the radio to the headline news. "Eight troops from Golani's 51st Battalion," the announcer said, "lost their lives on Wednesday during heavy fighting with Hezbollah terrorists in the southern Lebanese village of Bint Jbail. Another officer was killed in a clash at Maron a-Ras. Over twenty soldiers are wounded...."

Shachaf asked me to turn the radio off and give him spiritual inspiration instead before he heads to the front lines.

I shared with him thoughts that I heard and learned from my rebbe and teacher, the Lubavitcher rebbe, Rabbi Menachem M. Schneerson, of righteous memory. During past conflicts in the Land of Israel, and during times of danger for the Jewish people, the rebbe made practical suggestions of good deeds, mitzvot, that would elicit God's blessings and protection. I quoted him from the Torah that speaks of God protecting the land, and we discussed the need for us to understand the deeper truths as to why we have our permanent homeland specifically in Israel, as promised to us in the Torah.

Shachaf was very grateful to hear how Jews and non-Jews all over the world are praying for them and thinking of them every day now and wishing for their success and God's protection.

When we came to Jerusalem I opened my briefcase. I had a new mezuzah in a plastic case and I gave it to Shachaf. I told him, "I am giving this to you for protection, but you must return it to me when you come back and I will go to Beersheva and put it up in your bedroom."

Shachaf liked the idea. I said, "It says in the Torah, 'Emissaries of a good deed are not harmed.' You have a mezuzah—it will protect you."

Shachaf put the mezuzah in his front left pocket and promised me he would leave it there until he came back. He would also tell the story of our meeting to his fellow medic soldiers and tell them they have added protection.

I then pulled out an envelope with $500 that a member of my community gave me yesterday to give to distressed Jews in the North, and asked Shachaf to be my personal emissary to distribute these funds to wounded soldiers and civilians.

At first he refused to take it, but after we exchanged e-mail addresses and cell phone numbers he agreed, and promised to report to me exactly how he gave the funds to people who really needed it.

We had met only an hour before, but suddenly we were deeply connected to each other. We embraced, the mezuzah protruding from his pocket and his rifle strapped across his chest. I looked at him with tears in my eyes and said, "Rachamim, thank you for your protection"; and he looked me back in the eye while placing his hand over the mezuzah I gave him, and said, "Avraham, thank you for your protection."

I am writing this article on my laptop while sitting in the room at Hadassah Hospital while my wife rests. I look at the beautiful face of our little newborn daughter and thank God for the Divine's blessings and pray for divine protection for my child and all the rest of God's children.

As the Jewish world will pray this Shabbat for the protection of the soldiers of Israel, I will have in mind Rachamim Raviv. Please think of him and thousands more like him who need God's *rachamim*, mercy, and full protection.

Rabbi Avraham Berkowitz

Oath of Allegiance

The night before Sukkot, a number of Pardes students and faculty were at the Kotel for a swearing-in ceremony of the Givati Brigade of the Israel Defense Forces. For anyone who has attended such a program, you know that it is a moving one. For my family and the family of Rabbi Levi Cooper, there was personal significance: Levi's brother-in-law, and my son Shai, were among the soldiers taking an oath of allegiance to the State of Israel and its armed forces.

Shai was one year old when we made *aliyah* from Manhattan nineteen years ago. We always knew the day would come when he would be inducted into the army. Some parents think that by the time their children grow up, there will be peace. I don't think we ever really thought that; I think we just put it out of our heads, busy with raising him, our other three children, and dealing with the daily challenges of life, and life in Israel in particular.

Shai gave us two more years of respite when he decided to study in a yeshiva before doing his three full years of army service.

But there we were, at the Kotel, with hundreds of other Israeli parents: Sephardim, Ashkenazim, Russians, Ethiopians, Bedouins, and some other Anglo families as well. With a mix of pride and trepidation, we listened to the military trumpets, watched the procession of soldiers, then officers, and listened to a military chaplain (that means a rabbi in a uniform) speak movingly about the significance of the moment. Each young soldier was given a Tanakh (Hebrew Bible), and an M-16.

And then the base commander read their oath of allegiance. I had forgotten that it included the words "and if necessary, to give my life."

(There was a lump in my throat. Just giving three precious years of a young person's life, years that could be filled with fun, education, professional advancement, is a remarkable sacrifice. It brought me back to a few months ago, as Shai's induction neared, and my wife, Ricki, said something to him about how she feels a little guilty that we brought him here at age one, and it wasn't really his choice, and God forbid, if something should happen to him … Shai cut to the quick—I think trying to reassure her—and said: "Ima, if I have to give my life for this country, it would be a great honor." How do you respond to that?)

The answer to the officer's reading of the oath of allegiance came fast and furious: Each group of about fifty soldiers shouted in succession: "*Ani nishba! Ani nishba!*—I swear! I swear!"

The ceremony ended with *Hatikvah*. I don't know why, but tears welled up in my eyes as I sang the words "Od lo avda tikvatenu—Our hope is not yet lost." Maybe it was the events of the last three years, the terrorism, the fear, the repeated mourning—and yet we have not given up our hope. Maybe it was the fact that even though Shai's grandfathers and great-grandfather were soldiers, it was in the Polish, Russian, or Austrian army. Maybe it was because we were standing at the Kotel, site of the Temple and its destruction, the site to which our grandparents, and their grandparents before them, stretching back many centuries, prayed toward, and two thousand years later, we still have not yet given up our hope.

Maybe it was all of these.

David I. Bernstein, PhD

The Woman Who Mistook a Comb for a Fork

I have had a love affair with words ever since I can recall. My very first memory at the tender age of two is of holding my Aunt Emmy's hand and looking back over my shoulder at the pond we had just visited, departing with a profound "Bye, bye, wa-wa."

As a little girl I would whisper words to myself just to hear the sounds of them; magical words like *canopy*, *arithmetic*, and *Ethiopia*. As an adult, I have honored words as the precious tools of my trade. In my teaching, my writing, and my law practice, I have valued them as the finest of friends.

And so it was with great excitement in 1997, at the beginning of my sabbatical year in Israel, that I enrolled in a Hebrew language course at Hebrew University, ready to conquer the intricacies of a language that had intrigued and frustrated me since my youth. I entered the classroom as an enthusiastic, energetic forty-three-year-old, only to encounter a room filled with lethargic college students, most of whom were less than half my age and all of whom assumed that I was the teacher.

I was affectionately anointed the "sage," not because I knew more Hebrew than they, but because I knew how to get stains out of clothing and where to buy discount tennis shoes. While their primary concerns in class related to rock concerts and dating, mine were predictably geared toward conjugation and weekly quizzes.

I became obsessed with learning Hebrew, spending twelve to fourteen hours a day—in the classroom, on the streets, at home, on the bus, even in my sleep—learning the language. I was brazen and I was shameless. I insisted on speaking Hebrew to anyone and everyone who would listen, including a group of Japanese-speaking tourists who wanted directions to the Israel Museum.

Some people never leave home without a credit card; I never left home without my Hebrew-English dictionary. Such determination and diligence, while hastening my comprehension and ability to speak, came with a price. I became a walking, talking malaprop in Hebrew, the originator of more bloopers than Jerusalem has synagogues.

"The parade of horribles" began at one of my family's first dining-out experiences in Jerusalem. I proudly requested the menu in Hebrew and began ordering more food than we could possibly eat in a week. I was quite pleased with myself until my son asked for some ice for his drink.

"No problem," I said confidently turning to our middle-aged waiter, a man with absolutely no hair and a wide, open smile.

"Sir, may I have some ice, please?" I asked in my finest Hebrew.

He looked startled, then hurt as he scurried off. My Hebrew radar detector indicated immediate distress. What could I have possibly done to insult this gentle soul? I had only asked for some ice!

When a new waiter came to deliver the food, I knew I was in trouble. Slipping away from our table on the pretext of finding the bathroom, I headed straight for the dictionary hidden in my purse. It was on those worn pages that I discovered the error of my ways.

The trouble was that the Hebrew word for *ice* and the Hebrew word for *bald* are almost identical. I had told our unsuspecting waiter that I wanted him—and I wanted him bald! For a man with hair, this might have been funny but in my case, it was not. I felt humiliated. I was desperate to make amends and so returned to the table with renewed faith that I could make it right. I motioned to our hairless waiter and with a smile as big as Montana, asked for a *masrek*. Now he wasn't wounded but outraged. An Israeli called out, "She means a *masleg,* not a *masrek!*" This time I had asked the poor guy for a comb instead of a fork!

Embarrassed but undaunted, I never ceased using my Hebrew in public. I asked an attendant at the Jerusalem Forest if he wanted to marry me, described the biblical relationship between Rachel and Jacob as racy, and indicated that my lost luggage was fornicating. I told my daughter's pediatrician to tell me a joke instead of asking for a medical exam and asked the manager at a hotel if I could spend the night with him!

I might have thrown in the Hebrew towel if there hadn't been a breakthrough one Friday night at the shul we attended.

After several months of dedicated prayer, I still hadn't noticed much change in my ability to understand what was going on during services.

It came as a lovely surprise when I began singing the Hebrew words of *Yedid Nefesh,* the prayer that welcomes in the Sabbath. Suddenly, an awareness of what I was singing ran through me like a shiver. Never before had I understood the passion described in this song: Hebrew words depicting a most intimate love between humankind and the Creator. Never before had those words, this prayer, been mine.

The thrill raced through me and as I began to sing the opening paragraph of the *Shema,* I understood for the very first time the words that I had recited by memory my entire life. The *Shema* itself is a commandment to hear, to listen, and to understand. Suddenly I realized that in my efforts to learn Hebrew I had gained much more than knowledge of the aleph-bet. In learning Hebrew I had enabled myself to understand the true meaning of Jewish prayer.

Amy Hirshberg Lederman

Waiting in Line, a Cup of Tea, and Health Insurance

The State of Israel was founded on some pretty grand socialist ideals, but those ideals got a little mucked up along the way and, since 1948, the country's socialism has metamorphosed into some pretty abominable bureaucracy, bureaucracy that Israel has become famous, or perhaps infamous, for. But here's a story that just goes to show you that only in the Jewish state can the ancient Hebrew phrase "*Gam zoo l'tova*—Perhaps that too is for the best" apply to such exasperating bureaucracy as well.

It happened back when my friend Bobby was beginning a new life as an *oleh chadash*, a new immigrant to Israel. He had just officially declared citizenship and had to take care of a whole slew of bureaucratic chores that come with being a citizen of the Jewish State. One of these chores was signing up for a health plan that every citizen is entitled to as part of Israel's nationalized health care system. Bobby had heard stories about Israel's infamous red tape, but was determined not to let anything spoil his first days as a proud citizen of his new country. This is what happened, as Bobby tells it:

"I was walking into the main branch of the Kupat Cholim—the Israeli version of an HMO—renowned for its long lines, its busy doctors, and its languorous, tea-drinking office staff. After waiting in line for about an hour, I was finally received by a surprisingly pleasant woman of around sixty, who looked to be of Yemenite descent. I explained to her that I was an *oleh chadash*, and that I wanted to sign up for health care. Well, she flashed me a very pretty smile, had me fill out seven or so remarkably similar forms, and patiently explained to me that she would love to sign me up, but I would first have to go to the office of Bituach Leumi, Israel's social security system, and open up a file there before I could sign up at Kupat Cholim. It was, of course, Bituach Leumi that paid for health services, and a citizen couldn't get health insurance without their blessing, and funding.

"So I thanked her and waved good-bye and made my way over to the Bituach Leumi office, famous for its long lines, its busy managers, and its tea-drinking office staff. After about an hour on line, I was greeted by a pleasant receptionist, who, after having me fill out seven or so forms remarkably similar to those I'd filled out in Kupat Cholim, told me that I couldn't open a file at Bituach Leumi until I registered at the Ministry of the Interior. So I smiled, waved so long, and moved on to the Ministry of the Interior, also renowned for its long lines and its bustling, tea-drinking staff.

"Well, after an hour's wait at the ministry and after filling out seven or so forms unbelievably similar to those in both Kupat Cholim and Bituach Leumi, I was informed that before I could be recognized by the Ministry of the Interior, I would first have to sign up at the Ministry of Absorption, the only ministry that surpasses the Ministry of Interior in its perceptible bustle, its especially long lines, and the black Russian tea, usually drunk through sugar cubes by its staff, many of whom were former immigrants themselves.

"After a couple of hours of jostling around with other like-minded immigrants at the Ministry of Absorption, I was greeted at the door by a guard, a pleasant elderly man of around seventy, who had plenty of time to tell me that he, too, was an immigrant, albeit from Russia, and a veteran of the Red Army who had served in two world wars. He had me fill out seven or so extremely familiar forms, and explained that to sign up at the Ministry of Absorption I would have to make an appointment with one of the ministry's very busy counselors, and that because of the great demand for an appointment, I must put my name on a waiting list, which had no more than two weeks, worth of names on it. Well, after telling the guard what I thought about his waiting list and the rest of the bureaucracy in the country, I was told in no uncertain terms that I was a fine one to talk about bureaucracy, and that I should try living under communism for fifty years before I start lecturing him about bureaucracy.

"Down but not out, I trudged back to the Kupat Cholim, where, after another hour's wait, I was greeted by the same pleasant woman of Yemenite descent. Practically in tears from frustration, I described every step of my long day and explained that I couldn't possibly wait two whole weeks just to get the entire process started, because that would mean two weeks without health insurance, and what if, heaven forbid, what if I were hit by a car between now and then without health insurance—where would I be then?

"Well, the nice woman was very understanding, but unfortunately, she told me that rules are rules, and that I would just have to wait and hope for the best. But, she added, I seemed like such a nice, patient young man that she would take the liberty of giving my phone number, which I had penciled in on each and every one of the seven forms she had given me, she would take the liberty of giving it to her daughter, who was a true prize, and, she added, she wasn't just saying that because she was her mother."

Well, it took my friend Bobby six months before he got any health insurance, but only three before he was married—to a nice young woman of Yemenite descent.

Jonathan Elkins

Six Hundred Soldiers and a
Few Hundred Miracles

A year has passed but First Lieutenant M has not forgotten about the activities of Migdal Ohr, which had been discreetly accomplished. With minor changes, we publish here for the first time in English Lieutenant M's written recording of his experience:

I remember the two weeks of near face-to-face combat, the confused orders and insufficient combat gear, the intense hunger, physical and emotional exhaustion, and toughest of all, the self-imposed silence and disassociation with our surroundings. "Now is not the right time to complain, but when it is over," we thought to ourselves, when the air raid sirens stop and we are out of these fatigues, we can talk and the truth will be known.

When the news came that we were receiving a day off, our hearts soared. We had suffered so much stress and hardship. Where would we go? How should we take full advantage of this gift?

Rumors begin to circulate that we were going to some school in Migdal HaEmek. "This must be a joke! Who ordered ten buses to bring us to some yeshiva with some rabbi who is just going to try and brainwash us?"

Then, a few of the guys remembered. "Rabbi Grossman, that's the Disco Rabbi, right? The guys all give him great respect." But what do they know? He is still some rabbi.

Tired and emotionally drained, we got off the buses and stood face to face with an Old World–looking Jew, complete with a white beard, sidelocks, and long jacket. "So here it comes," I thought, "the push to put on *tefillin* or to say prayers together. Some day off."

"Boys," the rabbi's words thundered, "I suggest that first thing you do is take a dip in the pool and freshen up. In the meantime, we will make you something to eat."

In amazing simplicity, Rabbi Grossman heard in passing that the brigade was looking for a home for a day, and he immediately volunteered his campus. "What's the problem? Six hundred soldiers? They should all come. Of course we have room!"

With the echoes of war from the battlefield still in our ears, it seemed like a mirage or a hallucination. Soft music came from everywhere and flowing water and greenery surrounded us. Within minutes, the tables were set with cold, refreshing watermelon, cakes, and beverages, followed by cheeses, fresh vegetables, and soft rolls.

Then we heard, "Out of the pool, get dressed and eat something." We saw piles of new undergarments. Six hundred new undershirts and underwear appeared as if out of nowhere, laid out on tables for our choosing.

Rabbi Grossman sat with us and laughed. "Have a good time, boys! Have a great time! This evening, I will put on the most spectacular performance you have ever seen."

I am not a religious person by any means, but I can't help but envision the first Jew, Avraham, standing and personally serving his guests perfectly naturally and without the slightest hint of condescension. He respected each individual and cared for all their needs. Like Avraham, Rabbi Grossman saw in this an obvious act of kindness, a mission of a mitzvah that had fallen into his hands. As the evening continued, we learned quickly that this was the essence of who Rabbi Grossman is and what he is all about. He loves everyone and accepts everyone as they are with all his heart and soul.

"Tell me, friends," Rabbi Grossman said, "I heard you are lacking different pieces of equipment. Do me a favor. Here is a pencil and paper, just write down everything you are missing and leave the paper on the table." That night, we enjoyed the entertainment and afterwards, slept in soft beds and air-conditioned rooms.

As in a fairy tale, we awoke in the morning and could not believe our eyes. Mounds of gear which we so desperately needed had arrived at Migdal Ohr. Attached was a small note from Rabbi Grossman, "To my dear soldiers, from all my heart!"

Rabbi Grossman personally and immediately procured over $60,000 worth of equipment from friends—literally overnight! The essential equipment included ceramic bulletproof vests, helmets, canteens, kneepads, backpack water canteens, night-vision goggles, toothbrushes, socks, and more.

Interestingly, a few months before the war broke out, a special friend of Rabbi Grossman from France was interested in donating a new Torah scroll to the main Migdal Ohr Beit Midrash (school). For some reason, Rabbi Grossman requested to postpone the event until an unspecified later date.

"Now is the right time!" Rabbi Grossman realized. He immediately made arrangements and in an early-evening ceremony, we participated in the completion of writing the Torah. While the scroll was carefully laid on the table next to a special pen and ink, Rabbi Grossman addressed the soldiers.

"My holy ones! I am going to bestow upon you the merit of a holy mitzvah, which can be considered a once-in-a-lifetime opportunity. Each one of you will complete a letter in the Torah scroll. While you are executing this holy task, each one of you should pray the prayer of his heart and request from God that the merit of the letter he has completed will protect him in battle. Holy sparks will emanate from these sacred letters and disperse around you, creating a protective shield that will keep you safe and bring you home safely."

Those moments were the most exciting and emotional ones in my life. Shaking from the intensity of the immeasurable experience, still not believing, we held the edges of the Torah scroll while our hearts beat rapidly. There was complete silence all around. One after the other, we dipped the quill in the ink and completed a letter in the Torah scroll.

A bystander would have seen a breathtaking scene of incredible elation and spiritual exuberance. The world seemed as if shrouded in silence. The strings of our heart felt strummed and the tears flowed freely down our cheeks.

"Mother!" cried one of the soldiers into his cell phone, "You won't believe what I have done! I have written a letter in a Torah scroll! Mother, are you there? Can you hear?! Me, a shmutznik (a member of a nonreligious kibbutz) who can't differentiate between Shabbat and the rest of the week, who has not seen *tzizit* (ritual garment) in my life. Me, I wrote a letter in a Torah scroll! I can't believe it. I can't believe it."

After the completion of the Torah, the ceremony continued. Leading the procession was a decorated car with multicolored lights strung all over it and with a crown of lights spinning around on its roof. Following the car, bearers of a decorated canopy marched while people danced around it. Under the canopy, others held the Torah scroll, which was clothed in white and crimson with a silver crown at its top.

Six hundred soldiers and thousands of the town residents marched and danced in the procession, a loudspeaker accompanying them, playing traditional Jewish music.

As the ceremony came to a close, Rabbi Grossman approached every soldier and kissed him while placing a half-shekel coin in his hand and saying, "Shliach mitzvah aino nezok—Messengers of a mitzvah are not harmed." Rabbi Grossman concluded, "When you return, God willing, healthy and unharmed, you will fulfill this mission I am placing upon you, and you will donate this money to charity."

The night came. Twelve buses made their way atop the Galilee Mountains. Heavy darkness engulfed us, yet behind, in the growing distance, a bright flame pierced the night sky. In the midst of war and violence, we found love and unending human compassion at Migdal

Ohr, the educational center established in Migdal HaEmek by Rabbi Yitzchak Dovid Grossman.

Rabbi Grossman speaks

"This was an immense *Kiddush Hashem*. For a long period, I cried and was very emotional." Thus Rabbi Grossman recalled the moment when he first read the words above, written by First Lieutenant M.

Rabbi Grossman added this to the end of this exciting memoir. "A moment before they returned to Lebanon, I told the soldiers, 'In the merit that you said *Shema* and put on *tefillin*, wrote a letter in the Torah, and are messengers of a mitzvah, I promise you, that you will all return safe and sound. None of you will be wounded or killed.'"

"Weren't you scared to commit to six hundred soldiers that they would return home safe and sound?" I asked, as a journalist.

"That is what came out of my mouth word for word," he replied. "This was a moment of exuberance."

"I continued and told them," Rabbi Grossman relates, "if this does actually happen that you come back safely, the first place you must come back to—before you go home—is Migdal Ohr. We will thank God together and from there we will say good-bye." I told them, "Think of this as an emergency call-up. Do you accept?" The commanding officer replied in the affirmative.

Two weeks later, around midnight, Rabbi Grossman received a phone call. "Rabbi, your blessing has come true!" exclaimed the commander over the phone. "Everyone is safe and we are on our way to you. We will be there by two o'clock in the morning."

Rabbi Grossman immediately contacted the kitchen staff and asked them to prepare a meal while he worked to organize a band. People asked him, "You need a band at 2 a.m.? Is Moshiach (the Messiah) here?"

At 2:30 a.m. the soldiers disembarked from the buses, each one carrying sixty kilo of equipment on his back. The band started playing music and the soldiers approached Rabbi Grossman, each one lovingly received with a hug and a kiss. This continued for two hours. "I felt as I had never felt before," recalls Rabbi Grossman. "Each one told me his personal miracle."

One soldier, a kibbutznik and a lawyer in civilian life, relayed an incredible miracle. A group of soldiers were gathered in an empty house in a Lebanese village when one of them absentmindedly lit a cigarette.

Hezbollah terrorists immediately noticed the light and fired an antitank missile at the house. Coincidentally, two horses from the village ran in front of the house and were hit and killed. The missile, deflected by the horses, veered away from the house, landing elsewhere. Incredibly, the horses miraculously saved the soldiers inside the house.

After the warm reception, the soldiers recited *Birkat HaGomel*, and together with Rabbi Grossman, sang and danced until daybreak. "To this day," says Rabbi Grossman, "we maintain contact with each soldier and have thus become one family."

Rabbi Grossman is a recipient of the Award of Recognition for his Actions on Behalf of Soldiers of the Israeli Defense Forces and the Second Lebanon War.

Shula Wisper

Sulhita

Last month my friend Sarai and I sat at a gathering in the Negev desert in Israel called the Sulhita gathering. One hundred and fifty Jewish and Palestinian teenagers gathered together for five days in the desert to make and celebrate peace. No finger pointing. No blame game. Just some good old-fashioned peace making.

Sometimes we sit around and wait for politicians to tell us when we can and can't have peace. We decided not to wait for that. We can just do it. And we did. For five days. We sang each other's songs, and danced in each other's celebrations, and we sat at night around the camp fire and listened to each other's stories.

One story really grabbed me. It was told to us by a pair of peace-makers who came from a group of Israelis and Palestinians who had each lost dear family members from all the fighting. Most of the Israelis in the group had lost family members from bus bombings and shootings and most of the Palestinians lost family members from Israeli army activity. Yet they sat side by side and spoke of their yearnings for peace and reconciliation.

Ahmed grew up in Jenin. The only Israelis Ahmed had ever met wore green camoflauge, held huge guns, and sometimes drove tanks. This to him was what a Jew was. He said that he grew up hating Jews and during the intifada he was in the front lines throwing stones and who knows what else. He'd been in and out of Israeli jails several times.

One day there was an early curfew in town to keep people off the streets. Ahmed's thirteen-year-old brother went for a walk to his grand-mother's house just down the street. He heard shooting and started to run. Before he could make it to the door a rubber bullet made it to his chest. The bullet went through his little body and literally broke his heart. He died. Ahmed said that that day was the last day he saw his mother smile. Fueled with more rage, he hit the streets again looking for bigger stones to throw.

A few years later Ahmed needed a job and had looked everywhere in town but couldn't find one. His friends told him that there were good jobs in Israel. At first he was appalled at the idea of working in Israel for Jews, but eventually he had no other choice. So he got a construction job in a Jewish town working for a Jewish boss, the first Jew he ever met who wasn't wearing green. He was very bitter about the whole situation.

One day his boss stopped and asked him why his face was always so sad and bitter. They sat down under a tree, and Ahmed told the story of his brother's death and about his mother's grief. As he told the story, his Jewish boss began to weep and say how sorry he was that had happened to his brother.

Ahmed didn't really know what to do or what to think. He'd never met or seen a Jew expressing compassion and this behavior didn't jibe at all with the image he had in his head of his enemy, the "other" he'd been fighting against and trying to destroy.

Two weeks later a Palestinian man walked onto the number eighteen bus in downtown Jerusalem and detonated an explosives belt around his waist. The blast was so strong that the top of the bus peeled back like the lid of a sardine can. Seventeen Israelis were instantly killed and many more injured. After work that day Ahmed returned to his mother's house. When he came in, he found her on the ground crying beside the television set as the news was coming through. He said "Mom, why are you crying? Don't you know those were Jews who were killed, not Palestinians?" His mother looked up and said through her tears to him, "I'm crying because of all the mothers who are right now going through what I once went through."

Something began to change in Ahmed's heart and in his mind. He no longer could say that he hated Jews because he'd met one, just one, that he really liked. His mother showed him that pain and suffering transcends nationality and religion. And he had to reconcile this new information with his actions. He realized that throwing stones and plotting destruction were just perpetuating the struggle.

Eventually he found the Bereaved Families Group of Israelis and Palestinians and now he tours around Israeli towns and Palestinian communities side by side with Israelis and shares his story.

These people who lost their relatives have every excuse to live in hatred. Yet they choose love and reconciliation. If they can do it, we have no excuse.

Another thing that really struck me by this story is how it only takes a few small interactions to radically transform a person. So I'm trying to look at each moment as sacred and as having awesome potential for growth. In this life, with this body and with these eyes, we can barely see the ripples we are constantly sending out. We know so little about what effect we have on each other. The Jewish boss had no idea what impact he was having and neither did the mother. They were just being—being genuine and coming from a place of compassion. When we come from that place of compassion, especially for the "other," we send out beautiful waves of goodness.

Jeremy Pesach Stadlin

Acknowledgments

I would like to extend a debt of gratitude to my friend of over thirty years, Jack Canfield, who first set me on the path of collecting Jewish stories for the book we coedited in 2001, *Chicken Soup for the Jewish Soul.* Jack's friendship has been a source of joy and inspiration for a good part of my professional life.

Nick Ginsberg was very helpful in obtaining permissions. I would also like to thank all the kind and creative people whose stories are included in this collection, and who graciously consented to have their pieces reprinted here. I am particularly grateful to Dr. Blair Grubb, who not only contributed many of his own stories, but has led me to other sources as well.

I want to express deep appreciation to the staff of Jewish Lights Publishing. This is the fourth book of mine that they are publishing, and each experience with them has been filled with satisfaction, fulfillment, and ease. Their support, understanding, and professionalism have made each book better than the manuscript I submitted. For this book I am especially indebted to Emily Wichland, vice president of editorial and production, for her timely and friendly cooperation and support. Thanks also go to Kate Treworgy, whose skills, warmth, and professional skills have helped promote my previous books, and I am certain will do the same for this one. Special gratitude goes to Stuart M. Matlins, publisher of Jewish Lights, who has created in the last several decades the finest publishing house for Jewish books in North America. The range of outstanding books coming from Jewish Lights, the distinguished authors he has assembled, who make up a remarkable pantheon of the leaders of American Jewry, and his deep involvement with every aspect of every book, all make for the great success of Jewish Lights, raise the literary level of world Jewry, and go a long way toward enlightening the gentile world about things Jewish.

I am grateful to my son, Jonathan, whose creative literary skills have enhanced much of my work, including this book, to which he has contributed one of the stories. I am also grateful to my stepson, Jeremy Pesach Stadlin, for contributing his very moving story. My daughter-in-law, Vivian, helped with the cover design by providing preliminary suggestions; her intelligence, talent, and sweetness are always appreciated.

Finally, my loving wife, Maxine, is my best, most supportive, and most constant editor, critic, and partner in everything I do in my writing and in all matters personal and professional.

I give thanks to Almighty God that I have been able to complete this book at the same time that I celebrated my seventieth birthday ... *she-he-heyanu, ve-keymanu ve-heegeyanu laz'man hazeh.*

—Rabbi Dov Peretz Elkins

Credits

This page constitutes a continuation of the copyright page. Every effort has been made to trace and acknowledge copyright holders of all the material included in this collection. The editor apologizes for any errors or omissions that may remain and asks that any omissions be brought to his attention so that they may be corrected in future editions.

Grateful acknowledgement is given to the following sources for permission to use material:

Shula Wisper, "Six Hundred Soldiers and a Few Hundred Miracles," originally published through www.aish.com, a leading Judaism website. Reprinted by permission.

Rabbi Mitchell Wohlberg, "Anne Frank's Tree," © Mitchell Wohlberg.

Rabbi Gerald I. Wolpe, "The Reunion," © Gerald I. Wolpe.

Noam Sachs Zion and David Dishon, "The 'Seder' of Righteous Gentiles: A Family Liberation." Reprinted by permission from *A Different Night: The Family Participation Haggadah*, and *A Night to Remember: The Haggadah of Contemporary Voices*, © Noam Sachs Zion.

About the Contributors

Rabbi Bradley Shavit Artson (www.bradartson.com) is the dean of the Ziegler School of Rabbinic Studies at the American Jewish University, where he is vice president. The author of over 250 articles and six books, including *Everyday Torah: Weekly Reflections and Inspirations*.

James Auer is a writer for the *Milwaukee Journal Sentinel*.

Rabbi Aaron Benson grew up in suburban Chicago. He was ordained at the Ziegler School of Rabbinic Studies in May of 2003. He currently serves as rabbi at Congregation Beth Meier in Studio City, California, and is the recording secretary for the Rabbinical Assembly's Pacific Southwest Region Executive Board.

Rabbi Avraham Berkowitz is the executive director of the Federation of Jewish Communities of the CIS and Baltic States. Rabbi Berkowitz is responsible for the development and management of 450 Jewish communities that are members of the FJC. He is an expert with respect to the rebuilding of the emerging Jewish communities in countries of the former Soviet Union. He lives with his wife, Leah, and four children in Moscow, Russia. He can be contacted by e-mail at berkowitz@jewish.ru.

David I. Bernstein, PhD, holds a BA and an MA in history and a PhD in religious education from New York University. He also attended Yeshivat HaMivtar. Dr. Bernstein has been the dean of Pardes since 1998. Previously, he was the director of Midreshet Lindenbaum, popularly known as Brovender's, for twelve years. Dr. Bernstein was a Jerusalem Fellow at the Mandel School for Jewish Education in Jerusalem from 1996 to 1998. Before making *aliyah* in 1984,

Dr. Bernstein was the director of informal education at the Ramaz Upper School in New York City.

Miriam Newell Biskin, a retired English teacher, owes her talent to her beloved storyteller mother, Bessie, and her late beloved husband-listener, Irving. Her main interests are books, writing, and her great-grandchildren: Binyamin, Yonathan, Aleeza, and Naomi.

Jack H. Bloom, a rabbi and clinical psychologist, is one of a handful of rabbis who is a full member of both the Central Conference of American Rabbis (Reform), and the Rabbinical Assembly (Conservative). He has fulfilled his declared off-handed high school yearbook ambition of becoming an "athletic coach for rabbis" and has been honored for being the "quintessential rabbi for rabbis." He and his beloved wife, Ingrid, a retired German teacher and artist, are the parents of four children and the grandparents of seven. Rabbi Bloom and his wife reside in Fairfield, Connecticut.

The late **Rabbi Shlomo Carlebach** was a famous minstrel, composer, and charismatic teacher.

Sterna Citron is the author of *Why the Baal Shem Tov Laughed: 52 Stories About Our Great Chassidic Rabbis* as well as several children's books, including *Shlomo's Little Joke.* Presently Sterna edits a magazine for Jewish teenage girls called *Shoshanim.* Sterna and her husband, Rabbi Chaim Zev Citron, live in Los Angeles.

Rabbi Yitzchak Cohen serves in Dallas, Texas.

Debra B. Darvick's essays and feature stories have appeared in *Hadassah, Moment,* the *Forward,* and *Newsweek,* among others. She is the author of *This Jewish Life: Stories of Discovery, Connection and Joy.* Her website is www.debradarvick.com.

David Dishon made *aliyah,* emigrating from the USA to Jerusalem, during the Yom Kippur War in 1973 and teaches at the Shalom Hartman Institute, a pluralist Jewish think tank and teacher training center. He published, with Noam Sachs Zion, several contemporary Passover Haggadahs and Shabbat and Hanukkah Seder books. For selections see www.haggadahsrus.com.

The late **Rabbi Samuel H. Dresner** was a well-known congregational rabbi in the Chicago area, and author of several highly respected books.

Jonathan Elkins is a news anchor and television correspondent at Israel Television. He has interviewed top politicians across the globe including prime ministers, presidents, and Nobel laureates. He is also an author and filmmaker. He lives in Tel Aviv with his wife and family.

Cecelia Ostrov Euster is a wife, mother, grandmother, and educator who enjoys worldwide travel to historic Jewish locations.

Michael Feldberg, PhD, is director of research for the American Jewish Historical Society. His publications include a collection of essays, *Blessings of Freedom: Chapters in American Jewish History* (KTAV, 2002), from which his contribution to this book is taken.

Sam Fishman was a retired pharmacist, who wrote poetry and short stories. He and his wife, Mildred, were married for over fifty years. They lived in Marlboro, New Jersey. They were proud of their two children, Larry and Janet, and their five grandchildren, Mara, Lisa, David, Daniel, and Sara.

Stephen Flatow is a real estate lawyer, vice president, and counsel of Vested Title, Inc., a large title insurance agency. He is founder of Congregation Ohr Torah of West Orange, New Jersey, and a lecturer on Middle East politics, terrorism, and victims' rights.

Frieda Friedman went to Sweden after the liberation of the Nazi camps. There she met the man would marry, Salomon. They had two children, Rachel and Max. Before her death she lived in Mobile, Alabama, near her daughter.

Rabbi Melvin Glazer has been a pulpit rabbi and grief specialist for over thirty years. His recent publications, *And God Created Hope: Finding Your Way Through Grief with Lessons from Early Biblical Stories* and *When Grief Visits a Jewish Home: 99 Answers for Mourners* have helped mourners of all religions to navigate the difficult journey "from mourning to morning." He is the rabbi of Temple Shalom in Colorado Springs, Colorado.

Rabbi Elaine Rose Glickman, a writer, teacher, rabbi, wife, and mother, received her master of arts in Hebrew letters and ordination from Hebrew Union College–Jewish Institute of Religion. She is the author of *Haman and the Jews: A Portrait from Rabbinic Literature* and *How to Be a Great Parent*, and the editor of *B'chol L'vavcha* (revised edition) and *Living Torah: Selections from Seven Years of Torat Chayim.*

Irene Goldfarb is a wife, mother, grandmother, and a retired certified financial planner. She is active at her synagogue, the Jewish Center of Princeton (New Jersey), where she was honored as Congregant of the Year. She is also active in the Associate Alumnae of Douglass College, Rutgers University, and has received several service awards from Douglass College and Rutgers University.

Carole Orenstein Goldstein carries on the tradition of maintaining a Jewish home. She would like to dedicate her story to her mother, Leah Devorah Orenstein. Carole and her husband, Rabbi Nason Goldstein, have three adult children, Deena, Arnon, and Hana, and two grandchildren.

Steve Goodier is founder and publisher of Your Life Support System, an Internet newsletter of life, love, and laughter. He and his wife, Bev, currently live in Salt Lake City, Utah, with their two pugs.

The late **Rabbi Sidney Greenberg** preached from the pulpit of Temple Sinai, now in Dresher, Pennsylvania, for more than fifty years. He conducted sermon seminars and courses for rabbis and Christian clergypersons throughout America, and taught homiletics at his alma mater as well as at the Reconstructionist Rabbinical College in Philadelphia, and at Hebrew Union College–Jewish Institute of Religion in Manhattan. In 1992 the Jewish Theological Seminary designated him Rabbi of the Year. He was the recipient of the Simon Rockower Memorial Award for Excellence in Jewish Journalism in North America.

Blair P. Grubb, MD, a native of Baltimore, is a professor of medicine and pediatrics and director of Cardiac Electrophysiology at the University of Toledo Medical Center. He is married to Barbara Straus, MD, and has two children: Helen and Alex. He is an active member of B'nai Israel Synagogue in Toledo, Ohio.

Jeff Jacoby has been an op-ed columnist for the *Boston Globe* since 1994. In 1999 he became the first recipient of the Breindel Prize, an eminent award for excellence in opinion journalism.

Henia Karmel-Wolfe, a Polish Jew, was born in Krakow in 1921. She published two novels, *The Baders of Jacob Street* (1970) and *Marek and Lisa* (1984) as well as a number of anthologized short stories. She and her sister, novelist Ilona Karmel, wrote poems in Buchenwald that were recently translated and published in a *A Wall of Two*. She died in 1984.

Rabbi Paysach J. Krohn is a rabbi and fifth-generation mohel in Brooklyn. He is the author of *Echoes of the Magid: Heartwarming Stories and Parables of Wisdom and Inspiration* (Art Scroll/Mesorah Publications, 1999), among other collections of inspirational stories.

Rabbi Eugene Labovitz recently retired after serving for forty years in the same pulpit, Ner Tamid, Miami Beach, but he is still known as the "master maggid," having developed the use of holy stories to teach and to inspire. **Dr. Annette Labovitz** teaches all over the New York area. Together the couple have written five anthologies of holy stories, the newest titled *The Legendary Maggidim: Stories for Soul and Spirit.*

Amy Hirshberg Lederman is an award-winning, nationally syndicated columnist, author, Jewish educator, public speaker, and attorney. She lives in Tucson with her husband and two children (whenever they visit), and can be contacted at www.amyhirshberglederman.com.

Daniel N. Leeson was born and raised in Paterson, New Jersey. His degrees are in mathematics. He spent thirty years with the IBM Corporation, and is now retired. He is a professional musician and musicologist. He is married and has two children, and one grandchild.

Dr. Rafael Medoff is founding director of the David S. Wyman Institute for Holocaust Studies (www.WymanInstitute.org). He is the author of eight books about American Jewish history, Zionism, and the Holocaust, the most recent of which is *Blowing the Whistle on Genocide: Josiah E. DuBois, Jr. and the Struggle for an American Response to the Holocaust*.

Rabbi Daniel Moscowitz is the regional director of Lubavitch Chabad of Illinois, and vice-president of the Chicago Rabbinical Council.

Danielle Ofri, MD, PhD, is an assistant professor of medicine at Bellevue Hospital/NYU School of Medicine, as well as editor-in-chief of the *Bellevue Literary Review*. She is the author of two collections of essays about life in medicine: *Incidental Findings* (2005) and *Singular Intimacies* (2003). Her writings have appeared in the *New York Times*, the *LA Times*, *Best American Essays*, *Best American Science Writing*, the *New England Journal of Medicine*, and on National Public Radio.

Rabbi Stephen S. Pearce, PhD, is senior rabbi of Congregation Emanu-El of San Francisco. He is author of *Flash of Insight: Metaphor and Narrative in Therapy*, and coauthor—with Bishop William E. Swing, the Episcopal Bishop of California, and Father John P. Schlegel, president of the University of San Francisco—of *Building Wisdom's House: A Book of Values for Our Time*. The April 2, 2007, issue of *Newsweek* magazine ranked Dr. Pearce as one of the fifty most influential rabbis in America.

Alison Stern Perez was born and grew up in Seattle, and is a graduate of Brown University. She now lives in Beersheva, Israel. You can e-mail her at Alison_Golub@hotmail.com, and read more about her adventures on her website at www.alisonsterngolub.com.

Ingrid Peritz has been a news reporter and feature writer for Canadian newspapers for twenty-five years. She is currently a Montreal-based correspondent for the *Globe and Mail*.

Rabbi Joseph Potasnik is executive director of the New York Board of Rabbis.

Kenneth M. Prager, MD, is professor of clinical medicine at Columbia University College of Physicians and chairman of the Medical Ethics Committee at Columbia University Medical Center. He is a graduate of Yeshiva University High School in Brooklyn, Columbia College, and Harvard Medical School.

The late **Yitzhak Rabin** was prime minister of the State of Israel.

Rabbi Shlomo Riskin is chief rabbi of Efrat, and dean of Ohr Torah Stone Institutions.

Rabbi Yaakov Salomon, CSW, is a noted psychotherapist, in private practice in Brooklyn for over twenty-five years. He is a senior lecturer and the creative director of Aish Hatorah's Discovery Productions. He is also an editor and author for the ArtScroll Publishing Series and a member of the Kollel of Yeshiva Torah Vodaath. His speaking, writing, and musical talents have delighted audiences from Harvard to Broadway and everywhere in between. Rabbi Salomon shares his life with his wife, Temmy, and their unpredictable family.

Rabbi Eli J. Schochet was ordained at The Jewish Theological Seminary in 1960, received his doctorate in 1967 under Prof. Saul Lieberman, and wrote seven books on rabbinic thought and personalities. He was rabbi of Shomrei Torah Synagogue in West Hills, California, for forty years until his retirement, and is currently professor of rabbinics at the Academy for Jewish Religion in Los Angeles.

Peninnah Schram, an internationally known storyteller, teacher, author, and recording artist, is associate professor of speech and drama at Stern College of Yeshiva University. She is the author of ten books of Jewish folktales, including *Jewish Stories One Generation Tells Another* and *Stories Within Stories: From the Jewish Oral Tradition*. She has also recorded a CD, *The Minstrel and the Storyteller*, with singer/guitarist Gerard Edery. She is a recipient of the prestigious Covenant Award for Outstanding Jewish Educator (1995), awarded by the Covenant Foundation, and the National Storytelling Network's 2003 Lifetime Achievement Award "For sustained and exemplary contributions to storytelling in America."

Rabbi Byron L. Sherwin, PhD, is distinguished service professor of Jewish philosophy and mysticism at Chicago's Spertus Institute of Jewish Studies. He is the author of twenty-six books and over 150 articles and monographs.

Scott Simon is a reporter for National Public Radio.

Jeremy Pesach Stadlin is a world-traveling, truth-seeking, experiential educator who leads heart/mind/soul-expanding service/learning trips to Israel, Africa, Asia, and Central America. Having lived in redwood trees, in sailboats, in Tsfat (Safed) during the Lebanon War, and in a Kerouacian-style motor home named Mira, he uses the pen as a tool for inspiration and enrichment.

The late **Bea Stadtler** was devoted to educating Jewish children. The registrar of the College of Jewish Studies in Cleveland (now called the Siegel College of Jewish Studies), she was a prolific writer, whose work included *The Holocaust: A History of Courage and Resistance* (Behrman House), which is still used in many schools today.

Rabbi Reuven Taff serves as spiritual leader of Mosaic Law Congregation, a Conservative synagogue in Sacramento. He is a former cantor at Beth El Congregation in Phoenix.

Rabbi Hanoch Teller is a globe-trotting, modern-day *maggid* who lectures all over the world. He is the best-selling author of over twenty books, which can be found in virtually every Jewish community. He has also produced the award-winning film *Do You Believe in Miracles?*

Giorgina Vitale, who was born in Torino, Italy, arrived in the United States in 1949, after being forced to go into hiding during World War II. She and her late husband, Luciano, lived in New Haven ever since their arrival in the United States, and brought four daughters into the world. After her husband's premature death, Giorgina served in several professional capacities for the New Haven Jewish Federation before her retirement. Now she does volunteer work, travels, and enjoys her large family, including seven grandchildren and four great-grandchildren.

Wilhelm Weiner, PhD, lived under Hitler but escaped and maintains a practice as a psychoanalyst-psychotherapist in Brooklyn.

Chana Weisberg, the author of *Divine Whispers* and *Tending the Garden*, is the associate editor of chabad.org. She is a sought-after international lecturer who inspires and empowers her audiences on topics of faith, relationships, Jewish mysticism, and the Jewish woman.

Rabbi Avi Weiss is founder and president of Yeshivat Chovevei Torah—the Modern and Open Orthodox Rabbinical School. The school has already placed thirty-six rabbis across the country. Rabbi Weiss is the senior rabbi of the Hebrew Institute of Riverdale, a Modern and Open Orthodox congregation of 850 families. He is also national president of AMCHA—the Coalition for Jewish Concerns, a grassroots organization that speaks out for Jewish causes and Israel.

Elie Wiesel is a recipient of the Nobel Peace Prize, a writer, novelist, and lecturer.

Shula Wisper was born in Jerusalem and has worked at the Ministry for Foreign Affairs. She is a journalist, writer, and poet. She does volunteer work with autistic children and at nursing homes. She lives in B'nai B'rak with her husband, three children, and ten grandchildren.

Rabbi Mitchell Wohlberg has been the rabbi of the Beth Tfiloh Congregation in Baltimore for the past thirty years. The congregation is the largest Modern Orthodox synagogue in the United States. He also serves as the dean of its day school of 1,000 students.

Rabbi Gerald I. Wolpe has served as chaplain of the Second Marine Division and congregations in Charleston, South Carolina; Harrisburg, Pennsylvania; and for thirty years at Har Zion Temple, Penn Valley, Pennsylvania, where he is rabbi emeritus. He served as director of the Finkelstein Institute of Social and Religious Studies at the Jewish Theological Seminary. He also was first chairman of the Advisory Board of the Center of Bioethics at the University of Pennsylvania, where he now teaches as a senior fellow.

Noam Sachs Zion made *aliyah*, emigrating from the USA to Jerusalem, during the Yom Kippur War in 1973 and teaches at the Shalom Hartman Institute, a pluralist Jewish think tank and teacher training center. He adopted his Dutch wife Marcelle's last name when he married in order to preserve the family name of her Holocaust family. In the interest of promoting family story telling around the table on Jewish holidays, he published, with David Dishon and later with his oldest son, several contemporary Passover Haggadahs and Shabbat and Hanukkah Seder books. For selections see www.haggadahsrus.com.

Bar/Bat Mitzvah

The JGirl's Guide: The Young Jewish Woman's Handbook for Coming of Age
By Penina Adelman, Ali Feldman, and Shulamit Reinharz
This inspirational, interactive guidebook helps pre-teen Jewish girls address the many issues surrounding coming of age.   6 x 9, 240 pp, Quality PB, 978-1-58023-215-9 **$14.99**
   Also Available: **The JGirl's Teacher's and Parent's Guide**
   8½ x 11, 56 pp, PB, 978-1-58023-225-8 **$8.99**

Bar/Bat Mitzvah Basics: A Practical Family Guide to Coming of Age Together
Edited by Cantor Helen Leneman   6 x 9, 240 pp, Quality PB, 978-1-58023-151-0 **$18.95**

The Bar/Bat Mitzvah Memory Book, 2nd Edition: An Album for Treasuring the Spiritual Celebration By Rabbi Jeffrey K. Salkin and Nina Salkin
8 x 10, 48 pp, Deluxe HC, 2-color text, ribbon marker, 978-1-58023-263-0 **$19.99**

For Kids—Putting God on Your Guest List, 2nd Edition: How to Claim the Spiritual Meaning of Your Bar or Bat Mitzvah By Rabbi Jeffrey K. Salkin
6 x 9, 144 pp, Quality PB, 978-1-58023-308-8 **$15.99** For ages 11–13

Putting God on the Guest List, 3rd Edition: How to Reclaim the Spiritual Meaning of Your Child's Bar or Bat Mitzvah By Rabbi Jeffrey K. Salkin
6 x 9, 224 pp, Quality PB, 978-1-58023-222-7 **$16.99**; HC, 978-1-58023-260-9 **$24.99**
Also Available: **Putting God on the Guest List Teacher's Guide**
8½ x 11, 48 pp, PB, 978-1-58023-226-5 **$8.99**

Tough Questions Jews Ask: A Young Adult's Guide to Building a Jewish Life
By Rabbi Edward Feinstein   6 x 9, 160 pp, Quality PB, 978-1-58023-139-8 **$14.99** For ages 12 & up
Also Available: **Tough Questions Jews Ask Teacher's Guide**
8½ x 11, 72 pp, PB, 978-1-58023-187-9 **$8.95**

Bible Study/Midrash

Abraham's Bind & Other Bible Tales of Trickery, Folly, Mercy and Love By Michael J. Caduto
Re-imagines many biblical characters, retelling their stories.
6 x 9, 224 pp, HC, 978-1-59473-186-0 **$19.99** (A SkyLight Paths book)

Ancient Secrets: Using the Stories of the Bible to Improve Our Everyday Lives
By Rabbi Levi Meier, PhD 5½ x 8½, 288 pp, Quality PB, 978-1-58023-064-3 **$16.95**

The Genesis of Leadership: What the Bible Teaches Us about Vision, Values and Leading Change By Rabbi Nathan Laufer; Foreword by Senator Joseph I. Lieberman
Unlike other books on leadership, this one is rooted in the stories of the Bible.
6 x 9, 288 pp, Quality PB, 978-1-58023-352-1 **$18.99**; HC, 978-1-58023-241-8 **$24.99**

Hineini in Our Lives: Learning How to Respond to Others through 14 Biblical Texts and Personal Stories By Norman J. Cohen   6 x 9, 240 pp, Quality PB, 978-1-58023-274-6 **$16.99**

Moses and the Journey to Leadership: Timeless Lessons of Effective Management from the Bible and Today's Leaders By Dr. Norman J. Cohen
6 x 9, 240 pp, Quality PB, 978-1-58023-351-4 **$18.99**; HC, 978-1-58023-227-2 **$21.99**

Self, Struggle & Change: Family Conflict Stories in Genesis and Their Healing Insights for Our Lives By Norman J. Cohen   6 x 9, 224 pp, Quality PB, 978-1-879045-66-8 **$18.99**

The Triumph of Eve & Other Subversive Bible Tales By Matt Biers-Ariel
5½ x 8½, 192 pp, Quality PB, 978-1-59473-176-1 **$14.99**; HC, 978-1-59473-040-5 **$19.99**
(A SkyLight Paths book)

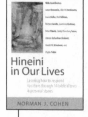

The Wisdom of Judaism: An Introduction to the Values of the Talmud
By Rabbi Dov Peretz Elkins
Explores the essence of Judaism.   6 x 9, 192 pp, Quality PB, 978-1-58023-327-9 **$16.99**
Also Available: **The Wisdom of Judaism Teacher's Guide**
8½ x 11, 18 pp, PB, 978-1-58023-350-7 **$8.99**

Congregation Resources

The Art of Public Prayer, 2nd Edition: Not for Clergy Only *By Lawrence A. Hoffman*
6 x 9, 272 pp, Quality PB, 978-1-893361-06-5 **$19.99** *(A SkyLight Paths book)*

Becoming a Congregation of Learners: Learning as a Key to Revitalizing
Congregational Life *By Isa Aron, PhD; Foreword by Rabbi Lawrence A. Hoffman*
6 x 9, 304 pp, Quality PB, 978-1-58023-089-6 **$19.95**

Finding a Spiritual Home: How a New Generation of Jews Can Transform the
American Synagogue *By Rabbi Sidney Schwarz*
6 x 9, 352 pp, Quality PB, 978-1-58023-185-5 **$19.95**

Jewish Pastoral Care, 2nd Edition: A Practical Handbook from Traditional &
Contemporary Sources *Edited by Rabbi Dayle A. Friedman*
6 x 9, 528 pp, HC, 978-1-58023-221-0 **$40.00**

Jewish Spiritual Direction: An Innovative Guide from Traditional and Contemporary
Sources *Edited by Rabbi Howard A. Addison and Barbara Eve Breitman*
6 x 9, 368 pp, HC, 978-1-58023-230-2 **$30.00**

The Self-Renewing Congregation: Organizational Strategies for Revitalizing
Congregational Life *By Isa Aron, PhD; Foreword by Dr. Ron Wolfson*
6 x 9, 304 pp, Quality PB, 978-1-58023-166-4 **$19.95**

Spiritual Community: The Power to Restore Hope, Commitment and Joy
By Rabbi David A. Teutsch, PhD 5½ x 8½, 144 pp, HC, 978-1-58023-270-8 **$19.99**

The Spirituality of Welcoming: How to Transform Your Congregation into a
Sacred Community *By Dr. Ron Wolfson* 6 x 9, 224 pp, Quality PB, 978-1-58023-244-9 **$19.99**

Rethinking Synagogues: A New Vocabulary for Congregational Life
By Rabbi Lawrence A. Hoffman 6 x 9, 240 pp, Quality PB, 978-1-58023-248-7 **$19.99**

Children's Books

What You Will See Inside a Synagogue
By Rabbi Lawrence A. Hoffman and Dr. Ron Wolfson; Full-color photos by Bill Aron
A colorful, fun-to-read introduction that explains the ways and whys of Jewish
worship and religious life.
8½ x 10½, 32 pp, Full-color photos, HC, 978-1-59473-012-2 **$17.99** *For ages 6 & up (A SkyLight Paths book)*

The Kids' Fun Book of Jewish Time
By Emily Sper 9 x 7½, 24 pp, Full-color illus., HC, 978-1-58023-311-8 **$16.99**

In God's Hands
By Lawrence Kushner and Gary Schmidt 9 x 12, 32 pp, HC, 978-1-58023-224-1 **$16.99**

Because Nothing Looks Like God
By Lawrence and Karen Kushner
Introduces children to the possibilities of spiritual life.
11 x 8½, 32 pp, Full-color illus., HC, 978-1-58023-092-6 **$17.99** *For ages 4 & up*

Also Available: **Because Nothing Looks Like God Teacher's Guide**
8½ x 11, 22 pp, PB, 978-1-58023-140-4 **$6.95** *For ages 5–8*

Board Book Companions to *Because Nothing Looks Like God*
5 x 5, 24 pp, Full-color illus., SkyLight Paths Board Books *For ages 0–4*

What Does God Look Like? 978-1-893361-23-2 **$7.99**

How Does God Make Things Happen? 978-1-893361-24-9 **$7.95**

Where Is God? 978-1-893361-17-1 **$7.99**

The Book of Miracles: A Young Person's Guide to Jewish Spiritual Awareness
By Lawrence Kushner. All-new illustrations by the author
6 x 9, 96 pp, 2-color illus., HC, 978-1-879045-78-1 **$16.95** *For ages 9 and up*

In Our Image: God's First Creatures
By Nancy Sohn Swartz 9 x 12, 32 pp, Full-color illus., HC, 978-1-879045-99-6 **$16.95** *For ages 4 & up*

Also Available as a Board Book: **How Did the Animals Help God?**
5 x 5, 24 pp, Board, Full-color illus., 978-1-59473-044-3 **$7.99** *For ages 0–4 (A SkyLight Paths book)*

What Makes Someone a Jew?
By Lauren Seidman
Reflects the changing face of American Judaism.
10 x 8½, 32 pp, Full-color photos, Quality PB Original, 978-1-58023-321-7 **$8.99** *For ages 3–6*

Children's Books
by Sandy Eisenberg Sasso

Adam & Eve's First Sunset: God's New Day
Engaging new story explores fear and hope, faith and gratitude in ways that will delight kids and adults—inspiring us to bless each of God's days and nights.
9 x 12, 32 pp, Full-color illus., HC, 978-1-58023-177-0 **$17.95** *For ages 4 & up*

Also Available as a Board Book: **Adam and Eve's New Day**
5 x 5, 24 pp, Full-color illus., Board, 978-1-59473-205-8 **$7.99** *For ages 0–4 (A SkyLight Paths book)*

But God Remembered
Stories of Women from Creation to the Promised Land
Four different stories of women—Lillith, Serach, Bityah, and the Daughters of Z—teach us important values through their faith and actions.
9 x 12, 32 pp, Full-color illus., HC, 978-1-879045-43-9 **$16.95** *For ages 8 & up*

Cain & Abel: Finding the Fruits of Peace
Shows children that we have the power to deal with anger in positive ways. Provides questions for kids and adults to explore together.
9 x 12, 32 pp, Full-color illus., HC, 978-1-58023-123-7 **$16.95** *For ages 5 & up*

God in Between
If you wanted to find God, where would you look? This magical, mythical tale teaches that God can be found where we are: within all of us and the relationships between us.
9 x 12, 32 pp, Full-color illus., HC, 978-1-879045-86-6 **$16.95** *For ages 4 & up*

God's Paintbrush: Special 10th Anniversary Edition
Wonderfully interactive, invites children of all faiths and backgrounds to encounter God through moments in their own lives. Provides questions adult and child can explore together.
11 x 8½, 32 pp, Full-color illus., HC, 978-1-58023-195-4 **$17.95** *For ages 4 & up*

Also Available: **God's Paintbrush Teacher's Guide**
8½ x 11, 32 pp, PB, 978-1-879045-57-6 **$8.95**

God's Paintbrush Celebration Kit
A Spiritual Activity Kit for Teachers and Students of All Faiths, All Backgrounds
Additional activity sheets available:
8-Student Activity Sheet Pack (40 sheets/5 sessions), 978-1-58023-058-2 **$19.95**
Single-Student Activity Sheet Pack (5 sessions), 978-1-58023-059-9 **$3.95**

In God's Name
Like an ancient myth in its poetic text and vibrant illustrations, this award-winning modern fable about the search for God's name celebrates the diversity and, at the same time, the unity of all people.
9 x 12, 32 pp, Full-color illus., HC, 978-1-879045-26-2 **$16.99** *For ages 4 & up*

Also Available as a Board Book: **What Is God's Name?**
5 x 5, 24 pp, Board, Full-color illus., 978-1-893361-10-2 **$7.99** *For ages 0–4 (A SkyLight Paths book)*

Also Available: **In God's Name video and study guide**
Computer animation, original music, and children's voices. 18 min. **$29.99**

Also Available in Spanish: **El nombre de Dios**
9 x 12, 32 pp, Full-color illus., HC, 978-1-893361-63-8 **$16.95** *(A SkyLight Paths book)*

Noah's Wife: The Story of Naamah
When God tells Noah to bring the animals of the world onto the ark, God also calls on Naamah, Noah's wife, to save each plant on Earth. Based on an ancient text.
9 x 12, 32 pp, Full-color illus., HC, 978-1-58023-134-3 **$16.95** *For ages 4 & up*

Also Available as a Board Book: **Naamah, Noah's Wife**
5 x 5, 24 pp, Full-color illus., Board, 978-1-893361-56-0 **$7.95** *For ages 0–4 (A SkyLight Paths book)*

For Heaven's Sake: Finding God in Unexpected Places
9 x 12, 32 pp, Full-color illus., HC, 978-1-58023-054-4 **$16.95** *For ages 4 & up*

God Said Amen: Finding the Answers to Our Prayers
9 x 12, 32 pp, Full-color illus., HC, 978-1-58023-080-3 **$16.95** *For ages 4 & up*

Inspiration

Happiness and the Human Spirit: The Spirituality of Becoming the Best You Can Be *By Abraham J. Twerski, MD*
Shows you that true happiness is attainable once you stop looking outside yourself for the source.   6 x 9, 176 pp, HC, 978-1-58023-343-9 **$19.99**

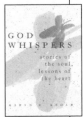

The Bridge to Forgiveness: Stories and Prayers for Finding God and Restoring Wholeness *By Rabbi Karyn D. Kedar*
Examines how forgiveness can be the bridge that connects us to wholeness and peace.
6 x 9, 176 pp, HC, 978-1-58023-324-8 **$19.99**

God's To-Do List: 103 Ways to Be an Angel and Do God's Work on Earth
By Dr. Ron Wolfson 6 x 9, 150 pp, Quality PB, 978-1-58023-301-9 **$17.99**

God in All Moments: Mystical & Practical Spiritual Wisdom from Hasidic Masters
Edited and translated by Or N. Rose with Ebn D. Leader
5½ x 8½, 192 pp, Quality PB, 978-1-58023-186-2 **$16.95**

Our Dance with God: Finding Prayer, Perspective and Meaning in the Stories of Our Lives *By Karyn D. Kedar* 6 x 9, 176 pp, Quality PB, 978-1-58023-202-9 **$16.99**

Also Available: **The Dance of the Dolphin** (HC edition of *Our Dance with God*)
6 x 9, 176 pp, HC, 978-1-58023-154-1 **$19.95**

The Empty Chair: Finding Hope and Joy—Timeless Wisdom from a Hasidic Master, Rebbe Nachman of Breslov *Adapted by Moshe Mykoff and the Breslov Research Institute*
4 x 6, 128 pp, 2-color text, Deluxe PB w/flaps, 978-1-879045-67-5 **$9.99**

The Gentle Weapon: Prayers for Everyday and Not-So-Everyday Moments—Timeless Wisdom from the Teachings of the Hasidic Master, Rebbe Nachman of Breslov *Adapted by Moshe Mykoff and S. C. Mizrahi, together with the Breslov Research Institute*
4 x 6, 144 pp, 2-color text, Deluxe PB w/flaps, 978-1-58023-022-3 **$9.99**

God Whispers: Stories of the Soul, Lessons of the Heart *By Karyn D. Kedar*
6 x 9, 176 pp, Quality PB, 978-1-58023-088-9 **$15.95**

Restful Reflections: Nighttime Inspiration to Calm the Soul, Based on Jewish Wisdom
By Rabbi Kerry M. Olitzky & Rabbi Lori Forman 4½ x 6¼, 448 pp, Quality PB, 978-1-58023-091-9 **$15.95**

Sacred Intentions: Daily Inspiration to Strengthen the Spirit, Based on Jewish Wisdom
By Rabbi Kerry M. Olitzky and Rabbi Lori Forman 4½ x 6¼, 448 pp, Quality PB, 978-1-58023-061-2 **$15.95**

Kabbalah/Mysticism/Enneagram

Awakening to Kabbalah: The Guiding Light of Spiritual Fulfillment
By Rav Michael Laitman, PhD 6 x 9, 192 pp, HC, 978-1-58023-264-7 **$21.99**

Seek My Face: A Jewish Mystical Theology *By Arthur Green*
6 x 9, 304 pp, Quality PB, 978-1-58023-130-5 **$19.95**

Zohar: Annotated & Explained
Translation and annotation by Daniel C. Matt; Foreword by Andrew Harvey
5½ x 8½, 176 pp, Quality PB, 978-1-893361-51-5 **$15.99** *(A SkyLight Paths book)*

Ehyeh: A Kabbalah for Tomorrow
By Arthur Green 6 x 9, 224 pp, Quality PB, 978-1-58023-213-5 **$16.99**

The Flame of the Heart: Prayers of a Chasidic Mystic *By Reb Noson of Breslov. Translated by David Sears with the Breslov Research Institute* 5 x 7¼, 160 pp, Quality PB, 978-1-58023-246-3 **$15.99**

The Gift of Kabbalah: Discovering the Secrets of Heaven, Renewing Your Life on Earth
By Tamar Frankiel, PhD 6 x 9, 256 pp, Quality PB, 978-1-58023-141-1 **$16.95;**
HC, 978-1-58023-108-4 **$21.95**

Kabbalah: A Brief Introduction for Christians
By Tamar Frankiel, PhD 5½ x 8½, 208 pp, Quality PB, 978-1-58023-303-3 **$16.99**

The Lost Princess and Other Kabbalistic Tales of Rebbe Nachman of Breslov
The Seven Beggars and Other Kabbalistic Tales of Rebbe Nachman of Breslov
Translated by Rabbi Aryeh Kaplan; Preface by Rabbi Chaim Kramer
Lost Princess: 6 x 9, 400 pp, Quality PB, 978-1-58023-217-3 **$18.99**
Seven Beggars: 6 x 9, 192 pp, Quality PB, 978-1-58023-250-0 **$16.99**

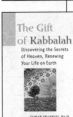

See also *The Way Into Jewish Mystical Tradition* in Spirituality / Lawrence Kushner

Holidays/Holy Days

Rosh Hashanah Readings: Inspiration, Information and Contemplation
Yom Kippur Readings: Inspiration, Information and Contemplation
Edited by Rabbi Dov Peretz Elkins with Section Introductions from Arthur Green's These Are the Words
An extraordinary collection of readings, prayers and insights that enable the modern worshiper to enter into the spirit of the High Holy Days in a personal and powerful way, permitting the meaning of the Jewish New Year to enter the heart.
RHR: 6 x 9, 400 pp, HC, 978-1-58023-239-5 **$24.99**
YKR: 6 x 9, 368 pp, HC, 978-1-58023-271-5 **$24.99**

Jewish Holidays: A Brief Introduction for Christians
By Rabbi Kerry M. Olitzky and Rabbi Daniel Judson
5½ x 8½, 144 pp, Quality PB, 978-1-58023-302-6 **$16.99**

Reclaiming Judaism as a Spiritual Practice: Holy Days and Shabbat
By Rabbi Goldie Milgram
7 x 9, 272 pp, Quality PB, 978-1-58023-205-0 **$19.99**

7th Heaven: Celebrating Shabbat with Rebbe Nachman of Breslov
By Moshe Mykoff with the Breslov Research Institute
5⅛ x 8¼, 224 pp, Deluxe PB w/flaps, 978-1-58023-175-6 **$18.95**

Shabbat, 2nd Edition: The Family Guide to Preparing for and Celebrating the Sabbath
By Dr. Ron Wolfson 7 x 9, 320 pp, illus., Quality PB, 978-1-58023-164-0 **$19.99**

Hanukkah, 2nd Edition: The Family Guide to Spiritual Celebration
By Dr. Ron Wolfson. Edited by Joel Lurie Grishaver.
7 x 9, 240 pp, illus., Quality PB, 978-1-58023-122-0 **$18.95**

The Jewish Family Fun Book, 2nd Edition: Holiday Projects, Everyday Activities, and Travel Ideas with Jewish Themes *By Danielle Dardashti and Roni Sarig. Illus. by Avi Katz.*
6 x 9, 304 pp, 70+ b/w illus. & diagrams, Quality PB, 978-1-58023-333-0 **$18.99**

The Jewish Lights Book of Fun Classroom Activities: Simple and Seasonal Projects for Teachers and Students *By Danielle Dardashti and Roni Sarig*
6 x 9, 240 pp, Quality PB, 978-1-58023-206-7 **$19.99**

Passover

My People's Passover Haggadah
Traditional Texts, Modern Commentaries
Edited by Rabbi Lawrence A. Hoffman, PhD, and David Arnow, PhD
A diverse and exciting collection of commentaries on the traditional Passover Haggadah—in two volumes!
Vol. 1: 7 x 10, 304 pp, HC, 978-1-58023-354-5 **$24.99**
Vol. 2: 7 x 10, 320 pp, HC, 978-1-58023-346-0 **$24.99**

Leading the Passover Journey
The Seder's Meaning Revealed, the Haggadah's Story Retold
By Rabbi Nathan Laufer
Uncovers the hidden meaning of the Seder's rituals and customs.
6 x 9, 224 pp, HC, 978-1-58023-211-1 **$24.99**

The Women's Passover Companion: Women's Reflections on the Festival of Freedom
Edited by Rabbi Sharon Cohen Anisfeld, Tara Mohr, and Catherine Spector
6 x 9, 352 pp, Quality PB, 978-1-58023-231-9 **$19.99**

The Women's Seder Sourcebook: Rituals & Readings for Use at the Passover Seder
Edited by Rabbi Sharon Cohen Anisfeld, Tara Mohr, and Catherine Spector
6 x 9, 384 pp, Quality PB, 978-1-58023-232-6 **$19.99**

Creating Lively Passover Seders: A Sourcebook of Engaging Tales, Texts & Activities
By David Arnow, PhD 7 x 9, 416 pp, Quality PB, 978-1-58023-184-8 **$24.99**

Passover, 2nd Edition: The Family Guide to Spiritual Celebration
By Dr. Ron Wolfson with Joel Lurie Grishaver 7 x 9, 352 pp, Quality PB, 978-1-58023-174-9 **$19.95**

Life Cycle
Marriage / Parenting / Family / Aging

The New Jewish Baby Album: Creating and Celebrating the Beginning of a Spiritual Life—A Jewish Lights Companion
By the Editors at Jewish Lights. Foreword by Anita Diamant. Preface by Rabbi Sandy Eisenberg Sasso.
A spiritual keepsake that will be treasured for generations. More than just a memory book, *shows you how—and why it's important*—to create a Jewish home and a Jewish life. 8 x 10, 64 pp, Deluxe Padded HC, Full-color illus., 978-1-58023-138-1 **$19.95**

The Jewish Pregnancy Book: A Resource for the Soul, Body & Mind during Pregnancy, Birth & the First Three Months
By Sandy Falk, MD, and Rabbi Daniel Judson, with Steven A. Rapp
Includes medical information, prayers and rituals for each stage of pregnancy, from a liberal Jewish perspective. 7 x 10, 208 pp, Quality PB, b/w photos, 978-1-58023-178-7 **$16.95**

Celebrating Your New Jewish Daughter: Creating Jewish Ways to Welcome Baby Girls into the Covenant—New and Traditional Ceremonies *By Debra Nussbaum Cohen; Foreword by Rabbi Sandy Eisenberg Sasso* 6 x 9, 272 pp, Quality PB, 978-1-58023-090-2 **$18.95**

The New Jewish Baby Book, 2nd Edition: Names, Ceremonies & Customs—A Guide for Today's Families *By Anita Diamant* 6 x 9, 336 pp, Quality PB, 978-1-58023-251-7 **$19.99**

Parenting As a Spiritual Journey: Deepening Ordinary and Extraordinary Events into Sacred Occasions *By Rabbi Nancy Fuchs-Kreimer*
6 x 9, 224 pp, Quality PB, 978-1-58023-016-2 **$16.95**

Parenting Jewish Teens: A Guide for the Perplexed
By Joanne Doades
Explores the questions and issues that shape the world in which today's Jewish teenagers live.
6 x 9, 200 pp, Quality PB, 978-1-58023-305-7 **$16.99**

Judaism for Two: A Spiritual Guide for Strengthening and Celebrating Your Loving Relationship *By Rabbi Nancy Fuchs-Kreimer and Rabbi Nancy H. Wiener; Foreword by Rabbi Elliot N. Dorff* Addresses the ways Jewish teachings can enhance and strengthen committed relationships. 6 x 9, 224 pp, Quality PB, 978-1-58023-254-8 **$16.99**

Embracing the Covenant: Converts to Judaism Talk About Why & How
By Rabbi Allan Berkowitz and Patti Moskovitz 6 x 9, 192 pp, Quality PB, 978-1-879045-50-7 **$16.95**

The Guide to Jewish Interfaith Family Life: An InterfaithFamily.com Handbook
Edited by Ronnie Friedland and Edmund Case 6 x 9, 384 pp, Quality PB, 978-1-58023-153-4 **$18.95**

Introducing My Faith and My Community
The Jewish Outreach Institute Guide for the Christian in a Jewish Interfaith Relationship
By Rabbi Kerry M. Olitzky 6 x 9, 176 pp, Quality PB, 978-1-58023-192-3 **$16.99**

Making a Successful Jewish Interfaith Marriage: The Jewish Outreach Institute Guide to Opportunities, Challenges and Resources *By Rabbi Kerry M. Olitzky with Joan Peterson Littman*
6 x 9, 176 pp, Quality PB, 978-1-58023-170-1 **$16.95**

The Creative Jewish Wedding Book: A Hands-On Guide to New & Old Traditions, Ceremonies & Celebrations *By Gabrielle Kaplan-Mayer*
9 x 9, 288 pp, b/w photos, Quality PB, 978-1-58023-194-7 **$19.99**

Divorce Is a Mitzvah: A Practical Guide to Finding Wholeness and Holiness When Your Marriage Dies *By Rabbi Perry Netter; Afterword by Rabbi Laura Geller.*
6 x 9, 224 pp, Quality PB, 978-1-58023-172-5 **$16.95**

A Heart of Wisdom: Making the Jewish Journey from Midlife through the Elder Years
Edited by Susan Berrin; Foreword by Harold Kushner
6 x 9, 384 pp, Quality PB, 978-1-58023-051-3 **$18.95**

So That Your Values Live On: Ethical Wills and How to Prepare Them
Edited by Jack Riemer and Nathaniel Stampfer
6 x 9, 272 pp, Quality PB, 978-1-879045-34-7 **$18.99**

Current Events/History

A Dream of Zion: American Jews Reflect on Why Israel Matters to Them
Edited by Rabbi Jeffrey K. Salkin Explores what Jewish people in America have to say about Israel. 6 x 9, 304 pp, HC, 978-1-58023-340-8 **$24.99**
  Also Available: **A Dream of Zion Teacher's Guide** 8½ x 11, 18 pp, PB, 978-1-58023-356-9 **$8.99**

The Jewish Connection to Israel, the Promised Land: A Brief Introduction for Christians *By Rabbi Eugene Korn, PhD* 5½ x 8½, 192 pp, Quality PB, 978-1-58023-318-7 **$14.99**

The Story of the Jews: A 4,000-Year Adventure—A Graphic History Book
Written & illustrated by Stan Mack 6 x 9, 288 pp, illus., Quality PB, 978-1-58023-155-8 **$16.99**

Hannah Senesh: Her Life and Diary, the First Complete Edition
By Hannah Senesh; Foreword by Marge Piercy; Preface by Eitan Senesh
6 x 9, 368 pp, Quality PB, 978-1-58023-342-2 **$19.99**; 352 pp, HC, 978-1-58023-212-8 **$24.99**

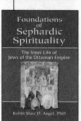

The Ethiopian Jews of Israel: Personal Stories of Life in the Promised Land *By Len Lyons, PhD; Foreword by Alan Dershowitz; Photographs by Ilan Ossendryver* Recounts, through photographs and words, stories of Ethiopian Jews.
10½ x 10, 240 pp, 100 full-color photos, HC, 978-1-58023-323-1 **$34.99**

Foundations of Sephardic Spirituality: The Inner Life of Jews of the Ottoman Empire
By Rabbi Marc D. Angel, PhD 6 x 9, 224 pp, HC, 978-1-58023-243-2 **$24.99**

Judaism and Justice: The Jewish Passion to Repair the World
By Rabbi Sidney Schwarz 6 x 9, 250 pp, HC, 978-1-58023-312-5 **$24.99**

Ecology/Environment

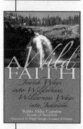

A Wild Faith: Jewish Ways into Wilderness, Wilderness Ways into Judaism
By Rabbi Mike Comins; Foreword by Nigel Savage
Offers ways to enliven and deepen your spiritual life through wilderness experience.
6 x 9, 240 pp, Quality PB, 978-1-58023-316-3 **$16.99**

Ecology & the Jewish Spirit: Where Nature & the Sacred Meet
Edited by Ellen Bernstein 6 x 9, 288 pp, Quality PB, 978-1-58023-082-7 **$18.99**

Torah of the Earth: Exploring 4,000 Years of Ecology in Jewish Thought
Vol. 1: Biblical Israel: One Land, One People; Rabbinic Judaism: One People, Many Lands
Vol. 2: Zionism: One Land, Two Peoples; Eco-Judaism: One Earth, Many Peoples
Edited by Arthur Waskow Vol. 1: 6 x 9, 272 pp, Quality PB, 978-1-58023-086-5 **$19.95**
Vol. 2: 6 x 9, 336 pp, Quality PB, 978-1-58023-087-2 **$19.95**

The Way Into Judaism and the Environment
By Jeremy Benstein 6 x 9, 224 pp, HC, 978-1-58023-268-5 **$24.99**

Grief/Healing

Healing and the Jewish Imagination: Spiritual and Practical Perspectives on Judaism and Health *Edited by Rabbi William Cutter, PhD*
Explores Judaism for comfort in times of illness and perspectives on suffering.
6 x 9, 240 pp, HC, 978-1-58023-314-9 **$24.99**

Grief in Our Seasons: A Mourner's Kaddish Companion *By Rabbi Kerry M. Olitzky*
4½ x 6½, 448 pp, Quality PB, 978-1-879045-55-2 **$15.95**

Healing of Soul, Healing of Body: Spiritual Leaders Unfold the Strength & Solace in Psalms *Edited by Rabbi Simkha Y. Weintraub, CSW*
6 x 9, 128 pp, 2-color illus. text, Quality PB, 978-1-879045-31-6 **$14.99**

Mourning & Mitzvah, 2nd Edition: A Guided Journal for Walking the Mourner's Path through Grief to Healing *By Anne Brener, LCSW*
7½ x 9, 304 pp, Quality PB, 978-1-58023-113-8 **$19.99**

Tears of Sorrow, Seeds of Hope, 2nd Edition: A Jewish Spiritual Companion for Infertility and Pregnancy Loss *By Rabbi Nina Beth Cardin*
6 x 9, 208 pp, Quality PB, 978-1-58023-233-3 **$18.99**

A Time to Mourn, a Time to Comfort, 2nd Edition: A Guide to Jewish Bereavement *By Dr. Ron Wolfson*
7 x 9, 384 pp, Quality PB, 978-1-58023-253-1 **$19.99**

When a Grandparent Dies: A Kid's Own Remembering Workbook for Dealing with Shiva and the Year Beyond *By Nechama Liss-Levinson, PhD*
8 x 10, 48 pp, 2-color text, HC, 978-1-879045-44-6 **$15.95** *For ages 7–13*

Spirituality/Lawrence Kushner

Filling Words with Light: Hasidic and Mystical Reflections on Jewish Prayer
By Lawrence Kushner and Nehemia Polen
5½ x 8½, 176 pp, Quality PB, 978-1-58023-238-8 **$16.99**; HC, 978-1-58023-216-6 **$21.99**

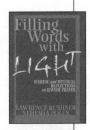

The Book of Letters: A Mystical Hebrew Alphabet
Popular HC Edition, 6 x 9, 80 pp, 2-color text, 978-1-879045-00-2 **$24.95**
Collector's Limited Edition, 9 x 12, 80 pp, gold foil embossed pages, w/limited edition silkscreened print, 978-1-879045-04-0 **$349.00**

The Book of Miracles: A Young Person's Guide to Jewish Spiritual Awareness
6 x 9, 96 pp, 2-color illus., HC, 978-1-879045-78-1 **$16.95** *For ages 9 and up*

The Book of Words: Talking Spiritual Life, Living Spiritual Talk
6 x 9, 160 pp, Quality PB, 978-1-58023-020-9 **$16.95**

Eyes Remade for Wonder: A Lawrence Kushner Reader   *Introduction by Thomas Moore*
6 x 9, 240 pp, Quality PB, 978-1-58023-042-1 **$18.95**

God Was in This Place & I, i Did Not Know: Finding Self, Spirituality and
Ultimate Meaning   6 x 9, 192 pp, Quality PB, 978-1-879045-33-0 **$16.95**

Honey from the Rock: An Introduction to Jewish Mysticism
6 x 9, 176 pp, Quality PB, 978-1-58023-073-5 **$16.95**

Invisible Lines of Connection: Sacred Stories of the Ordinary
5½ x 8½, 160 pp, Quality PB, 978-1-879045-98-9 **$15.95**

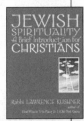

Jewish Spirituality—A Brief Introduction for Christians
5½ x 8½, 112 pp, Quality PB, 978-1-58023-150-3 **$12.95**

The River of Light: Jewish Mystical Awareness
6 x 9, 192 pp, Quality PB, 978-1-58023-096-4 **$16.95**

The Way Into Jewish Mystical Tradition
6 x 9, 224 pp, Quality PB, 978-1-58023-200-5 **$18.99**; HC, 978-1-58023-029-2 **$21.95**

Spirituality/Prayer

My People's Passover Haggadah: Traditional Texts, Modern Commentaries
Edited by Rabbi Lawrence A. Hoffman, PhD, and David Arnow, PhD Diverse commentaries
on the traditional Passover Haggadah—in two volumes! Vol. 1: 7 x 10, 304 pp, HC
978-1-58023-354-5 **$24.99** Vol. 2: 7 x 10, 320 pp, HC, 978-1-58023-346-0 **$24.99**

Witnesses to the One: The Spiritual History of the *Sh'ma* *By Rabbi Joseph B. Meszler;*
Foreword by Rabbi Elyse Goldstein 6 x 9, 176 pp, HC, 978-1-58023-309-5 **$19.99**

My People's Prayer Book Series
Traditional Prayers, Modern Commentaries   *Edited by Rabbi Lawrence A. Hoffman*
Provides diverse and exciting commentary to the traditional liturgy, helping modern
men and women find new wisdom in Jewish prayer, and bring liturgy into their lives.
Each book includes Hebrew text, modern translation, and commentaries from all
perspectives of the Jewish world.
Vol. 1—The *Sh'ma* and Its Blessings
   7 x 10, 168 pp, HC, 978-1-879045-79-8 **$24.99**
Vol. 2—The *Amidah*
   7 x 10, 240 pp, HC, 978-1-879045-80-4 **$24.95**
Vol. 3—*P'sukei D'zimrah* (Morning Psalms)
   7 x 10, 240 pp, HC, 978-1-879045-81-1 **$24.95**
Vol. 4—*Seder K'riat Hatorah* (The Torah Service)
   7 x 10, 264 pp, HC, 978-1-879045-82-8 **$23.95**
Vol. 5—*Birkhot Hashachar* (Morning Blessings)
   7 x 10, 240 pp, HC, 978-1-879045-83-5 **$24.95**
Vol. 6—*Tachanun* and Concluding Prayers
   7 x 10, 240 pp, HC, 978-1-879045-84-2 **$24.95**
Vol. 7—Shabbat at Home
   7 x 10, 240 pp, HC, 978-1-879045-85-9 **$24.95**
Vol. 8—*Kabbalat Shabbat* (Welcoming Shabbat in the Synagogue)
   7 x 10, 240 pp, HC, 978-1-58023-121-3 **$24.99**
Vol. 9—Welcoming the Night: *Minchah* and *Ma'ariv* (Afternoon and
Evening Prayer) 7 x 10, 272 pp, HC, 978-1-58023-262-3 **$24.99**
Vol. 10—Shabbat Morning: *Shacharit* and *Musaf* (Morning and
Additional Services) 7 x 10, 240 pp, HC, 978-1-58023-240-1 **$24.99**

Spirituality

Journeys to a Jewish Life: Inspiring Stories from the Spiritual Journeys of American Jews *By Paula Amann*
Examines the soul treks of Jews lost and found. 6 x 9, 208 pp, HC, 978-1-58023-317-0 **$19.99**

The Adventures of Rabbi Harvey: A Graphic Novel of Jewish Wisdom and Wit in the Wild West *By Steve Sheinkin*
Jewish and American folktales combine in this witty and original graphic novel collection. Creatively retold and set on the western frontier of the 1870s.
6 x 9, 144 pp, Full-color illus., Quality PB, 978-1-58023-310-1 **$16.99**
Also Available: **The Adventures of Rabbi Harvey Teacher's Guide**
8½ x 11, 32 pp, PB, 978-1-58023-326-2 **$8.99**

Ethics of the Sages: Pirke Avot—Annotated & Explained
Translation and Annotation by Rabbi Rami Shapiro
5½ x 8½, 192 pp, Quality PB, 978-1-59473-207-2 **$16.99** *(A SkyLight Paths book)*

A Book of Life: Embracing Judaism as a Spiritual Practice
By Michael Strassfeld 6 x 9, 528 pp, Quality PB, 978-1-58023-247-0 **$19.99**

Meaning and Mitzvah: Daily Practices for Reclaiming Judaism through Prayer, God, Torah, Hebrew, Mitzvot and Peoplehood *By Rabbi Goldie Milgram*
7 x 9, 336 pp, Quality PB, 978-1-58023-256-2 **$19.99**

The Soul of the Story: Meetings with Remarkable People
By Rabbi David Zeller 6 x 9, 288 pp, HC, 978-1-58023-272-2 **$21.99**

Aleph-Bet Yoga: Embodying the Hebrew Letters for Physical and Spiritual Well-Being
By Steven A. Rapp. Foreword by Tamar Frankiel, PhD and Judy Greenfeld. Preface by Hart Lazer.
7 x 10, 128 pp, b/w photos, Quality PB, Layflat binding, 978-1-58023-162-6 **$16.95**

Does the Soul Survive? A Jewish Journey to Belief in Afterlife, Past Lives & Living with Purpose *By Rabbi Elie Kaplan Spitz; Foreword by Brian L. Weiss, MD*
6 x 9, 288 pp, Quality PB, 978-1-58023-165-7 **$16.99**

First Steps to a New Jewish Spirit: Reb Zalman's Guide to Recapturing the Intimacy & Ecstasy in Your Relationship with God *By Rabbi Zalman M. Schachter-Shalomi with Donald Gropman* 6 x 9, 144 pp, Quality PB, 978-1-58023-182-4 **$16.95**

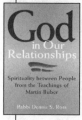

God in Our Relationships: Spirituality between People from the Teachings of Martin Buber *By Rabbi Dennis S. Ross* 5½ x 8½, 160 pp, Quality PB, 978-1-58023-147-3 **$16.95**

Judaism, Physics and God: Searching for Sacred Metaphors in a Post-Einstein World
By Rabbi David W. Nelson 6 x 9, 368 pp, Quality PB, inc. reader's discussion guide, 978-1-58023-306-4 **$18.99**;
HC, 352 pp, 978-1-58023-252-4 **$24.99**

The Jewish Lights Spirituality Handbook: A Guide to Understanding, Exploring & Living a Spiritual Life *Edited by Stuart M. Matlins*
What exactly is "Jewish" about spirituality? How do I make it a part of my life? Fifty of today's foremost spiritual leaders share their ideas and experience with us.
6 x 9, 456 pp, Quality PB, 978-1-58023-093-3 **$19.99**

Bringing the Psalms to Life: How to Understand and Use the Book of Psalms
By Daniel F. Polish 6 x 9, 208 pp, Quality PB, 978-1-58023-157-2 **$16.95**;
HC, 978-1-58023-077-3 **$21.95**

God & the Big Bang: Discovering Harmony between Science & Spirituality
By Daniel C. Matt 6 x 9, 216 pp, Quality PB, 978-1-879045-89-7 **$16.99**

Minding the Temple of the Soul: Balancing Body, Mind, and Spirit through Traditional Jewish Prayer, Movement, and Meditation *By Tamar Frankiel, PhD, and Judy Greenfeld*
7 x 10, 184 pp, illus., Quality PB, 978-1-879045-64-4 **$16.95**
Audiotape of the Blessings and Meditations: 60 min. **$9.95**
Videotape of the Movements and Meditations: 46 min. **$20.00**

One God Clapping: The Spiritual Path of a Zen Rabbi *By Alan Lew with Sherril Jaffe*
5½ x 8½, 336 pp, Quality PB, 978-1-58023-115-2 **$16.95**

There Is No Messiah ... and You're It: The Stunning Transformation of Judaism's Most Provocative Idea *By Rabbi Robert N. Levine, DD*
6 x 9, 192 pp, Quality PB, 978-1-58023-255-5 **$16.99**

These Are the Words: A Vocabulary of Jewish Spiritual Life
By Arthur Green 6 x 9, 304 pp, Quality PB, 978-1-58023-107-7 **$18.95**

Spirituality/Women's Interest

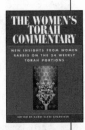

The Quotable Jewish Woman: Wisdom, Inspiration & Humor from the Mind & Heart
Edited and compiled by Elaine Bernstein Partnow
6 x 9, 496 pp, Quality PB, 978-1-58023-236-4 **$19.99**; HC, 978-1-58023-193-0 **$29.99**

The Divine Feminine in Biblical Wisdom Literature: Selections Annotated &
Explained *Translated and Annotated by Rabbi Rami Shapiro*
5½ x 8½, 240 pp, Quality PB, 978-1-59473-109-9 **$16.99** *(A SkyLight Paths book)*

The Women's Haftarah Commentary: New Insights from Women Rabbis on the
54 Weekly Haftarah Portions, the 5 Megillot & Special Shabbatot
Edited by Rabbi Elyse Goldstein 6 x 9, 560 pp, HC, 978-1-58023-133-6 **$39.99**

The Women's Torah Commentary: New Insights from Women Rabbis on the
54 Weekly Torah Portions *Edited by Rabbi Elyse Goldstein*
6 x 9, 496 pp, HC, 978-1-58023-076-6 **$34.95**

The Year Mom Got Religion: One Woman's Midlife Journey into Judaism
By Lee Meyerhoff Hendler 6 x 9, 208 pp, Quality PB, 978-1-58023-070-4 **$15.95**

See Holidays for *The Women's Passover Companion: Women's Reflections
on the Festival of Freedom* and *The Women's Seder Sourcebook: Rituals &
Readings for Use at the Passover Seder.* Also see Bar/Bat Mitzvah for *The
JGirl's Guide: The Young Jewish Woman's Handbook for Coming of Age.*

Spirituality / Crafts
(from SkyLight Paths, our sister imprint)

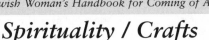

The Knitting Way: A Guide to Spiritual Self-Discovery
By Linda Skolnick and Janice MacDaniels
Shows how to use the practice of knitting to strengthen our spiritual selves.
7 x 9, 240 pp, Quality PB, 978-1-59473-079-5 **$16.99**

The Quilting Path: A Guide to Spiritual Self-Discovery through Fabric,
Thread and Kabbalah *By Louise Silk*
Explores how to cultivate personal growth through quilt making.
7 x 9, 192 pp, Quality PB, 978-1-59473-206-5 **$16.99**

The Painting Path: Embodying Spiritual Discovery through Yoga, Brush
and Color *By Linda Novick; Foreword by Richard Segalman*
Explores the divine connection you can experience through art.
7 x 9, 208 pp, 8-page full-color insert, Quality PB, 978-1-59473-226-3 **$18.99**

The Scrapbooking Journey: A Hands-On Guide to Spiritual Discovery
By Cory Richardson-Lauve; Foreword by Stacy Julian
Reveals how this craft can become a practice used to deepen and shape your life.
7 x 9, 176 pp, 8-page full-color insert, b/w photos, Quality PB, 978-1-59473-216-4 **$18.99**

Travel

Israel—A Spiritual Travel Guide, 2nd Edition
A Companion for the Modern Jewish Pilgrim
By Rabbi Lawrence A. Hoffman 4¾ x 10, 256 pp, Quality PB, illus., 978-1-58023-261-6 **$18.99**
Also Available: **The Israel Mission Leader's Guide** 978-1-58023-085-8 **$4.95**

12-Step

100 Blessings Every Day: Daily Twelve Step Recovery Affirmations, Exercises for
Personal Growth & Renewal Reflecting Seasons of the Jewish Year
By Rabbi Kerry M. Olitzky; Foreword by Rabbi Neil Gillman
4½ x 6½, 432 pp, Quality PB, 978-1-879045-30-9 **$16.99**

Recovery from Codependence: A Jewish Twelve Steps Guide to Healing Your Soul
By Rabbi Kerry M. Olitzky 6 x 9, 160 pp, Quality PB, 978-1-879045-32-3 **$13.95**

Twelve Jewish Steps to Recovery: A Personal Guide to Turning from Alcoholism &
Other Addictions—Drugs, Food, Gambling, Sex ...
By Rabbi Kerry M. Olitzky and Stuart A. Copans, MD; Preface by Abraham J. Twerski, MD
6 x 9, 144 pp, Quality PB, 978-1-879045-09-5 **$15.99**

About Jewish Lights

People of all faiths and backgrounds yearn for books that attract, engage, educate, and spiritually inspire.

Our principal goal is to stimulate thought and help all people learn about who the Jewish People are, where they come from, and what the future can be made to hold. While people of our diverse Jewish heritage are the primary audience, our books speak to people in the Christian world as well and will broaden their understanding of Judaism and the roots of their own faith.

We bring to you authors who are at the forefront of spiritual thought and experience. While each has something different to say, they all say it in a voice that you can hear.

Our books are designed to welcome you and then to engage, stimulate, and inspire. We judge our success not only by whether or not our books are beautiful and commercially successful, but by whether or not they make a difference in your life.

For your information and convenience, at the back of this book we have provided a list of other Jewish Lights books you might find interesting and useful. They cover all the categories of your life:

Bar/Bat Mitzvah	Life Cycle
Bible Study / Midrash	Meditation
Children's Books	Parenting
Congregation Resources	Prayer
Current Events / History	Ritual / Sacred Practice
Ecology/ Environment	Spirituality
Fiction: Mystery, Science Fiction	Theology / Philosophy
Grief / Healing	Travel
Holidays / Holy Days	12-Step
Inspiration	Women's Interest
Kabbalah / Mysticism / Enneagram	

Stuart M. Matlins, Publisher

Or phone, fax, mail or e-mail to: **JEWISH LIGHTS Publishing**
Sunset Farm Offices, Route 4 • P.O. Box 237 • Woodstock, Vermont 05091
Tel: (802) 457-4000 • Fax: (802) 457-4004 • www.jewishlights.com
Credit card orders: **(800) 962-4544** (8:30AM–5:30PM ET Monday–Friday)
Generous discounts on quantity orders. SATISFACTION GUARANTEED. Prices subject to change.

For more information about each book, visit our website at www.jewishlights.com